Bad Seed, Good Seed

A Novel

Ronald Lynn

Prologue

"Bad Seed, Good Seed" is a story about two boys who suffer through the divorce of their parents who were high school sweethearts and get married shortly after they graduate. The boys are placed in a religious home for children (the "home") for unwed parents when they are very young. One child is taken out of the home, one child is left behind, which is the start of how their two lives will dramatically go in different directions.

This is a story of reacting to actions that are outside of one's control and making choices in life based on the circumstances and situations that people may face in life. This is also a story of overcoming one's childhood and having a long and productive life that may include a loving relationship.

This story was written to give hope to young people living in the midst of a divorce, or any other form of disadvantage in their lives, that through effort, hard work, endurance, logical thinking and desire to better one's life, lives should not be considered to be ruined by the circumstances of their youth. Life's complicating circumstances are only potential obstacles that each of us can face and seek to overcome, on the path to adulthood. The complicating circumstances of childhood don't have to be barriers to a life of happiness. They will be barriers only to the degree that you allow them to be.

You can throw off the cloak of your problem childhood, regardless of the reason it was a problem, and grow beyond it. This is a message that I want to send all young people, including some in my own family. We are the masters of our future.

Chapter 1- The Nightmare, 1958

"Get into that corner and stand there until you come up with a story to tell me so I can sleep!" Charlie screamed at his younger brother. "And stop that damn sniveling, or I'll come over there and really give you something to cry about. And don't you lay down!"

It was 2:15 AM. Joey could see the time from where he stood in the corner of the room. His hands and knees shook out of fear of his older brother who had come to live with the family ten months earlier. Joey wracked his brain for some kind of story that he could tell his brother that would help Charlie fall asleep. But, at nine years of age, two years younger than Charlie, creative thoughts did not come easy – especially in the wee hours of the morning.

Finally, on his own, Charlie fell asleep. Hearing Charlie breathing deeply, Joey climbed quietly up into the upper bunk, being very careful not to make the bed squeak, which might waken his older brother.

Joey Lane laid under the covers thinking about how his life had gone so bad in the last eighteen months since his great grandmother, Luci, the womanly saint who had raised him for the last six years, had agreed to turn custody of Joey over to his mother and her second husband. That was before his stepbrother, Josh, Jr. was born and his older brother, Charlie, was brought into the home.

His mother, Maggie, was so happy. She now had her two boys from her first marriage with her and a beautiful baby from Josh, her second husband. In her joy for having her world turned right side up, she was oblivious to how Joey had become quiet and uncommunicative since Charlie had come into the home. Maggie did not see the fear in Joey's eyes every time Charlie entered the room. Somehow neither she nor Josh, a Detroit policeman, saw the bruises that Joey was beginning to show on his body. Bruises that were the result of beatings that Charlie would give Joey for the slightest reasons.

Charlie was a mean boy, an angry boy, a boy who hated Joey and would gladly spend the rest of his days handing out as much abuse as Joey was willing to take. And take it, Charlie believed, Joey would, because Charlie had something over Joey and was willing to tell all of Joey's friends and embarrass Joey to high heaven – Joey wets the bed.

That may not sound like a big deal to you, but it was to Joey. You see, other than when Joey was a baby, Joey had never wet the bed before. But since great grandma Luci had turned custody of Joey over to his mother and her second husband, Joey had developed a bed-wetting problem. He was very ashamed of it. After all, he was nine years old. Too old to be wetting the bed, and Charlie used that information to skillfully control his younger brother who he considered to be that little piece of crap who was taken out of the orphanage before Charlie was.

Joey closed his eyes and thought of his life with his great grandmother Luci before he had any real awareness of his mother or father or his abusive older brother. Joey's thoughts took him to when he was four years old and held tightly in the arms of his great grandma Luci, his mother's grandmother. Also in the family were Luci's daughter, Pauline, Pauline's husband, Ernie, and their daughter Danielle. The house was filled with love, compassion, trust and understanding. Joey didn't remember how he came to be there, but this home, in Roscommon, Michigan, was his home. These were the people he loved; this was the street that he knew, and life was wonderful.

Chapter 2 - The Meltdown of A Marriage – 1947-1950

Though Joey didn't remember it, his life before Luci had been turbulent and full of chaos. His mother, Maggie, was a Roscommon town beauty with smarts. She was the only daughter of a prosperous, local builder. Joey's father, Gregory Lane, was cute, smart, a good athlete, and was from the poor side of town. Maggie and Gregory had been high school sweethearts who married, against her father's wishes, as soon as they could afford to after graduating from high school. But then the United States entered into World War II, which pulled his father into the U.S. Navy.

When the war ended, Gregory came home, and he and Maggie started a family. Charlie was born first; two years later came Joey.

The war had changed Gregory and Maggie. Theirs was no longer a young, passionate love that could thrive on love alone. After the war, people wanted stuff, they wanted good times, long days and longer nights. They were no longer satisfied with living in a small town, they were drawn to the lights and vibrancy of Detroit. During World War II, Detroit, with its huge industrial base, became the arsenal of democracy. Its factories turned from car production to tank, jeep and airplane production. If the Army and Navy said they needed it, it came out of Detroit. Engineers, skilled tradesmen, and white color workers poured into Detroit. With their talent and skills that wanted something in return, a quality lifestyle of libraries, auditoriums, theatres, zoos, public transportation and on and on. And the people of Detroit built them. This new lifestyle was the American Dream, and Gregory and Maggie wanted a piece of it. Maggie stayed home with the kids while Gregory got a job at the Ford Motor Company factory in Highland Park.

But, just as the war had changed their feelings about where to live, it also created a distance between them that could not be bridged. Maggie, only 20 when she gave birth to her second child, Joey, felt trapped in her role as a mother. The man that she had married was no longer the loving, hard driving young man that he once was. He was now tempered by what he had seen in the service to his country. He now had two children, a job that paid the bills, and he was not going to risk what he had to chase after dreams that he had when he was a boy.

Regular arguments began to ensue between Gregory and Maggie. Gregory would come home from the factory where he had worked all day to find a wife who was bitter about where they lived and her role as a mother. "Oh, hell," she would say to Gregory when he walked through the door covered in factory oil, "you are dirtying up this little apartment that I worked my butt off to keep clean!" Throwing pots and pans and dishes around the kitchen, she would exclaim, "I'm damn sick of living like this! This is not how I was raised. I was not raised to live hand to mouth in a hell-hole like this with two crying babies grabbing at my ankles all day!"

Gregory, tired from a ten-hour day in the factory and stinking of factory oil, would respond in kind. Soon the childhood sweethearts were heading for the divorce court where it was decreed that Gregory would get custody of Charlie, and Maggie would get custody of Joey.

Chapter 3 - St. Mathew's Home For Children, 1950

With the divorce being final, Maggie had to get a job to pay her way through life in the capacity of a single mother. Not having anyone to babysit for the infant, she chose to put Joey in the St. Mathew's Home for Children in Southfield, Michigan (the "Home.") Gregory, faced with the same set of circumstances, and wanting to keep the boys together, chose the Home for Charlie as well.

Charlie, at five years of age, was already a rough and tumble little boy. He was old enough and scrappy enough to get his fair share of food. On the other hand, Joey, only three years old, had his food consistently taken from him (often by Charlie) became malnourished to the point where his Grandmother Harriett, his father's mother, became very distraught about the child's condition. As she held her grandson in the Home, she could feel his bones though his thin layer of skin. "Something needs to be done soon or this child isn't going to make it," she thought to herself. A strong woman who had made her way from Norway to America for a better life, Harriett was not going to see her grandchild die in her arms of malnutrition. Something had to be done.

That evening Harriett called Gregory and told him of her fears for Joey's survival given the amount of food he was getting. "Now listen, Gregory," she said, "this child is your son, even though you don't have custody of him. He is not doing well, and I am afraid that he may develop rickets (a bone disease caused by the lack of vitamin D) if he doesn't get more food and milk."

"Mother, I am absolutely aware of his condition, but as you just said, I don't have custody of him, and I can't make decisions concerning him. The only thing I can do is talk to Maggie and see if other arrangements can be made." He said good-bye to his mother then called Maggie to discuss Joey's condition and what other arrangements could be made for Joey.

Maggie recognized the problem as well. She too had felt the bones when she held her son. She saw the sunken eyes and the hollow cheeks of her child, but she had no answers. She was not going to give her child up for adoption and she was not going to ship her child up to Roscommon where she would seldom be able to see him.

Gregory persisted, "Maggie, you and I both know that things will not end up well if he continues to stay there. He is not getting enough food. Have you talked to them about increasing the amount of food they give him?"

Maggie said, "Of course I have, but they simply say that he is getting enough food."

"Not if other kids are taking it from him," Gregory interjected.

"They say that's not happening," replied Maggie.

"How do they know that?" Gregory scoffed. "Do they have someone monitoring activities at every table in the dining room?"

Maggie was getting more and more frustrated by the second. She retorted, "All I can tell you is what they tell me. If I push too much, they say that they know best. And then they add something like I got married too young and had a baby before I knew what to do with it."

"Did you tell them that I fought in the war for this country? If we were old enough to face a war together, we were certainly old enough to have children."

Maggie said that she had made retorts like that and was told that being old enough to die for your country did not mean that we were old enough to know how to raise children. "One woman actually said they may recommend that I am not fit to raise the child, and he should become a ward of the State."

"Well, that's bullshit, Maggie! All the more reason to turn custody over to your Grandma Luci. She at least will take the State and the Home out of the picture. And when you are ready to have Joey back, your grandmother won't fight it."

Maggie said, "That is just not an option. I will find another solution."

"But...,"

Maggie cut him off. "I won't discuss this anymore. I have custody of Joey. You don't. You worry about Charlie and leave Joey to me."

And that was that.

Maggie's response to Gregory did not sit well with Harriett. Harriett wrote a letter to Maggie's grandmother, Luci, in Roscommon, Michigan (a small town in central Michigan, about 180 miles north of Detroit.) She told Luci of Joey's condition and asked if Luci could prevail on Maggie to give up custody of Joey to Luci. If Maggie was willing to do that, then Luci could raise the child in Roscommon.

Luci was in her early 70's. She had raised her own family through very hard times. She did not believe in divorce and felt that a child needed to be raised by its mother and father. But the divorce had already occurred, and the child's health was at risk. The comment that the facility made about making her great grandson a ward of the State did not sit well with Luci. She bristled when governments began to forget that they served the people, not the other way around. Great Grandma Luci had immigrated to the United States from Germany and had seen in her lifetime too much aggression being taken by governments. Joey was innocent of any wrongdoing and deserved a chance to live and thrive, not be a ward of the State. She spit on the ground at the very suggestion, then made the sign of the cross for being so hostile. But, being a devout and practicing Roman Catholic, Luci could not allow Joey's health to be put at risk without putting forth an effort to help him, so she wrote to Maggie to see if Maggie would grant her custody of Joey.

Grandmother Luci had watched Maggie before and after school after Maggie's mother had left the family when Maggie was a child. She had read books to Maggie, cuddled Maggie, comforted Maggie, baked with Maggie and more. Luci had a great deal of influence over Maggie. The letters between Luci and Maggie regarding Joey went far better than Luci expected. While Maggie was reluctant at first to send Joey up to Roscommon, Luci was actually relieved knowing that her grandmother would be the custodian of her child. Joey would soon be going to live in Roscommon.

Chapter 4 - One Taken, One Left, 1950

Charlie would stay behind. No grandmother would come for him. No one would offer to take him to Roscommon, or anywhere else, to live. From a window in the Home, Charlie watched the scene down on the road as Joey was taken by his mother and placed into the arms of their great grandmother. Charlie, now four, was angry at the world. He did not trust anyone and scowled at the scene below. He felt true resentment - much of his resentment was directed toward Joey. It was Joey's fault. Joey was leaving Charlie alone in this place.

Charlie was too young to understand that Joey had no role in the matter. To Charlie, by leaving the Home, Joey was abandoning him. Charlie hated Joey for doing it. As the car carrying Joey drove away from the orphanage, Charlie said to himself, "I will get back at you, Joey. I will get back at all of them."

While Joey began to live in a wonderful family environment in Roscommon, Charlie remained at the Home – getting meaner, tougher and smarter every day. He would steal food from other children. He would find their flaws and fears and use them to his advantage. He would learn how to con those with more power than himself or who had something that he wanted. All of these skills he would develop for a lifetime of taking what he wanted. This was only fair, he would think, because the world owed him. Charlie became a child, and would become an adult, who had no sense of sorrow or remorse. He simply took what he wanted and did what he wanted because he was owed it for the life that he was being forced to live and the love that was being withheld from him.

Chapter 5 - Life With Grandma Luci, 1950-1955

The home that Joey went to live in was the home in which great grandma Luci had raised her own family years earlier. It was the home where she babysat Maggie as a little girl. Now it was Joey's home too. It was an old house within walking distance of downtown Roscommon. An old wooden outhouse still was functional in the back yard, even though the house had indoor plumbing and electricity.

Roscommon was a one-traffic-signal town in the late 1940's and early '50's and pretty much still is. It had a small downtown that consisted of certain types of stores that every small town has – a dime store, you might call it a general store, a hardware store, 4 gas stations, a hotel, a movie theatre showing the latest black and white movies, and a Dairy Queen on Main Street. In every store there were friendly owners and workers who would greet people coming in the door by their first name. Smiling, friendly faces greeted Joey every time he went downtown.

On Friday afternoons during lent, the Catholic Church and the Lutheran church would each have a fish fry consisting of deep friend white fish, perch and smelt. The whole town would emit the odor of fried fish until well into the weekend.

On the 4th of July, the town's one police car and the fire engine would come down the street with sirens blaring. Flat-bed trailers pulled by horses or pick-up trucks would go by with their horns blaring, waving a friendly "Hello" to everyone on the curb. All of this excitement was just a short walk away from Joey's house via a pathway between his backyard and the downtown. Joey's house was one of the oldest houses in town and was on the first street of houses away from downtown.

In the winter, the entire family would sit around an old, pot-bellied stove that sat in the middle of the living room. They would laugh and tell stories about their day. They had a small black and white television that got three channels, but those channels brought into the living room wonderful stories of The Lone Ranger, Roy Rogers, Gene Autry, Flash Gordon, and Charlie Chan. They were truly one very happy family.

Luci was a very religious woman. She and Joey would walk to Saint Michael Catholic Church twice a week - once on Sunday and once during the week - to attend church services. Joey attended grade school in Roscommon; played with kids in the neighborhood in Roscommon – including many cousins who lived nearby; learned how to ride a two-wheel bike in Roscommon; went to birthday parties and had birthday parties at their home in Roscommon. Joey was a very happy, little boy in Roscommon with his great grandmother, his Aunt Pauline, Uncle Ernie and cousin, Danielle. This was his home. He had no memory anymore of being at St. Mathews. After all, he was a little boy then, and now he was a big boy.

Within months of the divorce of Maggie and Gregory, in the spring of 1950, Josh entered Maggie's life. Josh was from a small coalmining town in Pennsylvania. He came to Detroit to get away from the coal mines and was now a proud member of the Detroit Police Department. Josh and Maggie had met in a bar in Detroit. He had just gotten off of his shift and was enjoying a beer with his squad car partner when he noticed Maggie sitting in a booth. Being a man who didn't let grass grow under his feet, shortly after they determined this was love, Josh and Maggie got married. It took four years after they got married to begin thinking about reuniting the family, but we shouldn't get caught up in the details. Many people are satisfied that they had good intentions even if they failed. Maggie and Josh likely weren't spending a lot of time thinking about any intentions other than their own happiness. The war was over, the city is alive, let's party. There is nothing so wrong with that but Maggie children were not being raised by Maggie. That maternal love that is highly touted was not occurring and neither boy was bonding with Maggie. She was just a picture on the wall.

Needless to say, when the good intentions came, they were a tad late.

Chapter 6 - An Unwanted Request, 1954

It was four years after the wedding vows of Josh and Maggie that a call was made by Maggie to Grandmother Luci. "Grandma, this is Maggie calling from Detroit. How are you, and how is Joey?" Luci hadn't heard hide nor hair from Maggie in four years. The fact that she would be calling and putting on this happy voice meant that she wanted something. Luci wasn't born yesterday. Luci took a deep breath, let it out slowly and said, "Everything is fine, Maggie. Joey is outside riding his bike with his cousins."

Maggie said, "He is really on a tricycle already?"

"No Maggie, he stopped riding a tricycle about the time you and Josh got married in 1950. He been riding a bicycle since he was 4 ½. Anyway, how are you?"

"Oh, Josh and I are doing fine, Grandma. We are planning on buying a house in a new neighborhood in Detroit. When it's done, we want to bring Joey down here to live."

This was what Luci feared. Luci was raising Joey like her own child, and Maggie's request felt like Maggie was asking Luci to give up her own child. Luci quickly put that first emotion aside. Maggie was her granddaughter, and of course she was pleased that Maggie wanted her son back. Luci, had met Josh in 1950 when they were married in Roscommon. He seemed like a pleasant enough fellow, certainly good looking, but she wanted to know more about him and about the home that want to move her great grandson into before she would ever agree to give up custody of Joey. She wanted to make sure that the picture that Maggie was painting was true before she agreed to anything. She needed to know that Joey's happiness and life in Detroit would be as happy for Joey as it had been for the past five years in Roscommon.

"Well, that's just wonderful!" Luci said to Maggie, "Please call me back when the house is ready for Joey. I don't want him being raised in an apartment in Detroit and he is in the middle of a school year." They talked a while longer and Luci said, "Do you want to talk to Joey? I can call him into the house."

Maggie said, "Oh, no, Josh will be home soon, and we are going out for dinner at a fancy restaurant. Only the best here in Detroit, Grandma. I still need to get my makeup on, but I wanted you to know what our thoughts were."

Luci said, "Ok, you have. You better hurry, you don't want to keep Josh waiting. Bye."

In April, 1955, another call came from Maggie. "Grandma, the house is completed, and we will be heading up next weekend to pick up Joey."

Luci said, "Slow down, Maggie. This little boy has lived up here for six years. He has friends and family up here. You can't just come up here and take him like he was just a puppy."

"Grandma, we had this conversation last fall. You knew bringing Joey here was our intention when the house was completed."

"But we also agreed that Joey and I would come down to look at the home and the neighborhood before a decision is made," Lucy stated.

"Grandma, the decision has been made, by me."

Luci stood strong, "Maggie, I love you, but it is not your decision to make."

"Of course, it is, Grandma. Joey's my son."

"Yes, he is, Maggie, but I'm his guardian. Remember?"

"Oh, Grandma, are you going to play that card?"

"It's not a card, Maggie. It's a sacred obligation. And you, my dear, gave it to me for the protection of Joey."

Maggie was silent. Then said, "When can we come up to get you and Joey?"

Not wanting to be indebted to Maggie, Luci said, "No, that's okay. During the Easter break, when Joey is out of school, we'll just take the Greyhound bus down to Detroit, then take a taxi to your home." Luci gathered the information that she needed from Maggie, said goodbye, laid the phone down, lowered her head and cried.

Luci knew in her heart that it was normally best for a child to be raised by the child's mother. But she loved Joey so much and didn't want to let him go. She would hold off making that decision until she saw the house and the living conditions. As she saw it, Maggie had failed both Charlie and Joey once before, and Luci was going to do her best to make sure that did not happen again.

Chapter 7- The Visit to Detroit, April, 1955

In April of 1955, Luci and Joey took a Greyhound bus on the 180-mile trip from Roscommon to Detroit. Before they left for Detroit, Luci bought Joey a pack of his favorite chewing gum to keep the eight-year-old occupied on the trip. Many years later, Joey wrote about their trip to Detroit in the poem "Black Jack Gum."

Black Jack Gum

**Black Jack gum cracked between my teeth
as I sat back against my seat.
I watched the moving countryside
as down the road, the bus did glide.**

**Around my shoulder wrapped an arm.
Upon it fell tears of alarm.
"Grandma, why do you have to cry?
It's only scenery passing by."**

**My grandma gave my arm a hug,
smoothed my hair, gave my clothes a tug,
and told me that she'd be just fine;**

forever she'd be only mine.

**Saying that I already knew,
I felt the brakes, our ride was through.
My stepdad stood outside the door,
and Grandma's tears fell on the floor.**

Luci and Joey stayed at Maggie and Josh's home for several days until Luci felt that she had a good understanding of the quality of the home and the couple that wished to have custody of Joey. She tried to find reasons for denying Maggie's request but could find little wrong with the house or with Josh and Maggie.

Josh was a big, handsome man, with a ready smile – which he often displayed. He seemed very thoughtful and showed tenderness toward Joey by putting his arm around Joey's shoulders when he asked Joey to sit by him on the couch. This could have been done just for show, but Luci didn't think so, and Luci had a keen eye for things that just didn't seem right. Josh's tenderness toward Joey seemed honest and real, and it also seemed right for Joey. Maggie had also matured since Luci had seen her last. Luci admitted to herself that the three of them, Josh, Maggie and Joey, seemed to be a picture-perfect family.

But one thing was bothering Luci a great deal, and she broached the topic delicately with Maggie.

Luci, Maggie and Joey were finishing up breakfast when Luci said, "Joey, could you go into the backyard and play a little while?"

"Why Grandma?"

"I just want to have a cup of coffee and talk to your mother a bit."

Joey got up from his chair and went outside.

Maggie looked at her grandmother and said, "Is there something wrong grandma?"

"Well, I don't know, but something is troubling me."

"Yes?" said Maggie.

"You and Josh seem pretty well established for the brief time that you have been married."

"Well, Grandma, it has been four years since we got married. We got married in Roscommon, remember?"

There was something in that "remember?" that stuck in Luci's craw a great deal, but being an elderly, church-going woman, and Maggie grandmother, she smiled sweetly, stirred her tea and said, "Oh, I remember most everything dear. I even remember the snacks that you used to like when you got home from school."

"You don't!"

"I do," Grandma said with a smile. "Saltine Crackers. They were your favorite."

"You're right. I haven't thought about that for a long time. But since you mention it, I do remember that," Maggie said.

"You see? My brain is still working," laughed Grandma. "Now what I am troubled about, Maggie, is this, why did you wait so long to ask for Joey?"

"What do you mean, Grandma?"

"What I mean is that you put him in the orphanage at a very early age. You seldom saw him."

Maggie interrupted her. "That's not fair, Grandma. I had to work."

"You seldom saw him," Grandma repeated with a little more emphasis.

"You got married four years ago and could have asked for him at any time, but you didn't, and I would like to know why not."

Maggie wasn't prepared for that she considered to be a full-frontal attack from her grandmother. Mentally she stepped back to give herself time to think. The problem all along had been Josh's hesitancy to take on a family that was not his own. He loved Maggie, but he wasn't excited about all the baggage that came with her – her two sons.

With the lack of response coming from Maggie, Luci added. "Is having Joey with you just something that you feel you have to do because it is the right thing to do?

16

Or do you really love him and miss him and want him with you? And if so, again, why did you wait so long?"

"Grandma, I am going to give you an answer, but I am afraid of how you may react to it."

"Just tell me the truth, Maggie."

"When Josh and I met it was virtually love at first sight. We wanted to be with each, and only each other, all of the time. When things cooled down a little bit that was when I wanted to reunite Joey and Charlie. Josh was OK with Joey, but Charlie is a much more difficult matter."

"Why?"

"Charlie is an angry child, Grandma. He is big, tough, defiant, and angry at me and Joey and the world in general for being put into the orphanage and being left there so long."

"So, it is Josh who has stopped you from bringing your child home?"

Maggie nodded.

"And you love this kind of man who stands in the way of a woman who wants to reunite her family? What kind of decent man would do that kind of thing, Maggie?"

"Josh is decent, Grandma."

"Stop it, Maggie! Stop it! Maybe it's the uniform that blinds you. Maybe its Josh's good looks. I don't know. I do know that no man worth marrying would deny his wife the chance to unify her family."

"Again, Grandma, it's not Joey so much as it is Charlie."

"Charlie, Charlie, Charlie. You don't even have custody of Charlie."

"Not now," said Maggie, "But Gregory is having a hard time dealing with Charlie and may turn custody of Charlie over to me."

"Would you want that kind of defiance in your family?"

"Josh knows how to handle kids like Charlie."

Grandma grimaced. "I just hope that kind of defiance doesn't rub off on Joey. Or have a bad effect on Joey. A weed can spread and destroy healthy plants. And a bad seed can destroy a good seed."

"I assure you, Grandma, it will never come to that."

"I worry, Maggie, that this tough man of yours may dole out punishment on both Joey and Charlie in order to get and keep Charlie in line."

"As the mother of both of them, Grandma, I will never let that happen. I will protect my children against any inappropriate aggression on anyone's part, even my husband's."

That seemed to put Luci's mind to rest. She hugged Maggie, and they both went into the backyard to spend some time with Joey.

When it was time for them to return to Roscommon, Maggie asked Luci if she was OK with letting Joey come live with her and Josh. Luci told Maggie that she wanted to go home and think about what was best for Joey, then she had Josh drive her and Joey to the Greyhound bus station for their return trip to Roscommon.

The fact that his great grandmother had his stepfather drive the two of them to the bus station when they had previously taken a cab from the bus station, suggested to Joey that she would soon be sending Joey to live with his mother and stepfather. Joey, sitting in the back seat of Josh's car, gulped deeply and choked back tears of anguish. He did not want to leave the life that he knew, the family that he loved, the friends that he had, to go all the way to this distant city and live with these strangers. Mother or not, Maggie was a stranger to him, and he somehow knew that life would not be as happy living in her house as it had been living with his grandma.

Chapter 8 - Luci's Decision, June 1955

After considerable thought and anguish, Luci decided that the environment in Maggie and Josh's home would work for Joey. Luci believed that having a mother and father was important to the health of a child.

Even if Josh was not enamored with Maggie's children coming to live with him, and there was a possibility that Charlie may not come, Joey was such a sweet boy that Luci knew he would win Josh over. Maggie and Josh displayed the attributes that she felt were necessary to successfully raise the little boy that Maggie had put into her care.

In the spring of 1955, Luci sadly, but willingly, told Joey that he would be going to live with his mother and his brand-new daddy. She put on a brave face and told her grandson what a wonderful life he would have in his new home. After they talked, Luci hugged Joey and told him it was time for him to go to bed. Then Luci went to her bedroom, pulled down the covers and cried softly into her pillow until she could cry no more.

As for Joey, later in life, when things were dim and Joey was lonely and scared in his new home, he would call on the memory of his great grandmother Luci and draw strength from the love he knew she had for him, but at this moment Joey's emotions were raw and his sorrow was overwhelming. But, being a good boy and not wanting to cause trouble, Joey bottled up his feelings, went to his room, crawled into bed and softly cried himself to sleep.

Once the decision was made to release Joey back into the custody of his mother and stepfather, Maggie wasted little time in coming to take Joey to his new home. Maggie and Josh came to Roscommon to get Joey the following weekend.

Joey wept when Maggie tried to pull him away from Luci. "I don't want to go!" he cried out over and over again. Josh physically had to pry Joey's fingers from around Luci's waist and take him to the car kicking and fighting. "Please Grandma, please don't let them take me. Please, please," Luci heard Joey cry out as the car pulled away from the house. Letting this sweet boy go was one of the hardest things she had to do in her life, but she believed it was the best thing for the child. She believed that Joey would have a good life with his mother and new stepfather. At least she hoped he would. Little did she know that storm clouds were already forming on the horizon of Joey's young life.

On the trip to Detroit, Joey sat on the floor in the front of the car and cried quietly for the entire trip. As far as he was concerned, he was being taken from the only home he had ever known, the family that he loved, the street and town that he knew, to go live in a far-away city with these people who he hardly knew.

Chapter 9 - Joey's New Home, 1955

Being taken away from his family in Roscommon was so upsetting to Joey that he developed a bed-wetting problem. The house made scary tapping sounds that Joey interpreted to be a witch walking up and down the hallway on a cane. Josh said the noise was from the heat expanding and contracting the ductwork of the furnace – but Joey didn't see it that way. It was a witch, and he was too afraid to go to the bathroom when nature called.

Joey would dream that he had to go to the bathroom. In the dream he would swing his feet out of bed, walk quickly to his door, open it, walk quickly down the hallway and into the bathroom and relieve himself like a big boy. He could feel the urine leaving his body and see the stream going into the toilet. He was so proud of himself for catching the need before he wet the bed. Then he would wake up and find himself still in bed laying on soaked sheets of urine. How did this happen? He was sure that he had made it to the bathroom on time and had relieved himself there. But here he was - in bed soaked in urine. This never happened in Roscommon. This never happened with at his grandma's house. Trembling and terrified that his mother would find the sheets and scream at him, which she often did, he would bundle the sheets together and throw them on the floor in the closet or under the bed until he could wash them in the wringer washing machine downstairs when his mom went to the grocery store. But no matter how hard he tried to hide what he had done, he would always get caught and more angry screams would rain down on him. He would sit at the kitchen table teeth chattering and hands and feet shaking out of fear of angry screams coming from his mother. He would sit at the kitchen table shaking in the middle of the night as Maggie would change the soiled sheets and yell at Joey that big boys did not wet the bed.

But there were good times too. Joey had a lot of friends in the neighborhood, and they would play catch with a baseball and mitt, play dodge ball in the back yard, trade baseball cards and chew the gum that came in the Topps wrapper. He was doing fine at the grade school which was a block away. He could run from his home to school in five minutes, after all he was the fastest runner in the third grade. Well, except for Suzie Fox, but she was a girl, so she didn't count. I know, it's a very sexist thing to say, but that is how most nine-year-old boys thought in 1956.

Joey had a brand new two-wheeled, red, Evans Colson bike which he rode everywhere – even up to Leslie's Drug Store where he could buy a small root bear in a frosted glass mug for a nickel. Sometimes he would splurge and get the larger mug of root beer for a dime. He was spending his money from money that he earned doing chores around the house.

He had two major chores. One chore was to dust and polish all the furniture in the house twice a week. His mom gave him a little calendar where he could keep track of things that he had to do. He would have to be very careful to get all the dust up and not break his mom's figurines – especially those glass figurines that were on the display case that separated the front door entry and dining room. He was so careful that he never broke anything. His second job was his favorite. He was responsible for pulling the weeds in the front and back yard and the flower beds. While dusting was kind of fun, Joey really liked pulling weeds – especially in the flower beds. He would even get angry at his mom when she made him stop weeding in hot weather.

Joey noticed one day that his mom's stomach was getting big. She was expecting a baby who would join the family in May of 1956. Joey was very happy that he was going to have a little brother or sister. He found that he liked to write and especially liked to write in rhymes like a lot of the books that he read. One day he sat at his steel frame desk and put pen to paper and came up with a masterpiece for his mother. He finished the little poem and proudly went into the kitchen to read it out loud to his mother. Maggie was in the middle of washing the floor on her hands and knees but she stopped when Joey said he had written a poem for her.

Nine-year-old Joey stood straight and tall and proudly read the poem:

**My mommy is as big as a barge,
When she tells me to do something
I say "Yes, Sir, Sarge!**

The sting of his mother's open hand on his face came faster than Joey could ever have imagined and was totally unexpected by him. His mother struck like a rattle snake. Whoosh, slap, sting. The anger that followed the slap was something that Joey never expected, after all he had written what he considered to be a nice poem for his mother.

His mother was screaming and crying all at the same time. Joey was so afraid that he began to get dizzy and almost fell.

"Why did you write something as mean as this?"

Joey mumbled, "The words just came to me. I thought you would like it."

"You thought I would like being told I was as big as a barge?"

Joey was now crying and shaking. "You're big with the baby and barges are big. I put sarge in because it sounds like sarge."

Maggie shook her finger at Joey and pinched his cheek. "Don't you ever write anything like this again. This is mean."

Joey broke down and wept and said, "I didn't mean for it to be mean. I thought you would like it."

"Well, I don't. Now get to your room and stay there."

He did.

In 1956, Maggie gave birth to Josh, Jr. Josh and Maggie were beyond themselves with happiness. Though still grieving for his Roscommon family, Joey found that he loved being around Josh, Jr. He would blow on Josh Jr's belly to make laugh. He would hug him and read him the picture book stories that his mother bought for Josh Jr. Josh found that he loved being an older brother.

Chapter 10 - Charlie's New Home, 1956

On the east side of Detroit things were changing in Gregory and Charlie's life as well. Gregory met Doris, fell in love with her and wanted to marry her. Doris had been divorced several times before, but Gregory believed that he could be the man that could make Doris happy and fulfilled. Doris had a boy and a girl (Bobby and Jamie) from each of her two previous marriages. Both of them were younger and smaller than Charlie.

Charlie had been living with Gregory since 1952. Living with his dad alone removed Charlie from all of the competition that he had at St. Mathews. Competition for more food if the workers liked him better than someone else; competition between him and other children for who got the bed closest to the window, who got the top bunk and on and one. St. Mathews was fraught with such competition. But, in his Dad's house the pecking order was simple – his Dad first, then Charlie, second. Doris and Gregory agreed that Gregory and Charlie would live in Doris' house once they got married.

Charlie had never been to Doris' house. She invited Charlie to join Gregory for dinner one weekend to see if

Charlie would get along with Doris and her kids in Doris' house. Charlie, now eleven, was on his best behavior. He hugged Doris and gave her a kiss on the cheek when they got to the house. Looking Doris straight in the eye, he said, "I hope you are going to be my new mother." Then he hugged and kissed her again.

"And this will be your own room," Gregory said. "You won't have to share your room with anybody. It's all yours." Charlie looked at the room with revulsion. It had cute, little, blue, yellow and red flowers on the wall, and Charlie was not a cute and flowery kind of kid. It was all he could do not to throw up. "Hold it down," he thought. "It wouldn't look good to puke right now." Instead, he took his dad and Doris by the hand, worked up some tears, and said, "Oh, it's so beautiful! I can't believe that you would go to all this trouble for me!" He looked at them both sharing his most angelic smile - while his inner soul ran cold inside of him.

After their wedding, Gregory brought Charlie home for good. The house was as neat as a pin. Charlie stood in the doorway to his room, looked at his dad and stepmother and said, "So, this is my room?"

"Yes, it is, Charlie," both parents said almost in unison, "and we are so happy that you are here," Doris added.

Charlie looked at the two of them as if he were sizing them up. He cocked his head and with a crooked smile said, "My room, to me, means I can have it the way I want it. Is that what it means to both of you?"

Doris jumped in and said, "As long as no ants or other living things come out of that room, Charlie, then you can keep it as you want it." Doris nodded to Gregory as she said it. Gregory showed a little surprise at Doris's gracious response to Charlie. He then also nodded and smiled at Charlie, "I agree with your mother, Charlie."

"Mother?" Charlie thought, "All of a sudden, she's my mother?" But he didn't say anything. He just gave a sweet smile and walked into the room - putting his duffel bag on the bed. He sat down and bounced on the bed a few times with a big smile on his face. "This whole room is mine? All of it? And the bed and other stuff? Mine?" I don't have to share the room with anyone even though you have two of your own children?" asked Charlie, addressing Doris.

Doris smiled and said, "Yes, it's only your room."

Charlie looked at both of them and said, "Could you close the door? I'm tired." Gregory closed the door, and he and Doris went into the kitchen. They agreed that it was a good idea to give Charlie some space and let him get used to his new life and new home.

Charlie, looked at the wallpaper with its pretty flowers and said, "If this room is mine, this crap's got to go." Then he thought about what other changes he would have to make to protect himself and his stuff. A cloud descended on his mind and he thought, "What is with all this lovey-dovey crap?" He opened his window, reached into his pants pocket and pulled out a pack of Camel cigarettes. Tapping the pack like someone who had done this many times before, he put the cigarette to his lips and lit it as he laid back on his bed and inhaled deeply – blowing smoke out through his nose. He got up, put out the cigarette and walked out of the room – closing the door behind him.

He went into the kitchen and found his dad and stepmother in quiet conversation. "Probably about me," he thought to himself. "They're probably already thinking about how they can get rid of me as soon as possible. It's all a game – a big f'ing game," he said under his breath.

When Gregory and Doris looked up from their conversation as Charlie entered the room, Charlie put on his biggest smile and said, "Hey, the room is great! Thank you for going to all the trouble for me."

"We're glad that you like it, Charlie," said his dad.

Charlie walked out of the house. Before the door closed, he looked back and said, "Dad, could you buy a lock for my door? I have never had a locked room before. Since this is my room, I want to be able to keep unwanted people out."

"Well, Charlie, we are all one big family here. There is no need for locked doors."

Charlie gave his dad a questioning look and said, "Dad, is it my room or not? You and Doris said it was my room. If it is my room, I want to be able to lock my door and protect my stuff."

"Well, okay son. If it's something you really want, that's what we'll do."

Charlie smiled and said, "Thanks, Dad. You're the best." Walking away from the house, Charlie smiled to himself, and said, "Just one day and I already have them eating my out of my hand."

As Doris watched Charlie walk down the street, she felt a little chill go up her spine. She turned to Gregory and said, "Does he always act like that, Gregory?"

Gregory said, "You know it seems like I hardly really know him at all. His behavior seemed peculiar to me too."

Chapter 11 - The Real Charlie Hidden, 1956

Charlie walked up to Cunningham's, a nearby drug store. He walked around the store touching this item, holding that item. After 15 minutes, he walked out the door with half of the items he touched or held in the pockets of his pants and coat. The lady behind the counter making chocolate shakes looked at him as he walked by, but Charlie just gave her a big smile, which she returned, and kept on walking. "This is going to be so much easier than living in the orphanage where they look at you suspiciously all the time," thought Charlie.

Charlie hid all of the items that he had taken from the store under the bed and in his closet. They were officially his now, because this was his room and everything having to do with his room was his – including the lock that his dad had put on the door while Charlie was "shopping." Charlie felt secure in his room. His dad showed him the box that the doorknob and lock system came in. The box said that it contained two keys. Charlie had both of the keys. What Charlie didn't know, and his dad didn't tell him, is that Gregory had a third key cut for the door just in case he needed access into the room.

Charlie looked around his room. Now that his room was secure, he could make the changes to his room that he desired. First, he moved everything to the center of the room so that he could access the walls. Then he proceeded to rip the wallpaper from the walls, piece, by piece, by piece. He threw the wallpaper into a corner of the room where no furniture was going to go.

Charlie walked quietly out of his room, locking the door as he left. He tiptoed into the kitchen, which he found empty. He grabbed a handful of Doris's steak knives from a drawer. With the knives, he returned to his room and locked his door. He pushed the bed into the middle of the wall where it had been in the corner before. No way was he going to be trapped in a corner of a room. On both sides of the bed, about a 1/3 of the way up the wall, he stuck one of the steak knives. He put a small desk and chair against a sidewall and again stuck steak knives into the wall on both sides of the desk. Another knife was put in the wall by the light switch. One knife went under his mattress. If anyone tried to come in and take anything away from him, they were going to pay a price for the intrusion.

Charlie had always wanted to protect himself like this at St. Mathew's where children stole from each other in the middle of the night all the time, but St. Mathew's had "rules" for everything, and one rule prohibited protecting yourself in this manner.

But this room was his room, and he would do with it as he wished to do. He had one more steak knife. He walked into his stepbrother's room and carefully placed it under his mattress, near the end of the bed.

That evening Doris tried to find her favorite steak knives. They weren't to be found anywhere. "Gregory," she called out, "have you seen my steak knives? The ones with the brown, wooden handles?"

"No, I haven't, but they must be around somewhere. Things like that don't just get up and walk away."

"Could you ask Charlie if he used them for anything?" Gregory went to open Charlie's door and found it locked. A little disgusted, Gregory called through the door and asked Charlie if he had seen Doris's steak knives. Charlie stepped out from behind the door, just opening the door enough to peek through.

"Why are you asking me, Dad?"

"Well, Mom just thought you might have used them for some reason and asked me to ask you. That's all."

"Did she ask you to ask the other kids first? Or did she ask you to check with me first because I'm the orphan, and orphan's steal?"

"Now wait a second, Charlie. Don't make a big deal out of this, because it is a simple question. Did you use the steak knives for anything?"

"Steak knives, Dad? Why would I use steak knives? Check with Bobby, I thought I saw him with something sharp today. Maybe he got into the knives." To get the attention off of his room, Charlie closed the door and began walking toward Bobby's room. His dad followed him.

Charlie and Gregory began searching Bobby's room. Charlie purposefully stayed away from where he had placed the knife. "Good grief," he heard his dad say. When Charlie looked at his dad, his dad was holding the steak knife that Charlie had hid under Bobby's bed. His dad, said under his breath, "Now, what the hell was Bobby doing with this?"

That night Bobby said over and over again, "I swear, Dad, I have no idea how that knife got in my room or under my bed." Bobby got so aggressive in his protests of innocence that Gregory spanked him with his hand for lying.

28

Gregory said, "Stealing knives and lying about it is a big thing, Bobby. I don't ever want to catch you stealing and lying to me again, or I will take the belt to you. Gregory stormed out of Bobby's room, leaving Bobby sobbing on the floor.

While Bobby was being spanked, Charlie had gone back into his room, locked the door, grabbed one of the knives and carved into the wall, "My dad is a fool. Doris is too, and Bobby is a bad boy." He laughed to himself on how witty he was.

When he heard his dad slam the door to Bobby's room, Charlie opened his door quietly, stepped out of his room locking the door behind him and stole down to Bobby's room. He knocked quietly on the door. Bobby, not having a lock, said, "Come in," hoping that it wouldn't be Gregory. He was relieved when Charlie's face peered in the room. Bobby motioned for Charlie to come in. Charlie sat down beside Bobby, who was only nine, and rubbed his hair with his hand. "I am sorry you had to go through all of that, Bobby. I know that you didn't put the knife under the bed."

Bobby said, "If you knew I didn't do it, why didn't you tell dad?"

Surprised by this aggression from Bobby, Charlie got right into the younger boy's face and said, "Listen, you piece of crap, I'm in charge here, and you'll do whatever I damn well ask you to do, or I will get even with you so bad that you'll be afraid to leave your room. Is that clear?"

Bobby was terrified, but he put on a bold face and said, "Why should I be afraid of you?"

Charlie's voice softened to almost a whisper, and he said, "I grew up in an orphanage, Bobby. I had to fight to survive. Do you know how I survived?"

Bobby shook his head slowly.

"I survived because I was the meanest, toughest son of a bitch in the orphanage, Bobby. That's how I survived. You know how I know that you didn't put the knife under your bed, Bobby? I know because I did it.

Do you know why I did it? Because I knew dad would blame you and possibly beat the crap out of you. That's why I did it. He's my dad, and he'll always believe me before he believes a stepson like you."

Bobby's eyes widened, and he asked, "Why would you want him to hurt me? I never did anything to you."

"Because I don't like kids like you, Bobby. You have never had to go without anything, have you? You have always had your mommy to love you, haven't you? I never had anything. I have always lived in fear, and I will do whatever it takes to make you live in fear too. I want you to be afraid. Afraid of your sister. Afraid of your mommy (he said with derision) and, most of all, embarrassed and afraid to be with your friends. I don't give a crap about you, Bobby, so don't make me do something you'll regret. And, Bobby, just like the knife I put in your room, I am capable of anything. Remember that. Anything."

Bobby shook his head knowingly.

"From now on, Bobby, when I say get something, you get it. When I say give me something, you give it, or I will really hurt you. Is that clear?"

"Yes," said Bobby.

"And, Bobby, if you ever tell anyone about what we are talking about right now, I will bury you. Have I made myself clear?"

Bobby nodded his head slowly, but in full understanding of what Charlie was saying. And he was afraid.

Charlie got up and went back to his own room, where he locked the door behind him and thought of how he would test Bobby's loyalty. He then got out his knife and scratched the following notes into the wall - "Bobby is a thief;" "Bobby likes little boys;" and "Bobby is under my thumb."

Chapter 12 - The Real Charlie Exposed, 1956

The next morning Doris made blueberry pancakes and called Bobby, Jamie and Charlie into the kitchen to eat breakfast.

Doris asked how everyone slept and other questions to try to get the kids to talk. Jamie and Charlie were very talkative and Charlie laughed like he didn't have a care in the world. Bobby just picked at his food, which surprised Doris, because Bobby loved blueberry pancakes.

"Bobby, are you sick? You are hardly eating anything? You love blueberry pancakes. Just try a couple of bites, and you'll want me to make another batch just for you."

"I guess I'm just not hungry, Mom."

"Well, if you say you aren't hungry, shoot those babies over to me!" Charlie exclaimed. "I'm as hungry as a horse!"

Without a second's hesitation, Bobby slid his plate over to Charlie, and Charlie wolfed the pancakes down like he hadn't eaten in days. "Thanks, little brother, that was so kind of you."

Bobby didn't look up. He simply asked his mom if he could be excused from the table.

After breakfast, Doris went to Bobby's room and asked if he was okay. Bobby said he was, "Just feeling a little tired, Mom." So, she left her son alone to rest. But she had a feeling that Charlie was behind all this, so she went to his room and knocked on the door. "Charlie," she called several times before he came to the other side of the door.

"Yes? What do you want, Doris?"

"Charlie, I want to come in and talk. Would you please let me in?"

"I'm busy, Doris. Can you come back later?" Charlie said as he carved on the wall, "Doris is a bitch, but she makes good pancakes."

"Charlie, I want to talk right now!"

"Geez, Doris, I'm not dressed. You don't want to see your little stepson naked, do you?"

"Get some clothes on and come to the door."

"No, Doris. I will not get some clothes on and come to the door. Go away!!"

Doris went to get the key to Charlie's door. Something was going on and she was going to find out what it was. She turned the key in the lock and turned the knob but Charlie had pushed his desk in front of the door and the door wouldn't budge. Doris decided to not do anything more until Gregory got home.

"So, the bitch has a key," Charlie said to himself. "The lying bitch said it was my room, but how can it be my room if the bitch has a key?"

Chapter 13 - The Eastside Standoff, 1956

When Gregory came home, Doris filled him in on what happened that day. About the pancakes, Bobby's reaction to Charlie, and Charlie not letting her in his room. Gregory went to Charlie's door and told him to open the door. "I want to talk about what happened between you and Mom today."

Charlie opened the door a crack, smiled at his dad and said, "Dad, she ain't my mom. She'll never be my mom. She's your wife, and that's all she is. Don't try to make me think she's my mom."

"Excuse me, son," Gregory shot back, "she may not be your mom, but you will show respect to her. Do you understand?"

"Excuse me, son?" Charlie retorted. "How can you say that with a straight face? All these years I was stuck in an orphanage to rot, and I'm supposed to all of a sudden be your loving son?"

Gregory was almost speechless. The hatred that spewed from Charlie was almost unimaginable. How could his son talk to him like that? What had happened to his little boy? What kind of evil had they brought into their house? Gregory looked at Charlie and said, "I don't get what going on Charlie."

"What do you mean, Dad?"

"We never had problems like this at our home, Charlie. You have been living with me for four years. You're acting like I just took you out of St. Mathews yesterday."

"It's different here. There is competition!" Charlie screamed.

"What competition, Charlie?"

Dad, don't you see? Her children. They are competition."

Doris had come close to Gregory while Gregory was having this exchange with Charlie. Shocked by the words and tone that were coming from Charlie, Doris whispered to Gregory, "I'm afraid of him, Gregory. Can you take him back to the St. Mathew's, or somewhere else out of our house?"

"Now, Doris…"

"No, Gregory, I think that he could be a danger to my children. I think he could be a danger to me. I want him out of here."

"Doris, let's just give it a while to calm down. He just came from a life of almost no freedom where he had nothing of his own. For the first time he is tasting freedom. This will run its course and be over with, you'll see. He's a good boy inside."

"Okay, but I am going to hold the reins tight on him, Gregory. I am not going to live in fear in my own house."

On the other side of the locked door, Charlie listened intently. He realized that he better cool it down or he could be sent back to St. Matthew's.

Chapter 14 - Life On The West Side, 1956

On the west side of Detroit, Josh, Maggie, Joey and Josh, Jr. were fairly happy although trouble was brewing on the horizon. When Josh, Jr. was born, Maggie contracted a staph infection at the hospital. The infection was so severe that she developed cysts all over her body. The staph infection left Maggie with scars on her skin that would never go away.

Josh had gotten emotionally and physically turned off by his wife's suffering. While he loved his wife, the cysts and the drainage from the cysts were more than he could handle. The two of them began to drift apart, and Maggie suspected that Josh was cheating on her.

At home, things were fine. Josh, Jr. was a beautiful boy with a gorgeous smile and a head-turning laugh. Joey loved his little brother and would play on the floor with him for what seemed to be hours. Joey would tickle him, blow on his belly, and wrestle on the floor with Josh, Jr. He would even take him for walks when Maggie would ask him to. After all, Joey was nine years old when Josh, Jr. was born, and that was certainly old enough to help his mother.

Joey was feeling much more comfortable in the home due to his tasks and friendships. Joey no longer had the problem with bed-wetting that he had when he first came to live with Josh and Maggie. Joey was beginning to believe that his great grandmother Luci had made a good decision after all.

Chapter 15 - The Con On The East Side, 1957

Things did calm down for a couple of weeks on the east side of the city. Charlie played with his new step-siblings and was respectful to his dad and Doris. Dad would come home to a far happier home than was previously the case. But Charlie did not have it in him to remain good for long.

Charlie began stealing the possessions of his step-siblings. He would always deny taking their things, but Doris knew something was up when she couldn't find their belongings anywhere. This kind of a problem never existed before Charlie came into the house, and it was just too much of a coincidence to think that Charlie wasn't involved. Doris just knew that if she could get into Charlie's room that all of the missing items would be found, but Charlie was spending most of his time locked in the room with his desk against the door now that he knew Doris and his dad had a key to his room.

One day Doris said that she was going to meet a lady friend for lunch and would be gone for a couple of hours. She left the house and parked her car around the corner from her house. Fifteen minutes had gone by when Doris saw Charlie come out of the front door of the house and walk down the street in the opposite direction from where she was parked.

Doris waited a few minutes to see if Charlie would turn around. When Charlie didn't, Doris drove back to her house. With key in hand, she opened Charlie's door. Charlie had moved the desk far enough away from the door so that he could squeeze out of the room, but Doris was bigger than Charlie, so the desk still partially blocked entry into the room. Doris pushed hard against the door, which moved the desk away far enough so that she could get in. She almost let out a scream when she saw the condition of the room. The wallpaper was stripped off and still laying in a corner of the room. All over the walls were written and carved angry comments about Joey, her children, and herself. She stooped low to look under the bed and saw many of her children's toys that had been missing.

Doris heard the door creek and saw Charlie standing in the doorway of the room. "What the hell are you doing in my room?" Charlie asked her in a low whisper. Rather than be defensive, Doris went on the attack. "It may be your room, Charlie, but this is our house. How dare you treat our house this way?"

Doris' verbal attack caused Charlie to pause, and Doris continued her assault. "What kind of kid are you, Charlie, to put all of these nasty comments about us all over the wall? What kind of perverse human being have you become?" Charlie flinched at this. Doris was so enraged that she grabbed a belt that was lying on the bed and began striking Charlie across the chest and arms, screaming, "I want you out of my house!"

Charlie put his arm up to protect himself from the sting of the belt. Then he grabbed Doris' arm and twisted it, causing the belt to fall to the floor. Twisting Doris' arm further, Charlie said, "Don't you ever touch me again, or I will beat you."

Gregory was just getting home from work when he heard the commotion in Charlie's room. Gregory ran into the room, saw Doris' arm being twisted by Charlie and struck Charlie across the face with the back of his hand – knocking the boy into a wall. Gregory pushed Doris out of the way, pushed Charlie to the floor and pinned him there until the fight was out of his son. As he was holding Charlie down, Gregory looked around the room and was disgusted with what Charlie had done to it. He saw the wallpaper on the floor, the writing on the wall and the knives strategically placed around the room – the knives that Charlie said his stepbrother had taken. He looked at Charlie and said, "My God, what a deceitful kid you are! You let your stepbrother take a beating from me knowing all the while that you had taken the knives!"

He told Doris to get the knives out of the room. When she did, he let Charlie get up from the floor. Gregory looked around the room in disgust. He said, "Charlie, I wanted this to work out. I never wanted to leave you in the orphanage as long as I did, but I didn't have the means to take you out earlier. I thought you understood that. But I can see that you have a level of hate for me that will never go away, and I don't see this ever working out. Doris doesn't trust you, for good reason, and doesn't want you here. And as much as I wanted you here, I don't want you here anymore either."

Gregory left the room to call Josh and Maggie to see if they would take Charlie in. This was a discussion that Gregory had been having with Josh and Maggie for a couple of weeks. Gregory had told Maggie and Josh that he was not ready to make the move yet because Charlie was acting better. But, he also promised Doris that if trouble began again, he would respect Doris'

36

concerns about her children and get Charlie out of the house. That time was now.

While Josh wasn't excited about it, Maggie wanted her family together. Maggie had convinced Josh that he could handle Charlie, because Josh was a Detroit cop and was used to dealing with hardened kids. Josh was also confident that he could control the child, even if he had to pistol-whip him to make him obey. That being said, Josh was not excited about taking Charlie in and only agreed to do it if he could handle Charlie his way, without any intervention from Maggie or Gregory. Maggie and Gregory both agreed.

The next day Charlie was on his way to a new house on the west side of Detroit. On the drive across the city, Charlie thought to himself, "Well, now at last I can get my hands on Joey."

Chapter 16 - Trouble Knocking On The Door, 1957

There was a knock on the front door. Joey looked through the curtain and saw his dad, who he could hardly remember, with an older boy who Joey did not recognize. Josh and Maggie invited them into the house, and Maggie began to cry as she went to her eldest son and smothered him with hugs and kisses. She sat down with Charlie on the couch. She looked at Joey, standing alone by the front door, and beckoned him to her other side on the couch. She sat there in tears with her arms wrapped around each boy sitting on either side of her. Charlie, now almost 13, was beaming with happiness while Joey had a look of confusion on his face. Maggie asked Josh to bring Josh, Jr. to her. When he did, Maggie burst into tears of joy. She had all of her children in her arms for the first time ever. This felt so good, so real, that she vowed to never see her children parted again. Her first and second husbands both looked on with tears in their eyes. It was difficult not to be touched by a mother's love for her children.

This is what nature intended, and the moment had finally come for Maggie.

Maggie said, "Children, from now on we are going to live together as a family. And nothing will ever break this family apart again. Nothing. We are all going to love and respect each other from this day on."

Charlie, though only two years older than Joey, was much taller and weighed much more than his younger sibling. Some of this was just the age difference, some of it could be genetics, but some of it could also be the lack of vitamin D that Grandmother Harriett had worried about when she thought that Joey had rickets at St. Mathews. Charlie took the size difference between himself and Joey as a badge of superiority over his younger brother.

In addition to the size differences between the two boys, Charlie's life experiences took his emotional age far beyond the two years that separated the chronological age difference between the two boys. Charlie had been forced to fight for everything he got. Charlie had a survival-of-the-fittest mentality. Because it was an eat-or-be-eaten environment at St. Mathews, Charlie had never developed any concept of tenderness. Accordingly, as we have seen, Charlie had become one tough kid and was a challenge for anyone who had taken responsibility for him.

As we have seen, Charlie had also developed a mean streak that was directed toward the world at large, an air of entitlement that was shown by an attitude of "the world owes me, because my life has been so bad." He also had developed a conniving nature that enabled him to shroud the mean streak and entitlement characteristics. His conniving ability enabled him to "play" others to get what he sought and take advantage of the weaknesses in others to control them and improve his own situation or give him the upper hand.

Charlie was very intimidating to Joey, and Joey became very concerned with surviving this social pariah who had entered their lives. It was not too long after

Charlie came into the home that Joey began to wet the bed again.

Third party reflection on what causes people to behave in a certain manner is a gift for those who are not in immediate threat of a destructive person or situation. Those who are in immediate threat of a situation are usually too busy trying to survive the person or situation to engage in philosophical questions on how this all came to be.

The characteristics that Charlie displayed were "survival" characteristics that were born out of being in the orphanage and having to fight for everything he wanted – necessities and niceties. Charles Darwin would say that they were natural instincts of someone who lived in a "survival of the fittest/eat or be eaten" environment.

Shortly after Charlie was brought into the home by Maggie and Josh, the warm, loving home that Joey's great grandmother hoped she was delivering Joey into took a step toward evaporation. Years later, Luci would die knowing that her decision to release custody of Joey had been a huge mistake.

One day, when Charlie and Joey were finishing lunch at the kitchen table, Charlie leaned over toward Joey and whispered, "I want your dessert, and if you don't give it to me, I will tell all of your friends that you wet the bed." Charlie had found Joey's weak spot. Joey did not want his bed-wetting problem to become known to his friends. So, Joey gave Charlie his dessert and many desserts thereafter. There began a long period of mistreatment that Joey endured because he didn't want his bed-wetting problem to be exposed. So much for his mother's assertion that from this day forward they will all love and respect each other.

When Joey did not cooperate to the degree that Charlie thought was appropriate, Charlie would make Joey hold out his hand (palm down) and rap the back of his hand with a stick that was 1 inch in diameter and 3 feet long. The stick was used for fishing clothes out of the washing machine before putting the clothes through a device called a wringer that squeezed the excess water out of the clothes, before hanging them up to dry. The pain that Joey felt from being hit by this stick was excruciating, but Joey would not cry out of fear that his mom or stepdad would hear.

Fear of having something exposed to the world can have a profound impact on one's life and how one chooses to live. The fear can make one do things that they are ashamed of but felt that they had to do it or the truth would come out. Joey and Charlie would often play baseball with kids in the neighborhood. The oldest, most athletic and dominant boys would be selected as captains and they would pick the members of their team one by one.

While Charlie was a big kid and accomplished in some sports, baseball was not a sport at which he was very good. He wasn't much of a hitter, couldn't catch and was a slower runner than most of the boys. Joey, on the other hand, was a pretty good ball player. He was only an average hitter, but he was a very good fielder. Put Joey in the outfield and if he could get to a ball, he would catch it. And Joey was fast so he could get to just about anything. It was as simple as that. If a ball was hit in the air to the outfield anywhere within striking distance of Joey, it was going to be caught.

One day Joey and Charlie were on opposing teams. Under his breath, Charlie said, "Joey, if I hit it in the air to the outfield, you damn well better not catch it, or else. The game began and the teams were playing good ball and having fun. Joey got a hit and helped the team score a run in the second inning. In the field, Joey was the combination of an eagle and a cat. Like an eagle he never lost sight of his prey, the ball, and like a cat. he swiftly would run his prey down and catch it.

Charlie struck out in the second inning and hit a soft ground ball to second and was thrown out in the fourth inning. In the sixth inning, Charlie got a solid hit that flew into right center field. Joey had a bead on the ball from time that it left Charlie's bat. He watched the trajectory of the ball and had a pretty good feel where it was going to descend and land. It would be a running catch but there was no doubt in Joey's mind that he could catch the ball, and his team had confidence that it would be caught as well. As he extended his glove to catch the ball he remembered Charlie's admonition and pushed his glove forward just enough so that the ball bounced off the heel of his glove and fell to the ground. Charlie scampered into second standing up for a double. Joey picked up the ball and threw it to the boy on third. Charlie was jumping up and down for joy that he had gotten a double, but Joey's team was livid at Joey and said that he had dropped the ball on purpose, and if that was how the game was going to be played then they might as well just end the game now – which is what they did. Joey's fear that Charlie would tell his friends about Joey's bedwetting problem caused Joey not to do the right thing, which in this case was to catch the ball. The fact that he didn't catch the ball, or do the right thing, was costing him the respect of his friends anyway, and if it continued, soon Joey would have no friends. Fear can stop one in their tracks. Fear can make you go backward when you should be going forward. Fear can stop one from doing what can and should be doing. Fear can be the tether around your neck that destroys your life. And fear is what bullies use to control the people they want to have under their control. If we can't control our fear, our fear will control us.

Chapter 17 - Why All The Hate? 1958

One day Joey asked Charlie why he hated him so much, and why Charlie couldn't treat him nice like other older brothers treated their younger brothers. Charlie said, "You left me alone in the orphanage, Joey. I had no one after you went away. I will never forgive you for that."

Joey, said, "I was taken out by our great grandmother Luci when I was small, Charlie. How can you blame me for something that adults did to me when I was small? Grandma Harriett told Mom that if I couldn't get more food I could get a bone disease or possibly even die. Don't you understand that?"

"You are a liar, Joey! You wanted to leave so you asked to be taken out so I would be alone. You could have had great grandma Luci take me too! You wanted her all for yourself!! You didn't care for me. Why should I care for you?"

"I was a child, Charlie! I could not have stopped anyone from taking me away. Is that so hard for you to understand?"

Now Charlie really got angry, "Are you calling me stupid, Joey? Are you?" He rushed over to Joey and grabbed him by the neck before Joey could get away. Then he threw Joey against the wall of stair going into the basement. Joey hit his head and fell to the ground. Charlie then grabbed him by the throat and said menacingly, "What I understand is that you left me alone, Joey, and I'll never forgive you for that. And you even imply that I am stupid again, you'll live to regret it."

With tears in his eyes, Joey got up and said, "I didn't say you are stupid, but you sure as hell are a bully."

"Watch yourself you little bed wetter. Keep up this crap and all your friends will know by tomorrow morning that you wet the bed. And you better not say anything to mom and dad about how you got that bruise on your head."

Joey slumped to the floor after Charlie bounded up the stairs. "I need to do something," he said, "before he kills me."

Josh and Maggie seemed to be totally unaware that Joey's demeanor had changed since Charlie came into the family. Neither one of them ever asked Joey if everything was okay. Bruises on Joey's body, bruises that got there from Charlie, were explained away by Joey saying that he had fallen down the stairs or he had bumped into a wall. Joey was too afraid to go to his parents about how Charlie was treating him because he knew Charlie would find out that he had said something to them and would tell his friends about his bed-wetting. So, he kept quiet and endured.

"What if I kicked his ass in while he's sleeping?" Joey said to himself. "What if I tell my friends what a prick he is? Nothing but a damn bully? What if I just say I don't need or want friends, Charlie, so go tell them. I don't care."

One idea after another came into Joey's mind. All of them would make him a different person than what he wanted to be. Joey finally got up, went into the bathroom and washed the blood off of his face and went upstairs.

At dinner, Josh looked at Joey and said, "What happened to you?"

Joey looked up from eating his dinner and said, "I was riding on a gravel road and my bike slipped out from under me and I fell."

"Did you get bruises on your legs and arms too?"

"No, I had a long shirt on and blue jeans. I didn't get my hands up fast enough to avoid getting my face hurt."

"Well, you be careful, Joey."

Maggie said, "That seems to be happening a lot, Joey. You need to slow down and pay more attention."

"Yes, Mom. I'll try to be more careful."

"Maybe we need to send Charlie out with you to make sure you don't hurt yourself."

Joey said, "Nah, Charlie's has his own friends. I'll be more careful."

Charlie said, "I don't mind tagging along with you, Joey, to help keep you from getting hurt."

Without showing any emotion, anger or hatred, Joey looked at that conniving, dishonest, deceitful bastard. What a liar he was. And he did it with so much ease and deception. It was like Charlie was the Devil himself. Then he smiled and said, "Charlie, I know you love me and want to protect me, but I'll be fine. You have your

43

own friends." Joey was learning how to play Charlie's game. Joey had a fleeting thought that he might be becoming like his brother – like the good seed was being corrupted and being taken over by the bad seed.

Charlie smiled at Joey's answer and thought "I'm corrupting Mr. Goody Two Shoes." Then Charlie responded to Joey in a like manner, "Well, little brother, that's what big brothers are for." Then he added, "This is a great meal, Mom." After which he smiled at Joey as if to say "That's how a pro does it"

Josh said, "I like seeing you boys getting along so well. Keep it up."

Eating his pork and beans, Joey wondered how he could ever get out of this and would his parents ever recognize the truth of what was going on under the roof of their home.

As if Charlie could read Joey's mind, he gave Joey a hard kick to shin, while smiling at Josh and asking, "How was your day today, Dad?"

Yes, Charlie was a professional at this game.

Chapter 18 - An Incident at Cunningham's Drug Store, Fall 1958

Joey was reading in his bedroom when he heard Charlie call out, "Mom, Joey and I are going to go up to Cunningham's and get a chocolate shake."

"OK, Charlie. Watch out for your little brother and be good."

"I always watch out for Joey, Mom."

"I know you do, Charlie. You are a very loving brother."

"I try to be, Mom."

Charlie walked down the hall and knocked on Joey's door.

"Hey, Joey, are you ready to go to Cunningham's?

Joey said, "I don't want to go, Charlie. I just want to stay home and read."

Charlie opened the door and said, "I'm not asking, Joey. Get your shit on."

Joey slammed his book shut and got to his feet.

Charlie came across the room and grabbed him by the hair and said, "Don't give me any attitude, Joey. I'm not in the mood."

"Owww!" Joey screamed out.

Maggie called from the kitchen, "Boys, what's going on in there?"

Charlie gestured to Joey and said, "Say something and make it good."

Joey called back, "Nothing Mom. Just playing around with my big brother."

"We're going now, Mom," Charlie added.

"Ok, Be back by 6:00 for dinner."

They got their bikes out of the garage and headed up the street. As they got near Cunningham's, Charlie pulled ahead of Joey and said, "Follow me."

Joey followed Charlie, who went to an alley behind Cunningham's. "We are leaving our bikes here."

"Why?" asked Joey.

"Don't ask why. Just do as I say. We are leaving them here, going into Cunningham's and getting a chocolate shake."

Joey said, "OK, I like that."

"After we have our shake, we are going to split up. I am going back to look at the records and you are going to take a battery-operated car in the toy section."

"What, steal it?" Joey asked.

"Yah, steal it," replied Charlie.

"Charlie, I can steal something. That's a mortal sin, and I don't want to go to Hell."

"You're not going to go to Hell for taking a $25.00 car, Joey. Anyway, you are just a kid and didn't know better."

"But I do know better, Charlie. Stealing is a mortal sin. I can't do that."

"Joey, you can and you will do that or I'll kick your ass in and tell your friends that you wet the bed."

Things had really gotten out of hand. Joey said, "Go ahead and tell my friends, Charlie. I won't steal for you."

"Dammit, Joey. You will do that or I will. But I am older and they'll be watching me more. If I get caught, I'll tell Mom and Dad that you begged me to take it because you wanted the car."

"I'll tell them you're a liar."

"They won't believe you, Joey. I am a much better liar than you are, and Mom likes me better than you anyway."

"She does not, Charlie. She likes us the same. She told me so."

"Of course, she is going to say that, you dumb-ass. All parents say that. But Mom has always felt guilty for not fighting to get custody of me. And she has always felt bad that I was kept at St. Mathew's so long, so she will believe me over you any time."

In his heart Joey knew that what Charlie said was true. He had sensed the difference in how his mom talked and dealt with Charlie. Charlie was the preferred son. He was trapped.

As they entered the Cunningham's, Charlie said, "So, you'll do it?"

"I'll try,"

The Cunningham's had a separate part of the store near the front where they offered breakfast, sandwiches, and ice cream. There was a large counter with stools and booths around the perimeter of the restaurant. The boys took a seat at the counter and ordered their milk shakes. Joey was so worried about what they were going to do that he hardly enjoyed his shake. After they were finished, they walked into the main part of the store and Charlie said loudly, "I am going to check out the records in back." Several store clerks looked at Charlie as he strolled to the back of the store. No one looked at Joey.

Joey went over to the toy aisle and found the car that Charlie wanted. Though he was afraid, Joey stuffed the box under his coat and headed for the door.

A store clerk called out, "Hey, you kids!!" Charlie came up behind Joey and said, "Run and fast!" They ran through the front door, made a quick left turn and ran down the side of the building toward the alley. Joey's heart was beating in his chest as Charlie ran behind him. They darted into the alley, and Charlie said, "Throw it behind the dumpster, get on your bike and follow me." Joey did as he was told and the two of them rode down the alley. As they were getting up to full speed on their bikes, the backdoor of Cunningham's store opened and several clerks came out and briefly gave chase on foot. But, the boys were too fast and the chase soon stopped.

The boys turned right on a sidewalk that led to an apartment complex that was in back of the strip center, and they were gone.

They made it home in time for dinner, but Joey said he felt sick and wanted to go to lay down. He was excused from the dinner table, went into his room and prayed to God that when he died God would not send him to Hell.

After dinner Josh came down the hall and heard talking coming from Joey's room. He stopped to listen and heard Joey talking to God to forgive him.

"That's curious," Josh said to himself. Then he heard Joey burst into tears. Josh opened the door and entered the room. Joey was on his knees on the side of the bed praying and crying.

"Joey, what is it? Is everything Ok?"

Joey thought, caught. Now what do I say? How much did he hear? Joey said, "I did something really bad today, and I was praying to God to not use what I did as a reason to keep me out of Heaven."

"Well, I'd say it must have been pretty bad if you are concerned that it will keep you out of Heaven."

Joey nodded.

Josh asked, "Was it something that involved your trip to Cunningham's?"

Joey's heart began to beat very fast. He knows. He's a policeman, and somehow, he found out.

"Joey, you can tell me. What did you do that was so bad?"

Got to think! Got to think, Joey thought. What came out was kind of ingenious. "When we were riding home a cat was running across the street. I hit it with my bike and killed it."

Josh said, "And that is what you are worried about? That God will blame you for killing the cat and keep you out of Heaven?"

Joey nodded.

"Did you mean to kill the cat or was it an accident?"

"An accident," Joey said.

"Accidents are part of life, Joey. Everyone has accidents. If God kept everyone who had an accident out of Heaven, there wouldn't be anyone in Heaven."

Joey probably should have stopped right there, but he couldn't; his guilt was too great. "What if I did a bad thing like that on purpose?"

"Did you?" Josh asked.

"No. But, what if I did?"

"Well, I think that if you did a bad thing on purpose, like kill an animal or a person, or hurt them, or steal something from someone, you may have something to worry about, unless you have asked God for forgiveness."

"Praying is asking for forgiveness," Joey said.

Josh looked at Joey close and said, "But, in the case of an accident like what you described, you don't need to be forgiven by God because you didn't do it on purpose. Right?"

"Right!" Joey said.

Josh got up, tussled Joey's hair and said, "You worry too much about these things, Joey. You are a good kid. Make sure that you stay that way. Don't allow yourself to be pushed into doing bad things."

Joey nodded.

"Do you know why, Joey?" Joey had a blank look on his face, and Josh said, "Because if you keep on doing bad things over and over again, God may not believe that your prayers are sincere and may not forgive you. Then you could be in real trouble. Understand?"

Joey nodded and said, "I understand."

"Good," Josh said and left the room.

Joey sat on the edge of his bed and knew that he had to learn to stand up to Charlie.

Charlie came into the room. "What was that all about? Did you tell him?"

"No, I said that I was upset because I ran over a cat."

"Ran over a cat? That's a good one, Joey. And he believed it?"

Joey frowned and nodded.

"Little brother you're getting to be almost as good of a liar as I am. I'm going to check on the dumpster. Let's go."

"I can't. Josh said I had to stay home."

"Sneak out the window. He'll never know."

"No, I can't."

"Suit yourself." Charlie closed the door and left.

"This lying gets easier and easier the more you do it," Joey said to himself.

Charlie rode his bike up to Cunningham's. It was getting a little dark, and he felt pretty sure that no one would notice him. He sat his bike down and walked behind the dumpster where he had seen Joey throw the box. There was nothing there. He got down on his hands and knees and looked under the dumpster. Nothing. Then two strong hands grabbed him from behind and pulled him to his feet.

"Are you looking for this?" The man had a badge on that said "Store Security," and he was holding up the box that contained the battery car so coveted by Charlie.

"Get your hands off of me, man. I don't know what you're talking about!" Another store employee had moved behind Charlie, still behind the dumpster. There was no way out, so the best defense was a good offense.

The security man said, "Oh, you don't know what I'm talking about, huh? I'm talking about you and another little creep taking this car and tossing it behind the dumpster before riding away on your bikes."

"This is the first time that I've been up here all day." Charlie continued his offense.

"Then what are you doing here looking behind this dumpster?"

Charlie said without a stutter or mis-step, "My friends and I were playing catch in the apartments in back and our ball went over the fence so I rode my bike over to find it. Do you have it?"

The security officer looked at the other store employee and said, "Is he one of the boys who ran out of the store?"

The store employee said, "It all happened so fast. I'm not sure."

"Look, man, it's getting late and I've got homework to do. All I want is to get my ball and go home. If you have my ball would you please give it back to met?"

The security officer's case was breaking down by the second. He turned to the store employee and asked, "Do you know anything about his damn ball? I don't have it?"

The store employee shrugged his shoulders and said he didn't know anything about a ball or see a ball.

The officer said, "Take him inside and let him pick out a ball."

As the three of them went into the store, Charlie said, "I am really thirsty can I have a chocolate shake too?"

The store employee looked at the security officer who nodded.

"And since you've kept me here so late, it's dark. I'm going to need a flashlight to get home."

The security officer said snidely, "Would you like a bag, too?"

"No sir. Just the flashlight." Charlie rode home on his bike slurping down a chocolate shake, with a baseball in one pocket and a flashlight in the other. All in all it was a good trip to Cunningham's, he thought to himself.

Chapter 19 - Stealing Money and Playing With Guns, 1959

Josh had a closet in the basement where he would hang his police uniform and put his wallet and other belongings – including his police revolver. Charlie would steal whatever money he thought he could get away with and play with Josh's police revolver. Charlie would pick up the revolver and twirl it on his index finger like he was Clint Eastwood starring in a spaghetti Western movie. There was never an accident, but Joey lived in fear that he would get shot by Charlie.

Josh got wise one day that money was being taken from the closet, so he took a number of coins that he had counted out and put them in his coin drawer in the closet. He placed his gun with a piece of paper propped against the trigger and went upstairs to bed. The following morning, Charlie took some of the money and played around a little bit with the gun, oblivious to the fact that it was a set-up.

Later that morning Josh went to the closet, saw that the gun had been moved and money was missing. He called the boys downstairs and asked them about the money and the gun. Joey honestly said that he didn't touch the money or the gun. Josh then turned to Charlie who also said he didn't know anything about the money or gun.

Josh removed his belt, bent down and looked Joey straight in the eye. "I know that money was taken, and I know someone was playing with my gun. I know it, period. I didn't take my money, your mom didn't take my money, and Josh Jr., sure as hell didn't take the money. So, that leaves only one of the two of you." Joey was scared out of his mind, but he was struck by the logic of how Josh reached his conclusion.

Josh then added, "If I don't find out who did it, I am going to whip both of you. Now, Joey did you touch the gun and take the money or do you know anything about it?" Joey knew that Charlie had taken the money and had played with the gun. He did not want to get beaten, but he was more afraid of Charlie than he was their stepdad. He gulped deeply and looked at Charlie.

"Don't look at Charlie. Look at me," Josh said jabbing his finger into Joey's chest.

"Dad, I don't know anything about it," he lied, trembling down to his bare feet.

Josh knew that Joey was lying and did not want to include Joey in the whipping, so he said, "Joey, I will whip you both if you don't tell me the truth," Josh warned – giving Joey one more chance to get out of a whipping. Joey just stood there trembling.

"Charlie, same question. Who stole my money and played around with my gun? Was it you?" Josh knew it was.

Charlie put on his most sincere and choirboy face and denied having any knowledge of the money or the gun. Josh's hand reached out and grabbed Charlie by the arm faster than a snake strikes its prey. Holding Charlie by the arm, Josh reared back and began whipping the boy with his police belt on his back and arms. Charlie ran in circles with Josh holding onto his arm, but he could not shake the hand that held him or the sting of the belt. It was Joey's turn next and rather than face punishment from Charlie, Joey took the punishment that Josh meted out until welts could be seen on the arms, legs and backs of both boys. Josh felt guilt about including Joey in the beating, but he had to break the cycle that he saw beginning.

Josh started up the stairs, turned around and glared at both of them and said, "You ever touch my crap again, the next time will make this look like a walk in the park."

When Josh got upstairs he told Maggie that he had to punish the boys and why.

Maggie had a hard time believing that Joey would do anything like that, but after hearing about what went on between Gregory and Doris and Charlie, she was not too sure that Charlie wouldn't steal from Josh and play with his gun.

Josh said, "You mark my words, Maggie, if that boy doesn't change his course and stop blaming things that happened to him in the past, he is going to end up in Jackson Prison."

"That's a hell of a thing to say, Josh."

"And it gives me no pleasure to say it, Maggie. The boy has a chip on his shoulder as big as a rock. I've seen these kids before. Kids who think the world owes them a living. Shit, I deal with them every day. They think they are so cool, so big and tough, but they' are nothing but punks. Charlie is one bad seed. What he will grow into won't be pretty, unless he gets his act under control."

Chapter 20 - Joey Runs Away, August 1959

Getting whipped like that for something that he didn't do and living in constant fear of Charlie, Joey got to the point that he trembled and quaked in the home his great grandmother thought would be his salvation. Things got so bad that one day Joey, at the age of 12, packed some clothes and food in a paper bag, snuck out the door and ran away. He had no particular plan in mind; he just knew he couldn't stay in the house another day. Leaving was a matter of self-preservation. He trudged down to Plymouth Road and was heading east into the city of Detroit. He passed Brennan Pools when it hit him just how stupid he was being. He had no money, little food, few clothes, no place to go, and no place to stay. It was getting dark, and he was afraid.

Joey turned back and found himself in a residential neighborhood. It was after 10:00 p.m., but he knocked on the front door of a small home. The porch light came on, then the door opened a little bit and two elderly people (a man and a woman) looked down at the small 12-year-old boy standing there with his paper bag of stuff. "It's late," the man said, "what do you want?"

With tears in his eyes and a tremble in his voice, Joey told the couple that things were really bad at home, and he was running away, but now he was scared and wanted to call his stepdad and go home.

The kindly couple let him come in and showed him to the phone. Joey called his stepdad and tried to talk in a whisper, because he was so embarrassed. He gave the address to his stepdad who said that he would come and get him.

The woman had gone into the kitchen and came back with a glass of milk and cookies for Joey. He thanked her and ate quietly, waiting for Josh to come.

The woman said, "Is there anything we can do for you?"

Joey said, "No."

"How bad is it at your home?"

Her kindness caused Joey to start crying, and he told what had been happening with his older brother. She came and put her arm around Joey as he talked, but that just made him cry more, because it reminded him of the life that he had with his great grandma Luci, and the love that she would show.

A car pulled up and then came a knock on the door. It was his stepdad in his police uniform. He talked with the family for a while and heard what Joey had told them. Then he thanked them for helping Joey, got Joey in the car, and left for home.

Joey shook uncontrollably in the passenger seat of the car. Josh said, "Well, that was sure embarrassing.

Why didn't you tell me you were having these problems with Charlie?"

Joey told Josh that he was more afraid of being beaten by Charlie than he was of Josh. He also told Josh about Charlie's threats to tell his friends that he wet the bed.

"Well, you are kind of old to be still wetting the bed, Joey. If you stop doing that, then Charlie won't have anything to hold over your head. I will talk to Charlie, Joey, but don't ever pull a stunt like this again."

And that was it. For whatever reason, Josh did not sit down with Charlie and read him the riot act. He kind of let it go. Because the abuse continued and the threats from Charlie did too. No magic wand was waved to make Charlie stop the abuse of Joey. Joey, more than ever, thought that he was alone in this situation with Charlie, because, to Joey, the fact that he had a bed-wetting problem shouldn't matter. How Charlie was treating him was the issue. Regardless of the reason, Joey did not deserve to be treated this way by anyone. And the fact that Josh didn't see it and try to stop it, made Joey believe that Josh didn't care. Was his mother in that category too? The thought that his mom might not care what happened to him, scared the daylights out of Joey. He knew his mother loved Charlie more than she loved him, but he thought his mother would protect him.

Chapter 21 - Devil's Night, 1959

When things are closing in on you, sometimes you look for any reason to have fun. Friends asked Joey to go out with them on devil's night, the night before Halloween, to ring doorbells and soap windows. These were things that all kids did at the time. While cleaning up any mess was troublesome for the homeowners or car owners, the kids were generally regarded as "just having a little fun." Nothing serious.

There was a house in the neighborhood where the

father would chase the kids if kids knocked on the door. That was a destination point in the neighborhood for those who knew the man's behavior. Joey and his friends all went to the house and knocked and knocked and knocked. They knocked on the doors, the windows - harder and harder until a large picture window broke. That wasn't supposed to happen, and the boys scattered in all directions.

Joey was running across a parking lot of a nearby monastery when he heard feet pounding on the pavement behind him. The person behind him was bigger and faster than Joey was. He caught up with Joey and tackled him to the ground. Joey knew the tackler. He was an altar boy from Joey's church. The tackler knew Joey too. He knew that Joey was soon to make his Confirmation as a member of the church. Joey and his friends had soaped the windows of the altar boy's house earlier in the evening. The altar boy had been on their trail ever since.

He dragged Joey back to the house with the broken window and rang the doorbell – calling out to the people inside. After a few minutes of quiet knocking on the door, a woman and two small children came to the door. They were in tears. While Joey and his friends had been banging on the door, the woman and her children hid in a back bedroom of the home. They had no idea why people had been banging on their door and were terrified. The woman's husband was on a business trip out of town.

Joey cleaned up the mess and told them how sorry he was for what they had done. Joey said that they were just out trying to have fun, but things got out of hand. The altar boy who tackled Joey drove him home and threatened to tell the priest and Joey's parents if Joey ever did anything like that again. Joey told him he wouldn't, then Joey crept into the house and went to bed in fear that the altar boy would tell his stepdad or the priest. The altar boy never did. "Thank God!" Joey thought later. "What a whipping that would have been."

56

It has often been said that a family does not raise their children alone – the whole community often takes a part in raising children. The mailman, the old man next door, the clerk at the local drug store, can all be teachers. In Joey's case, that night a woman with two scared children and an altar boy from his church were his teachers and helped him grow up to be the person he became.

Chapter 22 - Joey Reveals The Truth, December 28, 1959

Gregory had gone through a messy divorce from Doris and was living in a small home on the east side of the city. Near Christmas, Gregory called Maggie and asked if he could have Joey for a week or so over the Christmas holiday, and Maggie said, "Yes." Father and son had one whole week together. One week where Joey did not have to think about the troubles at home. The night before he was to go home, Joey and his dad sat in the kitchen eating cookies and drinking milk.

A tentativeness in Joey's demeanor concerned Gregory, and he asked Joey if everything was okay at home. Joey didn't want to say anything because of how Josh had behaved when Joey ran away and told the older couple what was going on at his home, but the warm encouragement of his father caused Joey to tell everything about what was going on at his house. As Joey talked and cried, Gregory took notes. After about an hour, they stopped, and Gregory said he was going to call Joey's mother.

Joey panicked, "Please, Dad, don't say anything to Mom or Josh! I will just get into trouble for telling you." Tears dropped from Joey's eyes, and his dad held him close and said, "Joey, what is happening is wrong. It has to stop. I cannot allow it to continue."

The next morning, Gregory called Maggie and talked about the abuse going on in her house. Maggie was truly shocked, but at the same time she was defensive because her former husband was telling her something that she should have seen – and didn't.

When Gregory brought Joey home, all five of them – Gregory, Maggie, Josh, Charlie and Joey, talked about Joey's charges. Charlie glared at Joey from across the room, and Josh took on an attitude of "boys will be boys." Maggie, knowing that something had been going on but not wanting to believe it, looked at Charlie with a pained expression. Had the divorce or her behavior caused Charlie to become the way he was? She did not want to believe it, and she didn't want to believe the accusations that Joey had made against Charlie.

After Gregory left, Maggie, who was very embarrassed by the discussion that they had just had with Gregory, said, "Joey, you can go to your room."

Josh piped in, "And Charlie, you can go outside." With the living room cleared except for Josh, Jr., Maggie said, "I can't believe what I just heard, Josh. I know that Charlie is kind of a tough kid because of his background, but I have a hard time believing that he is the monster that Joey is saying he is. Is it possible that Joey is lying?"

Josh said, "Well, I know that Joey has lied to me. I never told you this, but when I realized that money was missing from my closet and someone was playing with my gun, Joey said he didn't know anything about it. But he did know. He knew it was Charlie. He sat there and looked me in the face and told me he knew nothing."

No consideration was given by Josh or Maggie to the possibility that maybe Joey had lied out of fear of Charlie.

Later that day, Maggie, Charlie and Joey all went to get ice cream. Joey was about to get in the front seat with his mom, but Maggie quickly said, "Oh, no. Joey, you get in the back seat. Charlie, you come up here with me." Both boys knew exactly what that meant. Things were not going to be any different tomorrow from what they were like yesterday. Joey's heart sank. Before Mom got into the car, Charlie turned around in his seat and quickly brought his index finger across his neck. Joey was screwed. The worst of it was that there was nothing that anyone of power and authority in his life was willing to do to protect him from his older, much bigger and abusive brother. Any relief from punishment that Joey was going to experience would be from running away from the problem or confronting the problem directly, which could have dire consequences. For the time being Joey thought that the best path to take was to just be a part of Charlie's fan club. Laugh at his jokes, do what he did, support and serve his wishes to the best of Joey's ability.

Chapter 23 - Altercation At Church, 1960

Joey had a deep regard for propriety in church. Due to the upbringing of his great grandmother, Joey attended church on a regular basis – each Sunday. Josh, Maggie and Charlie would generally go to church on special holidays like Easter or Christmas. But otherwise, they were not inclined to go. One Sunday, Charlie told Joey that he would go with him. On this particular Sunday, the church was installing a new priest for the outgoing priest who was retiring. All of the pews were taken. Ushers were directing church members to go down the center and the two side aisles where they would be standing for the entirety of the service.

As the mass progressed Charlie realized that it was going to be an extra-long service and began pressing Joey to walk to the front of the church and leave the service through the side door. The badgering began during the new priest's homily. While most of the members of the church were paying rapt attention to the priest's message, a half dozen babies were crying and Charlie was badgering Joey to leave.

Joey whispered for Charlie to keep quiet, that he was not going anywhere and Charlie was disturbing parishioners who were trying to hear the priest. Charlie put his hand on Joey's shoulder and said in a voice too loud for a quiet church:

"Joey, I swear to God, if you don't walk out that door in two minutes, I am going to make your life a living hell."

"Shhhh," came from the parishioners around them.

Joey whispered, "I'm not leaving, Charlie. You want to leave, leave."

Charlie said, "You'll be sorry." He turned around and went back to the main entry to the church. On the way to the exit, Charlie passed by a donation box for the outgoing priest's retirement. There was no one there, so he took the opportunity to tip the money in the box into his pocket and was out the door. It is said that the honesty of an individual is measured by how they behave when no one is around.

Chapter 24 - Charlie Fights Lloyd, 1960

Charlie and Joey were at the playground of Healy School in Detroit. They were going on the swings and playing on the Jungle Gym, which had a number of curved vertical and horizontal bars that kids could climb on. Truth be told, Charlie at 15 was a little on the big side to be going on the playground equipment. Joey was 13, so he was fine. They were having fun with other kids around Joey's age when something that Joey did, who knows what it was, a look, a smile, a gesture, whatever, set Charlie off and he began to push Joey around. It was almost like he was trying to make his younger brother look foolish in front of the other children. It continued until Joey said, "You've taken all the fun out of being here, Charlie, I'm going home."

"Just like the cry baby that you are," Charlie said.

The other kids started laughing at Joey, which was exactly what Charlie wanted.

"Go ahead, go home cry baby," Charlie said, "run home a to your mommy."

An older voice yelled out, "Why don't you leave the kid alone, you bully."

Charlie wasn't used to being dressed down like that. He swung around and saw an Asian boy standing by the swing set.

"What did you say, man?" Charlie said.

"You heard me," the Asian kid said. "I've seen you around here before picking on all the little kids, especially him" (pointing at Joey). "Why don't you just leave him alone? He wasn't doing anything to you."

Charlie smiled a malevolent smile, and said, "He's my brother. I can say and do anything to him that I want to do. It's none of your business."

"I'm making it my business. Why are you picking on someone you should be protecting? He's your family."

"You should just walk away from this, and I won't kick your ass in," Charlie said.

"You punk, do you think I'm afraid of you?"

Charlie huffed and said, "If you had a brain in your head you would be."

"Let's go, then, punk."

The kids in the playground all gathered around saying "Fight, fight, fight!"

Even Joey, joined in, but he was silently cheering for the Asian boy, whose name was Lloyd.

Charlie put his fists up and began circling Lloyd who kind of went into a cat-like crouch and moved to the left.

Charlie threw the first punch, a lefthanded jab, which Lloyd easily avoided. Then Charlie threw and uncontrollable looping right fist that got half way to its target, when Lloyd snapped a high precise kick to Charlie's mouth and nose that sent Charlie reeling backwards and landing on the ground six feet away.

Joey, seeing Charlie get hit so badly called out, "That's enough, Charlie, let's go home."

With tears welling in Charlie's eyes and a big lump beginning to grow on the side of his face, Charlie yelled back at Joey, "Shut up, Joey." Then he turned to Lloyd and said, "What the hell was that, man? Are you going to fight like a man or kick like a girl?"

"Lloyd smiled and said, "You fight your way, you little prick, and I'll fight mine."

Charlie began to turn away and said, "I'm not going to bother with someone who fights like a girl."

Lloyd taunted Charlie, "Doesn't feel so good to fight someone your own size, does it you little crybaby."

The taunt did what it was meant to do, it turned Charlie around. Charlie lunged at Lloyd with both fists flailing in the air, leaving Charlie wide open for a left footed kick to Charlie's gut followed by a flying kick to Charlie's head, which snapped back and lead Charlie's body to the ground.

Charlie tried to get up when Lloyd put his foot on Charlie's shoulder and said, "Stay down. You're done."

Lloyd took his foot off Charlie's shoulder and like a cat began to move away. He turned and said, "Leave your brother alone."

"Hah," Charlie said, "Lucky kick. You won't be so lucky next time."

"Nothing lucky about it, man. I mean it, leave the kid alone."

Joey wanted to let out a cheer. Lloyd was like Superman to him. Seeing Charlie defeated started a seed to grow in Joey's mind. He thought, "Charlie is not indestructible after all."

Chapter 25 - Dangerous Exploits, Summer 1960

One day in the following spring, the two boys walked down the railroad tracks near their home to the Rouge River. Charlie was now 15 and Joey 13. A bridge crossed over the river that was made of a steel grid. It had vertical support columns on the side with a six-inch lip at the bottom of the grid that ran across the river.

Concrete finished off the structure of the bridge. Train tracks ran along the top of the bridge. Down below the tracks ran the Rouge River. When it rained hard, the river was a mighty force that carried anything in it down to the Detroit River. When it didn't rain, the water in the river would reduce to virtually nothing more than a trickle, which was the case now.

Charlie looked at the bridge and said to Joey, "I am going to walk along that 6" lip on the side of the bridge. Follow me."

"Charlie, that bridge is too high, and if we fall, we'll die," said Joey. "Don't you see how shallow the river is?"

But the older brother ignored the arguments being presented by Joey, and stepped out onto the ledge of the side of the bridge with his back to the bridge. He inched along until he was half way across the river and then inched back again without incident. "See, you little chicken," he said to Joey, "If I can do it so can you. Or, maybe you want all of your friends to learn about your bed-wetting."

Joey hadn't wet the bed in months, but the threat still felt like someone held an ax over his neck. With shaking knees he ventured out onto the side of the bridge, matching the path that Charlie had taken. Joey got to the center of the bridge and turned back, like Charlie did. With about 10 feet to go, he heard the sound of a train as it entered onto the tracks on the bridge. The bridge began to shake with the weight of the train, and Joey raced to get back to safety. But before he knew it the train was over where Joey was on the ledge. Joey was still four feet away from safety. At three feet from safety, Joey leaped to the ground at the side of the bridge as the train went by overhead shaking the side of the bridge where Joey had been only seconds earlier. Had Joey still been on the side of the bridge, he would have likely been shaken off the small ledge that he was on and would have fallen to his death.

Having survived the life-threatening experience with the train, an inner strength came out in Joey that he didn't realize he had. If he could survive walking along a ledge of a bridge that crossed an empty riverbed 80 feet below, he could certainly handle the teasing that he would receive from his friends if Charlie told them about Joey's bed-wetting. In fact, Joey knew that he could even handle losing some, or all, of his friends, if their learning about his bed-wetting broke their friendship apart, then the friendships weren't worth saving anyway, Joey decided. The ironic thing is that Charlie was responsible for most of the anguish in Joey's life anyway, and here he was using it as a sword over Joey's head. If Out of Joey's fear of being embarrassed in front of his friends, he was letting Charlie put him on a glide path that could lead him to death or serious injury. Joey's fear of being embarrassed in front of his friends was giving power to Charlie to control, and potentially destroy, Joey's life. This had to stop.

Chapter 26 – Joey's Rebellion, August 1960

Several weeks after the train incident, Joey was reading a book in the backyard when he heard Charlie calling his name. Joey didn't answer. He didn't want to be bothered at that time, and he didn't want to be at Charlie's beck and call anymore. Charlie came around the corner of the garage and saw Joey lying in the grass, reading. Charlie spat out, "Joey, are you deaf? I was calling you!"

"I was busy," was Joey's response. Charlie had never heard that kind of a comment from his little brother. He didn't know where Joey was getting the strength to talk to him that way, but Charlie knew he had to lay down the law again. Charlie ran over and knocked the book out of Joey's hand. Then he slapped Joey across the face, pushed Joey onto his back, and jumped on him, pinning his shoulders to the ground. Holding Joey's arms down and sitting on Joey's stomach, Charlie said, "Who in the hell do you think you are? When I call you, you come. Do you understand me? I don't give a damn what you are doing. You just stop doing it and come when I call."

A storm began to grow in Joey's chest. Charlie saw the defiance in Joey's eyes. He leaned over Joey's face and began to drool on his younger brother. Joey wriggled under Charlie's grip, but Charlie successfully held the smaller and younger boy down and continued to let his saliva drip onto Joey's face. Charlie taunted Joey. "Oh, aren't you the defiant one," he chided. "You won't be so damn defiant when I tell your friends that you wet the bed." Charlie laughed and continued to spit on Joey's face - getting spit in Joey's eyes, nose and mouth. Then he pulled up grass and dirt and rubbed them into the spit that covered Joey's face. "What are you going to do about it, Joey? Tell mommy and daddy? They don't give a crap what I do to you. They love me more than you anyway."

The hopelessness of his situation and how this really bad kid was getting away with everything he did, brought fury into Joey's heart. While Charlie was laughing over the situation, suddenly Joey's right arm broke free from Charlie's grip, and Joey's arm came up with a fist at the end of it. The fist landed squarely in the middle of Charlie's face. A cracking sound could be heard from Charlie's nose as the nose flattened against Charlie's face. Charlie rolled off of Joey, holding his bleeding nose. Joey could have stopped right then, but years of pent-up anger took over, and he lost all self-control. With the stunned Charlie lying on his back in a pool of blood coming from his broken nose, Joey got on top of Charlie and rained punch after punch onto Charlie's face.

Charlie screamed out, "I give! I give!" But, those words of surrender fell onto deaf ears, as Joey gave way to all of the mistreatment that Charlie had doled out. Joey's hands went to Charlie's throat, and Joey pressed down on his hands with all of his weight. He squeezed his hands as hard as he could around Charlie's neck – choking off the air supply. Joey began to get back his self-control. He put his mouth next to Charlie's ear and hissed, "Don't you ever touch me again, you prick! If you ever threaten me again, I will beat you with a baseball bat in the middle of the night as you sleep!"

Joey let his grip loosen, allowing Charlie to take in some air. Then Joey said, "Say it!"

Charlie, crying and wetting his pants, said, "Say what?"

"Say what?" Joey mimicked him. "You always hold yourself out as being so damn smart. But you aren't, Charlie. You're a dumb ass and a bully! I want you to say you will never touch or threaten me again."

Charlie nodded and said the words that Joey demanded to hear. "I will never touch you again, and I will never threaten you again."

"I swear to God," Joey chimed in.

"I swear to God," Charlie repeated after Joey. Joey got off of Charlie and walked away. Charlie, never expecting retaliation from Joey, sobbed in the backyard. Maggie heard the sobbing from the house and ran to the backyard to see her oldest son covered with blood. "Charlie, what happened to you? Who did this?"

Charlie said, "I was on the roof of the garage, Mom, and I fell off."

Neither Maggie or Josh ever believed Charlie's story about falling off the roof, but they had a hard time believing that Joey could have done such damage to Charlie. The situation was never brought up again. From that day on Charlie never again put a hand on Joey, and Joey's bed wetting soon stopped for good.

The aggression that Joey exhibited toward Charlie was not pre-planned. It was not a contemplated act looking for a reason for aggression. Joey had taken all other actions that he could think of, to no avail. This was a flight - or - fight situation and nothing else had ever worked against this older, stronger predator. In the situation that Joey was in, the fury just overcame him.

Sometimes bullies only react to force or the threat of force.

The end result was a positive one - Charlie stopped bullying Joey, and the two of them went on to have a better relationship after that. They never had a good relationship, just better. With the threshold that Joey just crossed, he decided that Joey did not work for him anymore. At dinner he told the family that he now wanted to be called Joe.

Chapter 27 – The Baby Crow, Summer 1960

Once Charlie learned to have respect, and maybe a little bit of fear of Joe, the two boys had a period of time in their mid-teens where they did have fun together. This wasn't necessarily the fun that one would espouse as a parent, but they got a kick out of it.

One such good time was back by the Rouge River again. The two boys saw a crow going into its nest high up in a tree. Once there, the crow began to feed its babies in the nest. When Charlie saw the crow leave the nest after one feeding frenzy, Charlie scampered up the tree to the crow's nest. The adult crow was off getting more food for its babies. At the nest, Charlie called down to Joe to catch what he was throwing down. Down from the tree came a crow's egg that Charlie had taken from the nest. Joe held out his hands to catch the egg. When the egg hit his hand, it broke, and Joe had broken crow egg all over his hands, arms, shirt and pants.

Mr. and Mrs. Crow got quite angry as Charlie spirited another egg from the nest and was dropping limb by limb down the tree, much like Tarzan. Circling him and cawing were Mr. and Mrs. Crow.

Charlie made it down the tree, and he and Joe took the egg home. Now what to do with the egg?

The boys decided that the best spot for the egg was in the fruit cellar that Josh had built in the area under the stairs leading to the basement. (In this fruit cellar, their mom stored all of her canned sauerkraut, peaches, pears, etc.) So, there the egg was placed under a towel to keep it warm, and off they went to school.

Well, the egg finally hatched. Josh was the first one to hear the bird. As he walked down the stairs, he heard noises from the pantry. Noises that shouldn't be there. What he found when he walked in the pantry was a baby crow, batting its wings, and little bits of white bird poop all over the shelves containing the canned goods. Under the sting of Josh's belt, the boys agreed that the pantry probably wasn't the best hiding spot that they could have selected. Much of what their mother had canned had to be thrown out, which made their mother especially angry since she had endured many injuries to her hands in slicing up the cabbage to make the sauerkraut. Each of them was in the doghouse (or maybe I should say birdhouse due to the incident.)

The boys rigged up a shelter for the baby crow in the garage, and during the day they tied its leg to a bush in the backyard.

Maggie was terrified of birds. She was in the backyard sunbathing one day when the baby crow somehow got free from its tether and began strutting across the backyard cawing at her. This threw Maggie into such a panic that she crawled backwards on her hands and knees screaming from the backyard to the back door.

It was agreed by the entire family, and Mother Nature, that the crow had to go. I say Mother Nature because the next morning most of the people on their street and for several blocks around awoke to the cawing of dozens of crows circling their house. The crows were responding to the caws of the young crow ready to join the flock. The boys let the crow go free and off it flew.

Chapter 28 – Charlie Leaves Home, February 1961

Shortly thereafter, Charlie moved out of the house. He was now 16 years old, had dropped out of high school and wanted the freedom to come and go as he pleased. He rented a room from a widow who lived about three miles away and got a job at a small grocery store in Detroit. He would often go over to Gregory's house. One such time, he waited until his dad left the house, snuck into the house quietly and stole Gregory's television set.

When Gregory came home from work and found that his television was gone, neighbors described a fairly young man who was seen hanging around in Gregory's back yard. The description closely matched that of Charlie, and Gregory presumed that his own son had stolen his television set from him. Suspicion became proof when Gregory was at a nephew's house and saw the television in his nephew's living room. The nephew said that Charlie had been by earlier in the week and had sold him the television set. Gregory knew that his son was on a glide path to a life of crime, and it would be best to nip it right now and call the police, but he could not do that to his own son.

Chapter 29 - Bad Choices, April 1962.

Charlie was driving in his 1955 Chevy Bel Air one afternoon. He stopped into a hamburger stand and had a couple of burgers with an order of fries and a coke. A very attractive girl came up to Charlie and said,

"What's a good-looking guy like you doing in a dump like this?"

Charlie said, "Just slumming it. You never know when you are going to find a diamond in the rough, like you."

"Ahh, I love a sweet-talking man. I'm a little on the hungry side, do you mind if I join you for a bite to eat?"

"Not at all," Charlie said. "Squeeze in here with me although it's a bit tight, but I like it tight." Charlie said with a wink.

"Well, I'll just bet that you do. You're like most men in that way. Let me properly introduce myself. I'm Darlene, and you're?"

"Charlie. Darlene, up until you came up to me and said 'Hello' the day was not one of my finest days, but you have made it do a 180."

Darlene smiled and said, "That sounds like a good thing."

"Yes, it is, and I hope that it will get nothing but better." Charlie flashed her a big smile and gave her shoulders a hug.

"Darlene, do you want to party?"

"What do you have in mind, Charlie?"

I was thinking about heading down to Toledo. Minimum age down there is only 18. You are 18, aren't you?"

"I am," she smiled and that was good enough for Charlie. Darlene, from head to toe absolutely looked 18. Well, 18 was actually stretching credulity a little bit, but Charlie's ruler was at attention and wanted to be served, so Charlie accepted the representation as legitimate. She was well endowed, if you know what I mean, very attractive, her makeup was outstanding, her hair was perfect and she carried herself with so much poise that she just couldn't be any younger than 18. But she wasn't 18. She wasn't even close to

18. She had ID that said she was 18. But she was only 14 ½.

Now a lot of people lie about their age, Charlie did, he was only 17 but said he was 18, and had fake ID. Sure, it was dishonest but didn't stagger the imagination as does someone who was 14 ½ but claims to be 18, but while Charlie's falsehood only shaved a year off his age, Darlene's falsehood, changed her from being at the age of majority – to being a minor. If Charlie was to let the ruler have what it craved, Charlie would be committing statutory rape.

They were in Charlie's car heading south to Toledo. She sat next to Charlie in the front seat as Charlie drove south on I-75 across the Michigan/Ohio state line. Charlie's plan was to buy beer, get the girl drunk, have sex with her either in the car or elsewhere, drop her off somewhere. A complete evening out.

Darlene was all over Charlie while he was driving. It came to his mind that if he pulled into a rest stop, he could satisfy the ruler right then and there and save the beer money. But he stayed true to the plan. He had promised Darlene that they would party after all.

True to the plan, Charlie stopped at a beer and wine store and bought a six pack of beer, which he shared with Darlene in a 2 to 4 ratio. Two for Charlie, four for her. Darlene thought that Charlie was really a considerate guy, but that had nothing to do with it. He wanted the ruler to stay at attention and anything more than two bears would cause the ruler to want to go to sleep. That was not part of the plan.

The sky was beginning to light up with lightning and a pretty steady rain began to fall, mixing with oils that were always on the street from all of the vehicle traffic. Charlie slowed the car down due to the conditions of the road and was fine until he came to a swerve in the road and the tires lost their grip on the road, and he ended up in a ditch on the side of the road. This was obviously not a part of the plan, but sometimes you have to improvise to keep the ruler happy.

"Darlene, let's get into the backseat and rest for a while until the rain stops."

"Are we stuck?"

I don't think so, said Charlie, but we could get stuck if we go off the road again. It's better to wait the rain out, let the road dry and continue."

They crawled into the backseat and got under a blanket that was waiting for their use and Charlie went to work. Soon clothes were off legs and arms were inter tangled with each other, moans and releases were heard by the silent car. The couple dosed off to sleep. The ruler was no longer at attention, but it did have a smile of its face. Because Darlene's age was younger than her fake identification, Charlie had just committed statutory rape with a 14-year-old girl.

We live in the moment it's said, and moments change. One moment our brain is under control by a lesser member and, in this case, the next moment is under the harsh bright light coming from a floodlight shining into the car that was held in the hand of an Ohio State Highway Patrolman. The elation of just several hours ago, crumbled in the light of the officer's flashlight.

The officer told them to get dressed and get out of the car. The officer took Identification and discovered two sets of ID on the girl. One, a poor rendition of a driver's license and obviously fake, that said she was eighteen, and the real ID, a stamped birth certificate that indicated that Darlene was fourteen. The officer immediately put cuffs on Charlie, read him his rights then pushed him into the back of the patrol car. Charlie was arrested for statutory rape of a minor, giving alcohol to a minor, aiding and abetting juvenile delinquency, taking a minor across the state line and failure to have his motor vehicle under control. Charlie was taken to the nearest police station, photographed, finger printed and tossed into a cell, all the while contesting that he knew the girl was underage.

The girl was taken to a room at the station and questioned by a female member of the Ohio State Highway Patrol. The girl confirmed to the officer everything that the male officer had written up in the ticket that was given to Charlie. She had no intention of having sex. Heck no! She was only 14 years old and was just out for some fun, but she had no plans on leaving Michigan, drinking or having sex with a stranger- all of that was forced on her by Charlie.

Charlie was told that due to the seriousness of the charges against him, there would be no bail. An officer told Charlie that he should get a good attorney. Charlie said that he didn't know anyone and that he could not afford an attorney. Because of that, a preliminary hearing before a judge was set up as soon as possible.

Charlie was arraigned before a judge at the Municipal Court of Toledo. The judge read off the charges against Charlie who vehemently contested the fact that he had taken an underage girl across the state line. He also told the judge that the rape charge was wrong – that the girl had consented to having sex with Charlie.

The judge tossed the girl's driver's license over towards Charlie and said, "The license is a fake, boy. You had sex with a fourteen-year-old girl. That's statutory rape in this state."

"Oh, God," was all that Charlie could utter. He was a tough kid, but this was a whole new ballgame.

"Judge, honest to God, I had no idea. She looks older, and she told me she was 18 years old.

She approved me in a restaurant in Michigan. She came on to me. I asked her if she was 18 and wanted to go to Toledo, and she said yes to both."

"Did she tell you it was ok to rape her?" The judge's voice went cold.

"Judge, we were joking around in a sexual manner. Both of us were. I thought she was willing to get involved."

"Charlie, a 14-year-old is not of an age where she can be held responsible for agreeing with a sexual event."

"Again, judge I had no idea she was 14. And she was all over me while I was driving. I thought she wanted to do it as much as I did. She willingly and with a great deal of passion got into the back seat with me where we had sex. She didn't 'No,' she didn't try to stop me or tell me to stop, it was 'let's do this' all the way"

"I hate to keep repeating myself, Charlie, but since she is so young, she can say whatever she wants, in the eyes of the court the guilty party is still the older male who bears the guilt and must face the consequences."

Charlie said, "That just doesn't seem fair. The girl is given license to totally deceive the male, even entrap the male so long as she is underage."

As the judge was considering what direction to take in this matter, he tried to take Charlie's situation into the equation. While Charlie was already a hardened kid, he did not have a criminal record. Because of that fact, and the fact that the girl did have fake ID, if what Charlie said was true, that she did come on to Charlie and lied to Charlie about her age, then he would not allow the case to go to trial on one condition - Charlie needed to sign up to serve in the military and get his GED High School Equivalency Certificate. If Charlie proved to the court that he had signed up for the military, passed boot camp, and passed his GED, the charges would be dropped. Otherwise, the charges would stand. Charlie agreed.

The judge called Darlene to his office with a court officer. He told the girl that her fake ID was responsible for much of the problem that Charlie was in.

Darlene said, "I don't care what kind of trouble he's in. He shouldn't have taken me out of Michigan."

"Charlie said that you came on to him in Michigan. Is that true?" Asked the Judge.

"Well, I thought he was cute so I did approach him. There's nothing illegal about that is there?"

"No. We're you also flirting with him in a sexual manner?"

"Well, Charlie said that you wanted to go party in Toledo. Are you denying that you said that?" asked the judge.

"I don't think it is fair that you are siding with that guy who raped me, judge."

"Young lady, all I am trying to get at the facts. Did he or did he not ask you to come down to Ohio with him to party?"

Darlene said, "He told me we would party in Toledo, not Ohio."

The judge asked, "And where is Toledo?"

"South of Detroit," Darlene said.

"Might it be in Ohio?" asked the judge.

Darlene said, "I suppose so."

"You suppose Toledo, Ohio may be in Ohio?"

"Ok, Ok, stop badgering me. I knew Toledo was in Ohio."

"You play pretty careless with the truth, don't you, Darlene."

"Judge, I just want to go home."

The judge ignored her protest. He said that the State of Ohio could charge her for having false ID and being in the illegal possession of alcohol. He added, "Charlie said that you were all over him when he was driving down on the expressway and you were giving every indication that if there was going to be sex it was going to be consensual. Is that true?"

"Is what true, judge?"

The judge was getting annoyed with her antics, and said, "Darlene, try to follow what I am saying. Try to pay attention. OK?"

Darlene nodded.

"Did you give Charlie strong indication that you wanted to go to Ohio and party and have consensual sex?"

"Yes, but I'm a minor and I can't give consent."

The judge said, "That true, Darlene, but you sure think you can purposely deceive, tease and leave," don't you?"

"I like to have fun if that's what you mean."

"Darlene, this minor law doesn't apply to girls like you who are conniving and vengeful. I could throw the book at you, Sweetie. I could hit you with false identification, sexual entrapment, collusion to commit a crime, but you drop this charade, and I won't send you to jail or drag your folks down here for a trial. You are a deceitful, little bitch trying to take advantage of a low that was designed to protect young girls like you. Drop the charges and go home. If you come back without your parents before you're are 21, I'll throw the book at you."

"She agreed to drop the charges and arranged for her older sister to drive down to Toledo to take her back to Michigan.

On the following Monday, Charlie was taken by the police and dropped off outside of a U.S. Navy recruitment office in Toledo, Ohio. Charlie came out of the recruiter's office as an inductee into the U.S. Navy. He went to boot camp in San Diego. He graduated from boot camp, qualified for his G.E.D. and was told to report to the Norfolk Naval Base in Norfolk, Virginia. The year was 1962.

Chapter 30 - Cuban Missile Crisis, 1962

The United States, via spy planes flown over Cuba, had spotted a lot of construction activity with large military trucks bringing missiles to the north end of the island. Further investigation confirmed that they indeed were missiles and that if left in place they could likely hit the capitol of the United States and many other large cities in the central, southern and eastern states.

The United States President John Kennedy ordered a naval fleet to block and turn-back any Soviet ships attempting to gain access to Cuba. Charlie was a part of the call to arms serving on the United States battleship USS Abbot. Tensions ran very high on all sides for several days as President Kennedy negotiated with the Soviet Union's Prime Minister Nikita Khrushchev about the future of Cuba, the future of the Soviet Union's relationship with the United States, and the removal of missiles from Cuba.

The world stood at high alert as President Kennedy and Prime Minister Khrushchev postured back and forth until finally Khrushchev told his naval commander to stand down and return his ships and men to the Soviet Union.

Charlie had signed up for a 4-year stint with the Navy in April of 1962, but he was discharged and came home in December of 1963. He never talked about why he was sent home before the four years were up, but one day he was in the bar with some friends, and they began talking about Charlie's experience in the Navy. Charlie got very quiet and said, "I learned a lot from the Navy. They taught me how to make my bed and tuck in the corners in a very precise manner. They also taught me how to fold my clothes in such a way as to minimize any excess space in my carrying bag. But, when I have to stand at attention in the middle of a stand-off like the Cuban Missile Crisis and salute some asshole with a sub 90 IQ, that's where I draw the line. You know what I mean?"

His friends nodded, but they really didn't know what Charlie meant.

Charlie went on. "Here I am with a 135 IQ, and I'm only in the Navy because some lying little bitch says she's 18 when she is only 14, and I come face to face with a jail sentence for statutory rape, so I cut a deal to join the Navy and serve my country, and I have to deal with some friggin petty officer who barely comes up to my shoulders, who I could snap with my left hand, and who read comic books, who I have to call "Sir." Well, shit, that wasn't for me."

"So, what did you do Charlie?" one buddy asked him.

"I worked out a deal to be discharged early after I put a pile of shit under that petty officer's sheets. They never caught me but given my attitude toward that little cumquat they kind of came to the conclusion that I had a hand in the matter. We ultimately determined that me and the Navy were not a good fit, so I was discharged early.

"Did they give you a dishonorable discharge?" one of the guys asked.

"Hell, no. I was a pretty good Navy man except for certain things that I couldn't tolerate. The Navy and I agreed that it wasn't a real good fit, so I got what is called a general discharge. I still got to keep my Naval benefits. Sometimes it's best to just shake hands and go quietly into the night. Which we did."

Chapter 31 - President Kennedy Shot, 11/22/1963

The assassination of President John Fitzgerald Kennedy (JFK) was a life changer for Joe, as it was for most people who lived through it. Joe was 16 when President Kennedy was assassinated. The announcement of his assassination came over the loud speaker in his English class. His teacher, a female, threw up her hands, lowered her head and wept when it was announced that President Kennedy was dead. Joe and most of the students in his class were doing the same.

That night, while delivering the Detroit News to his customers, Joe listened to his transistor radio and wept over the coverage of President Kennedy's life, times and death. For the next week, Joe was glued to the television set watching the coverage of the fallen President lying in state and the funeral. If the divorce of Josh and his mother hadn't made Joe somewhat jaundiced about the state of the world, the death of JFK, pushed Joe closer to that line.

In his great novel, "Sea Wolf," Jack London wrote about how the people, places, experiences and events in a person's life play a significant role in molding a person into who they become. The essence of it is that we all begin our lives as smooth lumps of clay, (not literally, of course) and we are molded into who we become by people, places, experiences and events that we come into contact with or have an effect on our lives. The assassination of President John Fitzgerald Kennedy was one such event. It tended to end the age of innocence and opened the door into the harsh realities of life for many people. Joe was one of them. He became a little jaded on the concept of the goodness of mankind and putting one's life into God's hands. That was a place where Joe had been before JFK's assassination, but he would never go back to that place again.

Chapter 32 – The Family In Trouble, March1963

The battle that Maggie had fought against the staph infection which started in 1956, and the slow breakdown of the love that Josh felt toward her was escalating to the point where the marriage was in severe trouble, and possibly beyond saving. Josh began to come home later and later each day. He had his job on the police force and also had a construction business. He was difficult to keep track of, and Maggie had long been suspicious of his whereabouts. She would often follow him in her car when he left home (many times with Joe and Josh, Jr. in the backseat) trying to catch Josh cheating on her. She never caught him, but she was highly suspicious that he was cheating on her.

Maggie had always been a social drinker, but now she turned to alcohol to comfort her from the emotional pain she was suffering from her dying marriage. "Two can play this game," she would say bitterly and go out "on the town" herself.

Maggie had been taking a home-study program to become a bookkeeper. She was very bright and very good with details, logic and numbers. She got her bookkeeper certification after completing the program with an "A" average. The certificate of completion led to her being hired as a bookkeeper at a nightclub in Livonia, a Detroit suburb.

The pressure of working full time as the bookkeeper for the nightclub, trying to maintain a household, and the stress that existed in her marriage, resulted in Maggie drinking on a regular basis. She was now far past the point of having a drinking problem – she was now an alcoholic.

She did not deny her addiction to alcohol. She recognized that she was an alcoholic and attended Alcoholic Anonymous (AA) classes. Telltale AA signs were all around the house encouraging her to stay clear of alcohol – "one day at a time." But she knew that Josh was running around on her, and that was like an open wound in her heart. She would often walk around the house, with a mixed drink in her hand, singing, "crying over you" along with Roy Orbison on the stereo.

Joe was not immune to all of the chaos in the house. He would hear Josh and Maggie arguing in the wee hours of the morning. Often their words were slurred, because both of them had been drinking. They would scream at each other and throw things at each other. In his heart and mind, Joe knew this would not end well. He just hoped Maggie and Josh could work their problems out, because if they got divorced, among other concerns that he had was where he would live and what would happen to Josh, Jr.? The marital relationship between Josh and Maggie was like a dry forest during a heat spell. All it needed for it to turn into a blazing fire, was someone with a match.

Chapter 33 – Maggie Gets Caught, Fall 1963

Joe's mom began to go to steam baths on a regular basis. She became friends with the owner of the steam bath. This was not something that she kept from Joe. In fact, Joe was very much aware of what Maggie referred to as the "friendship" that she had with the male owner of the steam bath. One day, the owner of the steam bath came home with Maggie and gave Joe a mixed breed German Short Haired Pointer puppy that Joe named Thor. Maggie's friend also gave Joe a doghouse that was kept in the back of the garage. Thor was kept on a half- inch thick chain that was connected to a metal stake that was kept by the opening of the doghouse.

Joe didn't have any idea that anything other than friendship was going on here, so he wasn't terribly surprised a few weeks later when he came home and saw his mom and Josh playing cards in the living room with the owner of the steam bath and his wife. Joe went in and said, "Hi." The steam bath owner asked about the dog, and Joe said he named him Thor and everything was cool.

Drinks were flowing along with the dealing of the cards, and Josh began to get the idea that the man sitting at the card table in his living room was a little more than just a friend of his wife. A comment here, a smile there, a giggle, a wink all convinced Josh that this friend was having an affair with his wife. But he kept his suspicion to himself and allowed the evening to play out. By the end of the evening, Josh was convinced of his suspicion, and very angry that his wife would wave her infidelity right under his nose, in his own house. Keeping his own counsel, Josh said nothing of his suspicion.

Maggie was figuratively holding a burning match at both ends. If the flames got to her fingers from both sides, she risked the chance of getting burned very badly, and burning down the forest that was her marriage. That risk became a reality several days after the card game.

Joe became aware that something was terribly wrong when Maggie came rushing into the house frantically gathering her belongings. She told Joe that she had to get away from Josh who had come to the steam bath and was going to kill her. She ran in one door, collected some items that she needed, went out the back door and never came back.

Later that evening, Josh came home. "Where's your mother, Joe?" Josh asked. Joe had put Josh, Jr. to bed and was in the living room. Joe's knees began to shake, and his voice got dry. Josh could tell the boy was terrified and sat down on the couch next to him. "Joe, you have nothing to be afraid of, I promise you. I will not hurt you in any way. Do you understand me?" Josh said. Joe nodded. yes.

"Where is your mother?" Josh asked again.

Tears welled up in Joe's eyes, and he said, "She came home a couple of hours ago and said you were going to kill her. She left in her car."

Josh lowered his head in his hands. "I am not going to say bad things about your mother, except I caught her with another man."

Joe sucked down his sniffles and looked at his stepfather waiting for him to continue.

Josh looked at the boy and said, "And I did what any man would do. He will not be messing around with anyone's wife soon. I will not hurt your mother. You don't have to worry about that. Now, it's late. You get to bed."

A divorce settlement was soon reached ending the marriage of Josh and Maggie, and leaving a scorched forest behind. Josh got the house, belongings, and Josh, Jr. Joe was not addressed in the divorce settlement. An open question in Joe's mind was, "What is going to happen to me?"

Chapter 34 – Life After Mom, 1963

After the divorce, Joe felt totally lost. Would he be living with his real dad, Gregory? Would his mom want him? Did he want to be with her? What about her drinking? Joe didn't know if Josh would allow him to stay with him. Joe was in the tenth grade and did not want to go to live with his real dad, because Gregory lived on the east side of Detroit, and Josh lived on the west side of Detroit – over an hour's drive from each other. All of Joe's friends, and everything he had come to know, were on the west side of the city.

Joe's concerns increased when he came home a couple of days later and Thor was nowhere to be found. Josh simply said that Thor had broken the chain and had run away. Thor never came back. Joe wondered if the same thing was going to happen to him.

Josh put an end to all of Joe's concerns, saying that Joe could live with him and Josh Jr if Joe wanted to. Joe said he did. Josh laid down some conditions. Joe would cook most of the meals, maintain the house and take care of Josh Jr. It was an offer that was better than Joe's alternatives, so he nodded and said, "Okay, I understand." Joe never enjoyed cooking and never was a good cook, but he made a lot of chili and hamburgers. He learned how to do the wash and iron clothes as well as anyone.

Chapter 35 – Josh and Jane Marry 1964

Josh and Jane had been seeing each other and Josh had been bringing Jane to the house for quite some time. Josh would take Josh, Jr. aside and say, "Jane is going to be your new mother, is that ok?" Joe thought it was kind of a ridiculous thing to ask the poor kid. Whatever Josh Jr, at the age of eight, said wouldn't make a bit of difference in what Josh was going to do. So just stop the crap and say "We're going to get married Josh Jr. I don't care if you like it or not. Get with the program." Parents think kids are stupid when they ask a question knowing the kid has only one answer to give if he or she has a brain in his or her head. Don't be condescending to kids was what Joe wanted to say, but he wouldn't dare say it because he might get kicked out of the house. So "sure, sure, sure, whatever" was what he thought when he heard Josh ask the question of Josh Jr, and if the question was put to him. But it wasn't put to him because Josh didn't give a damn how Joe felt about it. Joe was just part of the custodial staff after all and was lucky to have a roof over his head. He thought Josh could say, "Gather your shit up, Joe, I'm taking you to live with your real dad." But Joe knew that Josh wouldn't do that; Joe was too good of a worker.

Anyway, it was hardly a surprise when Josh came

home with Jane on his arm and told Joe and Josh Jr that they were married. Joe wondered if Jane was one of the women that his mother believed that Josh was fooling around with, but it really didn't matter. Maggie was gone with all of her alcohol trappings and signs, with all of her drunken, stumbling, Crying Over You." Joe felt bad for her but that crap was upsetting for the neighborhood and upsetting for Josh Jr. As for Joe, he missed his mom, but he couldn't control her implosion and life had to go on.

Jayne owned a bar in Detroit. Jayne had two children, Ray and Andrea, from two previous marriages. She had already been married three times. Each of her husbands had coincidentally died of a heart attack. "Josh better lose some weight," Joe thought. Jayne and her two children moved into Josh's home on the northwest side of Detroit.

Jayne was looking for someone to clean her bar every night. Joe, now 16 years old and able to drive, asked Jayne if he could have the job. Jayne was a little concerned that Joe may not be up to it because Joe was still in high school and already had a paper route. Plus, the bar needed to be cleaned between when it closed at 2:30 am and before it opened at 11:00 am. But Joe said that he could do it, and Jayne knew that Joe was a hard worker, so she agreed to try him. For the first time in his life, Joe had an adult-person's job.

Was it the best situation for Joe? Probably not. He was a junior in high school and had to be at school at 8:00 AM. Joe found that it took about two hours to clean the bar and fill the beer. If he finished by 6:30 AM in the morning, it gave him enough time to get home, take a shower and leave for school at 7:20 AM.

Joe's day looked like this:

- Go to bed at 10:00 PM

- Wake up at 4:00 AM
- Get to the bar at 4:30 AM
- Leave the bar at 6:30 AM
- Shower and get dressed for school at leave at 7:15 AM
- Get to the school at 8:00 AM
- School ended at 2:30 PM

Joe had from 3:00 pm to 10:00 PM to get his homework done, do his evening paper route, do his chores around the house such as cut the grass, weed the flower beds and lawn and clean the garage. There was not a lot of time in there for a personal life, but Joe found that he could make the time. Hard work was something that he lived with all of the time, but he had a lot of energy and was able to make it all work.

Chapter 36 - Bullies and Weakness. November, 1964

In an English class that fall, Joe, now 17, gave a speech about bullies and weakness. He stood in front of the class and said, "It is said that the weak will inherit the earth. That has never been my experience. It is my experience that the strong will gladly walk all over the rights of the weak if the weak allow the strong to do so and not fight back. It is the fear of a rebellion from the weak that often keeps the strong from acting out their worst aggression. Bullies will do what you let them do." There was more to the speech, but the reader gets the idea.

Mrs. Watson, the teacher, took issue with parts of Joe's talk and asked him to stay behind at the end of the class, which was the last class of the day.

When the class ended, she asked Joe to sit by the side of her desk so she had sight of the door.

Mrs. Watson started out saying, "Joe, you gave an interesting talk, but I am troubled with the idea that the victim of bullying is somehow responsible for the bullying that was inflicted on them by the bully. Could you explain that to me?"

Joe said, "Sure, I believe that if the victim of bullying does not do something to stop the bullying they are actually encouraging, not intentionally, but encouraging the bully to behave badly."

"So, Joe, you are endorsing and supporting the notion that the victim should stoop to the bully's level and fight back?"

Joe said, "By fighting back himself, Mrs. Watson, the victim of bullying is not sinking to the bully's level. The bully is picking on, traumatizing, an innocent party. If the bully believes that there will be no consequences for the bully's bad behavior, and the bully is being rewarded emotionally, financially, psychologically, whatever, by the one being bullied, and if the bully doesn't have any sense of remorse for his or her behavior, what tools are there for the victim to stop the bully's behavior other than fight back or acceptance? If the bullied is going to allow the bully to bully him because of the belief that the bully might eventually leave him alone, the bullied will find that he or she is wrong. The bullying will continue, because there is no incentive for the bully to stop. This to me is acceptance and will not stop the bullying."

Mrs. Wilson asked, "What about going to a parent, a trusted teacher, a friend with their concerns about being bullied?"

"That's great," Joe said, "as long as the person they go to acts on the information to protect the victim. My experience is the primary person who benefits from stopping the bully is the victim of the bully. Oh, the others may care and may try to stop it, but they don't have the personal interest in stopping it, like the one who is being bullied. I believe that the bully must recognize that their behavior is potentially or, even more so, probably putting themselves in harm's way. Only then will the bully consider a change of their bullying behavior."

Mrs. Watson said, "Interesting answer. I am guessing that you have firsthand experience."

"I have, as the victim of a bully."

"Joe, are you being bullied now? Because I can help you if you are."

"No, I stopped the bully myself."

"By going to your parents?"

"I went to my parents. They did not stop it. To some extent they held it against me for bringing it to their attention. Like it embarrassed them."

"So how did you stop it?"

"I fought back." I beat the crap out of him and made him promise to never do it again."

"And what if he had?"

"I told him that I would make him very, very sorry if he did."

"Hmmmm," Mrs. Watson uttered. "I guess I'll leave that alone."

"Well, I wouldn't have killed him," Joe said. "But he would have learned that there would be consequences for his bullying."

"I'm curious, having gone through what you went through, did you ever fear that you would become a bully."

Joe laughed, "Oh, God, no. Just the opposite. I know what being the victim feels like.

"Have you yourself ever been a bully?" She asked.

"I have played mean-spirited practical jokes, but I don't believe I have ever been a bully."

"Do you mind saying what the mean-spirited practical joke was?"

"I don't mind. It was kind of cruel in retrospect, but when I did it I thought it was funny."

"Uh huh. Go on."

Well, my younger brother, Josh, Jr., is nine years younger than I am. We shared a bedroom with pull-out beds. His bed was the pull-out on the bottom. Josh, Jr. was very afraid of seals."

"Seals?"

"Yes, you know the black water mammals that catch fish, have flippers that they can use to move around out of the water.."

"Yes. Yes. Seals."

"He said that he had a nightmare that seals were in the closet while he was sleeping, and they jumped on his bed and began tickling him. So, I put on a long black raincoat one day. You know, the kind with a hood?"

Mrs. Watson nodded.

"Well, I hid in the clothes closet that is near the foot of Josh Jr.'s bed. Mom always reads Josh Jr bedtime stories when he went to bed. So, I hear Mom come in with Josh Jr. He gets into bed and Mom reads him three bedtime stories. I'm in the closet being really, really quiet. I hear Mom kiss Jos Jr. good night, and she closes the door."

Joe starts to giggle.

"Yes?" says Mrs. Watson. "Then what?"

"I started moving around in the closet and began making seal noises, something like erk, erk, erk. Well, Josh Jr hears it and says, 'Ron? Ron? Is that you, Ron?'"

Mrs. Watson giggles and says, "That's awful."

Joe laughs and says "I know. So, I throw open the closet door and come into the room on my hands and knees wearing my slicker, with my head covered, going erk, erk, erk. I jump onto the bed, go over to Josh Jr's belly and start tickling him." Josh Jr. is screaming and the door suddenly opens and it's my step dad. He screams out, 'What the hell is going on in here?'"

Mrs. Watson is silent then says, "What did your step-dad do?"

"Well, by then Josh Jr knew it was me because I took off my raincoat, and Josh, Jr. began laughing." Before Josh could say or do anything more, I said something to the effect, 'See Josh Jr there's no seal in the closet, it's only me.' Josh Jr laughed some more and hugged me. Josh looked at us and said, 'Enough playing around. Get to bed.'"

"Was that your intent? To teach your little brother that there was nothing scary in the closet?" Mrs. Watson asked.

"No. I thought that scaring him would be funny. And it was. I just got lucky that Josh Jr started laughing, or I would have been given the belt."

Mrs. Watson said, "Does your step dad give you the belt often?"

"He tended to bunch my older brother and I in together. If something in my step dad's mind deserved the belt, he would try to determine who did the bad thing. If we didn't say or maybe didn't know, he would beat us both. I was more afraid of my older brother than I was my stepdad, so I didn't tattle on my brother even though I knew I would get a beating."

"Getting back to what you did to Josh, Jr., do you think that was bullying?"

Joe said, "I would call it a mean thing to do or a practical joke, but I wouldn't call it bullying. To me bullying is much more physical or mental with the intent of really hurting the other person. It is more of a continuous thing meant to tear someone down."

Mrs. Watson looked at her watch and said, "Oh, my goodness. Look at the time. I've got to get going. I enjoyed this conversation, Joe. Remember what bullying feels like when you have your own family someday, Joe. Don't allow your own children to have to suffer like you had to suffer.

"I won't. Mrs. Watson. I know how it feels, and I know what to look for."

They went their separate ways after saying a quick "good-bye."

Chapter 37 - The Beatles and Austin Healey, 1964

Joe was ironing one day while listening to the radio. The disc jockey said that the next song was from a British band called the Beatles. The song was, "I Want To Hold Your Hand."

The beat of the music, the harmony, and the message of the Beatles immediately hooked Joe. He idolized John Lennon and Paul McCartney, because of their mastery of song writing. He even bought John's book, "John Lennon, In His Own Write," which he didn't understand at all, but it was cool to carry the book around at school.

All of a sudden it was "everything British." When Joe was 17, he bought a 1959 Austin Healey 100 – 6 – a British made sports car, the precursor to the Austin Healey 3000. It had a slick design, a convertible top, a stick shift with an overdrive switch, and a black and yellow paint job that looked like a honeybee coming down the highway. Joe loved the car at first sight, bought it and drove it home.

When Joe brought the car home, he took Ray out for a ride through the neighborhood. Joe took one turn a little too fast, and the passenger door flew open, the convertible top came down around their heads and the car stalled out. Ray yelled, "Let me out of this thing!" Ray jumped out of the car and walked home. Joe smiled, and said to himself, "I guess he just doesn't appreciate British sports cars."

The Austin Healey would get up to 128 miles per hour, which Joe proved one day on the I-96 expressway heading out for a day of swimming at Kensington. A good friend from down the street was in the car when Joe said, "Let's see what this thing can do." Joe took the Healey up to 120 miles per hour, then flipped the overdrive switch, which kicked it up to 128 miles per hour. At that speed, the convertible top was pulling away from the frame on the front window of the car. His buddy put one knee on the floor and begged Joe to slow down, which he did. A jerk of the wheel, if something came into the road, a blow out of a tire, and they would have been imbedded into I-96. But Joe, at 17 years old, just didn't think about those things. Like most teenagers, Joe lived in the moment.

Joe often had a girl on his arm while driving this hot

little sports car with the convertible top down and listening to the songs of John, Paul, George and Ringo on the radio. For a high school kid, life just couldn't get any better than this.

Joe later wanted the Austin Healey to look like the Austin Healey 3000 – a later model. So, he removed the rearview mirror from the two front fenders. Also, he wanted the Healey to be a one-tone car, instead of two-tone. Always watching his money, Joe prepped the car for a paint job himself. He diligently sanded down the car in preparation for the final baby blue color that Earl Scheib Auto Painting on Schoolcraft was going to apply to the car. The only problem was that Joe sanded the Healey down with a disc sander rather than a vibrator sander. Even though the surface of the car felt smooth to the touch, the disc sander left hundreds of small grooves on the surface of the car – small grooves that could only be seen after it was painted.

When Joe got the car back from the paint shop, it looked like someone had painted it with a broom. With the new baby blue paint job, he could see every uneven swirl the sander made in the old paint. But it was still one of the coolest cars at school, so the bad paint job didn't stop Joe from appreciating the car.

The Healey had one major flaw; it had a bad habit of stalling out at the most inopportune time. One time, it stalled out while Joe was making a left-hand turn coming home from school. Joe was in the middle of an intersection when the Healey's motor went silent. Joe put his left foot on the clutch, his right foot on the accelerator and turned the key. All he heard for his efforts was "click, click, click," and the car wouldn't start. Joe believed the problem was a short somewhere in the electrical system. The engine, in the front, was not getting juice from the battery, located in the trunk.

With cars honking and people screaming, Joe got out and pushed the car out of the intersection to the side of the road. He walked two miles home and came back with a friend with jumper cables and vowed that once he had enough money, he was going to get that problem fixed.

Chapter 38 - Writing and Equality, 1965

In high school, Joe began to seriously look at his adult employment options. While he loved to write and thought that he could be a journalist one day, he really didn't see much of an opportunity to go to college. Accordingly, he had primarily taken business classes in high school. His mother had been a bookkeeper and had told Joe that all companies needed to have an accounting staff to determine if the business was profitable. Accounting was also valuable for the future planning of the company and for the determination of taxes. All of this excited Joe, and he worked really hard at the business curriculum. Joe was getting all "A"s in his bookkeeping and accounting classes and was pretty confident that he could get a bookkeeping job once he graduated from high school. But Joe wondered if a job like that would satisfy his desire of creativity and personal expression.

Writing was his first love. He had started to write poetry in his early teens. He liked to write poems that had surprise endings. One of his favorite writers was Edgar Allen Poe (whose writings came alive to him when Joe was in an English class and the teacher read a fantastic rendition of "The Raven.") Joe also enjoyed Alfred Hitchcock. From Hitchcock's influence came "Hiding In The World," which Joe wrote when he was fifteen.

Hiding In The World

**Flowing through a dreamland
of life that's wavy blue;
a surrounding of blue heaven;
a life away from you;**

> streaking into good times,
> away from times so gray;
> streaking into tomorrow,
> leaving yesterday;
>
> leaving everything behind
> that's representative of you;
> passing by and away from objects
> that remind me so much of you;
>
> swimming happily
> through the water all around,
> someone screams, "You're dreaming!"
> I wake up and I drown.

Lines of poetry would come into Joe's mind all the time. They just seemed to float in at any time. Joe would often have to scurry around to find something to write with and on, so that he could capture the thoughts before he forgot them. Joe had lines of poetry on little pieces of paper, shopping bags, white spaces in magazines and newspapers, and receipts that he kept in his wallet. Whatever he found that could hold the lines that his brain and mind were hearing were used to capture the verses. Often full poems would come into his mind, but more often he would hear or think of a line or two of the verse and the rest would be written around those original lines of the poem.

Joe was very caught up in the civil rights desires of African Americans, and would read books like "The Man," and "Black Like Me." The fact that there were laws and practices in the country that treated a race of people differently just because of their skin color caused Joe deep sorrow. Something was very much wrong and out of sync between the reality of life in America and the lines of the "Pledge of Allegiance" which read "one nation, under God, indivisible with liberty and justice for all." These words in America's Pledge of Allegiance were totally out of sync with the fact that in America there were "whites-only" bathrooms and water fountains, and Blacks were forced to sit at the back of the bus.

Joe would get into debates with Josh about this inconsistency between the ideal of America and the reality of America. The debates would always end with Josh saying something to the effect of, "Come back and talk to me when you grow up." As if Joe's "growing up" would give him the skill to understand that there is nothing inconsistent between the claim that all people were free, and the lack of freedom afforded to Blacks. Joe felt that this period – prior to and through Martin Luther King and the Civil Rights Movement – to be one of the most shameful periods of our Republic's history.

Chapter 39 – After High School - What? Spring 1965

High school graduation was right around the corner. In the high school yearbook Joe said that he intended to go to college in the fall. He hoped that he would be able to do that, but he wasn't sure. More than anything he wanted to have something in that book that would make his future look bright. Joe wasn't aware that most high school yearbooks, within six months of graduation, end up on the top of book shelves or under the bed, likely to never be seen again. Looking at yearbooks paled when compared to thinking about Viet Nam which was ramping up, the draft that was going on, girls, college and work.

Joe had not given college much of a thought. He didn't know if he could get into a college, because he hadn't applied anywhere.

On the chance that a college would accept him, Joe sat down and reviewed how much he had in the bank after years of selling greeting cards door to door, having two paper routes and working in the bar for two years. The money he had saved didn't come near what the cost of college would be. He called up his dad and asked if Gregory could give him any assistance with college. "Not give it to me," he made clear, "but a loan." His dad said that because of all of his divorces, he didn't have money to help.

Joe brought up the matter with his stepdad, Josh, who promptly said, "Geez, Joe, you're not my kid. I let you live here rent-free, isn't that enough?" Joe assured Josh that it was and how much he appreciated Josh allow him to stay.

Josh's terse rejection of any help for college, even a loan, caused Joe to look back at the life that he and Josh had lived together, after his mom had left the home. While Josh had provided Joe with a place to stay, which Joe appreciated, the offer was only good if Joe cleaned the house, cut the grass, cooked the meals, washed and ironed the clothes and took care of Josh Jr. Josh did not offer Joe the ability to stay with him out of love. Joe began to feel like he had been a little bit like an indentured servant in the house.

In spite of the whippings over the past years, Joe loved Josh and always felt that Josh loved him as well. Joe knew that he had been a loyal son to Josh. He had lived up to his side of the deal with Josh allowing him to stay. Joe had helped raise Josh, Jr. He had done all of the gardening and housework at Josh's home in exchange for being allowed to live there. That had been their deal, but Joe always thought there was some love there too. But now Joe was being told, in no uncertain terms, that he was not Josh's kid. Of course, he knew that! He wasn't stupid! But, to have Josh slam it in his face like that was a rude awakening for Joe.

Joe thought that sometimes a person's desire to have something be true (being regarded as a member of the family) can cloud us to the reality of what really is occurring. It gave Joe a greater appreciation for his real father, Gregory, who only denied Joe the help Joe requested because divorces had left him without the money to help pay for college for his son.

"To be fair," Joe thought, "his stepdad did allow him to remain in the house when the divorce went through. He didn't have to do that. And Josh made no mention that Joe would have to pay rent now that his high school years were coming to an end.

Joe also appreciated the fact that Josh, regardless of the reason, kept him as a part of the family. Josh knew that Joe was very close to Josh Jr. It would have been hard on Josh, Jr. and Joe if Joe had been forced out of the house.

But the "You're not my kid" comment hit Joe so hard that it did cause Joe to think of other situations where Josh's lack of caring was shown. Josh's inclusive beatings of Joe, when Josh knew it was Charlie stealing his money and playing with his police revolver, should never have happened. Josh knew the nature of Charlie. He knew what Charlie did at Gregory's house before he agreed to take Charlie in. That Josh had treated them with equal guilt, given Charlie's history, was shocking to Joe.

Josh's inability to recognize that Joe's denials of knowledge of the taking of the money and playing with the gun was also shocking to Joe. Here Josh had a good kid living with him without incident and then a troubled kid comes into to the house and incidents began. Josh's focus should have always initially been on Charlie. This is now called profiling, but whatever name you give it, it just makes sense that you focus your attention on the person or group that has been responsible for similar actions in the past. You don't go after everyone as if you had no history. Humans are intelligent mammals and to not act intelligently goes against the nature of intelligent mammals.

Joe also remembered the time when he was working night crew at a local grocery store. While standing on a box putting items on the top shelf, Joe slipped off of the box and landed on what was called a j-hook that extended out from the shelf with the curved portion of the "j" pointing up. Small items with holes in the packaging were put on j-hooks to save shelf space and for display purposes. When Joe slipped from the box his left nostril landed on the j-hook and made a one-inch tear all of the way through his nostril. The night crew workers were locked in the store until a manager came in the next morning, so Joe wrapped gauze around his nose and, bleeding profusely, kept on working. When management opened the store in the morning, they were shocked to see the condition that Joe was in and told Joe to stop what he was doing and go immediately to the hospital.

Joe's house was in between the store and the hospital, so he stopped at his house hoping that Josh would be home and would drive him to the hospital. Joe was exhausted from working all night in pain. Josh was home and having breakfast when Joe walked in the door and told him about the injury. Josh initially seemed concerned but then he said, "You better drive yourself to the hospital." There was no mention of him driving Joe to the hospital. The concern for Joe's well-being just wasn't there.

As Joe drove to the emergency room, Joe was dismayed that Josh would not drive him to the hospital. He thought, "I will never do that when I have children of my own one day. I will be the opposite of that."

As he continued to drive, Joe again thought back to Jack London's "The Sea Wolf." Joe remembered that London wrote that our minds are a smooth hunk of clay at birth and all of a person's experiences molded each person into who that person would become.

The situation with Josh not helping him, made Joe think about London's premise. "While life's events do impact us," Joe thought, "people still have a personal choice to do the right thing." He continued thinking about the book and Josh. "In spite of how Josh was molded by his life's events, Josh should have still realized that Joe needed help and should have helped him." Joe's reflection of the book flipped again when he thought, "Jack London would argue that caring for others had not been molded into Josh's personality by previous events in life."

"This whole clay molding scenario, somewhat takes personal choice right out of the equation," Joe said to himself as he drove. "Based on my life, my lump of clay should be in pretty bad shape," Joe thought, "but I would never let that act as an excuse not to help someone who was in need. I know I wouldn't."

With these thoughts in his mind, Joe walked into the emergency room where doctors performed surgery on his nose. One doctor later asked, "Where is your driver?" Joe was too embarrassed to tell him that no one at home cared enough to help him.

Chapter - 40 - Coming Of Age, 1965-1966

After Joe graduated from high school, he knew that going to college immediately was not an option. His high school grades had been pretty good but did not warrant a scholarship, and he didn't have money or a patron (parent or otherwise) willing to fund college. So, he applied for, and got, a job at a Detroit factory.

Joe continued working in the bar, cleaning the bar and restocking the beer from 5 AM to 7 AM. Then Joe would go to his factory job, where he worked from 8 AM. to 5 PM. When you are young you can work these kinds of hours and still thrive. At least Joe could. After all, he had done it all the way through high school

At the time Joe was listening to a lot of Beatles, Bob Dylan and Peter Paul and Mary, who did a lot of Dylan covers. Bob Dylan was the inspiration for many of Joe's earlier poems.

Joe was often moody and experienced periods of loneliness and detachment especially in his later teenage years. He just wasn't sure what kind of path he wanted to follow with his life. Would he have a life? Or, would he be drafted, sent to Viet Nam and die in some rice paddy? And for what?

Joe thought that his chaotic thoughts and moods may have something to do with his being a child of divorced parents, but he never wanted his parents' divorce to be an excuse for how he felt. When he felt low he could usually find something in his life to take away the feelings of sadness and loneliness.

Joe especially liked to employ positive self-talk and forced himself not to feel sorry for himself. This, he found, helped him fight his sadness and loneliness. He knew that people around the world had lives that were a lot worse than the life he was living. "Charlie feels sorry for himself," Joe thought. "I will not be like Charlie."

Chapter 41 - Lightning Strikes, Summer 1965

When Joe was eighteen, he went into the hospital for a few days for an operation on his foot. It was nothing serious, just infected "ingrown toenails." He felt that it was a good opportunity to get the stalling problems of the Austin Healey fixed at a gas station that Josh recommended. The owners of the station said they would check what was causing the stalling problem in the Healey. Josh knew the owners well and assured Joe that they would find and fix the problem.

After the operation on his foot, Joe was driven home from the hospital by Ray. While driving down their street, Joe saw the most beautiful girl he had ever seen in his life. It was a "lightning strikes" moment because if Joe had gone by 30 seconds earlier or later, he may have never seen the girl who was destined to take a major part in his life. Joe turned his head almost 270 degrees to look at the young beauty as they drove by. She had dark brown hair, cut in a Sassoon style and was wearing a pink top and white bell-bottom slacks. Joe was 18 years old and was dating someone already, he had had other girlfriends before, but he had never been struck by lightning as he was with this girl.

When Joe got home, he stood in the driveway,

leaning on a cane and watched her as she had gathered with her friends in front of her friend's house, down the street.

She noticed Joe looking at her and ignored him, but he kept on staring. Ultimately out of annoyance, embarrassment, interest, whatever, she smiled and waved at Joe. Joe was like a frightened deer, caught in the headlights of a car. He quickly retreated to the house. From that first encounter, Joe wrote "You Smiled."

You Smiled

You smiled.
In that moment I froze.
You smiled.
In seconds my heart closed.
It was yours.

You smiled.
In that instant I was yours.
You smiled.
Life lost clarity.
Its moves were in blurs.

I wasn't unhappy
with my life.
I had playful moments,
without strife.

I wasn't prepared
for this turn.
But now that I've seen you,
I burn.

"What's your name?"
danced on my lips.
I longed to touch
your fingertips.

**Your smile
permeates my brain.
Since I've seen you
I've gone quite insane.
And I like it**.

Chapter 42 - Finding The Girl, 1965

Joe needed to find the girl who he had seen on his street. He would not give up until he found her. Joe rode around the neighborhood on his bike hoping to see her. He stopped the paperboy in the neighborhood, told him that he used to be a Detroit News carrier and needed some information on a girl he had seen. Joe described the girl to the paperboy. The paperboy said that he thought he knew the girl who Joe was talking about. He pulled out his route book and gave Joe the family name, the address and telephone number. The paperboy thought her name was Carol.

Late that afternoon, Joe called the number that the paperboy had given him. A man answered the phone, and Joe asked for Carol. The man said, "You've got the wrong number" and hung up on him. Joe called again, and a girl who sounded like a teenager answered the phone. He said, "Please don't hang up. Are you the girl who waved to me a couple of days ago on Hazelton?"

"Maybe, but how did you get my telephone number?" she asked.

"I have my ways," Joe laughed.

"Well, I've got to go. It's dinner time," she said.

"Wait, what is your name? Is it Carol?" Joe asked.

"No, it's Kate. And I've got to go."

"Wait!" Joe was desperate, "Can I meet you sometime?"

"Hmmm," Kate said, "we'll see." She then hung the phone up softly.

Several days had gone by when Joe saw Kate

walking down Glendale, a street in the neighborhood. Joe was on his bicycle. He hit the brakes, and he and Kate began talking.

Kate said, "Hello, when you asked if we could meet sometime, the whole family was listening. That is why I hung up."

Joe said, "I understand."

"Since you live on this street, I told my mom I was going to my friends who live down the street from you."

Joe nodded, "So this is your answer to my question of meeting you."

"Bingo." Kate said.

"My coming down here on my bike was just a lucky chance," Joe said. "Can I have your last name and address?"

Kate was a little hesitant about giving Joe that information. They had just met, and she really didn't know him. But she knew where he lived and her friends knew him so she said, "My name is Katheryn but everyone calls me Kate. My last name is Jones. She gave Joe the address.

Joe said, "I know that house. You have a beautiful flowering tree by the front door."

"Yes, my dad's prize Magnolia Tree."

"With the pink flowers and it blooms around Easter. That's where you live?"

Kate nodded, surprised that he knew the house so well.

"I use to have a newspaper route and you were one of my customers. Let me think, your dad's name is Jules and your mother's name is Nancy."

Kate laughed. "You have a very good memory. But I need to get going."

"Kate, I would like to see you again. Can I come to your house? It will give me a chance to see that cool tree," he joked.

Kate blushed and said that she would have to check with her parents, but that she thought that it would be okay. Joe called Kate that evening, and she said that he would be allowed to come over to her house.

Kate lived three blocks from Joe's house, so on the day that he and Kate set up, he walked over to her house. Kate's dad was sitting on the front porch, wearing only a pair of walking shorts and reading a newspaper. He had arms the size of Joe's thighs and it looked like you worked out with weights incessantly. Joe was so nervous that his heart almost exploded in his chest when he walked up to her dad and said, "Hello, sir. My name is Joe. Is Kate home?"

Jules Jones, Kate's dad, did work out with weights and was kind of in a perpetual flex. Joe didn't think that Kate's father was sitting on the porch by accident. The dad's message, without being uttered, was clear, "Young man, this is my beloved daughter – treat her with care." Kate's dad got up from the chair, opened the front door, and called Kate.

The afternoon went well. Kate had an interest in Joe, and Joe was off the charts crazy about Kate. Her parents agreed that she could go out with him as long as they told her parents where they were going and were home when her parents said they wanted her home. Joe was fine with hat. Anything to be with this girl who had him under her spell. And, of course, there was her dad to think about with his biceps strong enough to crush Joe's skull if he was crossed.

Their first date was a fall fair at a nearby church. The conversation came easily, laughter resounded, and Joe was hopelessly in love with a girl three years younger than him. Kate went to a prim and proper all-girls' private school and intended on going to college after high school. Joe had gone to public schools from kindergarten through the 12th grade. There was absolutely nothing wrong with his education, but it was different than what Kate had experienced. Here was Joe with his factory job and his part-time job working in a bar- both very honorable jobs – going out with this ravishing beauty with her private school education. Joe felt just a little unworthy of Kate, and he decided immediately that if he wanted to have any chance of a future with such a girl that he would have to go to college. College was in his forecast, but he decided that he needed to move the clock forward.

Although Joe was three years older than Kate, her maturity effectively narrowed the years that separated them. This maturity was a result of Kate being the oldest of five children in her family. Being the oldest, Kate, to some extent, had helped her mom and dad raise her younger siblings – resulting in the maturity she displayed. She was also very smart, and she was the nicest girl that Joe had ever met. He just couldn't mess this one up.

Chapter 43 - Broken Promises, Summer 1965

Now that Joe had seen the girl of his dreams, he had two major concerns in his life. He needed to get his Austin Healey back from the gas station, and he had to find out who the girl was who waved at him from down the street.

His foot was soon healed enough where he did not need his cane, so Joe went to the gas station to get his Austin Healey. To Joe's great disappointment, he found that someone had backed into the rear of the Healey - causing significant damage to the trunk and back fender. The owner of the gas station denied any knowledge of the damage and said it was not the station's responsibility. They had, according to the owner of the station, fixed the stalling problem and parked the car outside for customer pick-up. No, their insurance company would not cover the damage to the car.

Joe called Josh about the position that the owners of the station were taking, but Josh said there was nothing he could do to help. Josh told Joe about a good bump shop on Plymouth Road, west of the Southfield Freeway, in Detroit. Josh said he would talk to the owner of the bump shop about getting a good deal on fixing the car.

As Joe drove the Healey to the bump shop, the

Healey stalled out twice at two intersections. Joe was totally disgusted. He had paid good money to have the electrical problem fixed, which wasn't fixed, and in the process had suffered an accident to the car, because they had stored it on a back alley. He wondered if they had even looked at the car. Joe asked Josh to intercede with the gas station, which Josh chose not to do.

While the car was at the body shop, thieves jumped over the barbed wire fence, took a crow bar to the Healey's hood and removed the engine from the car. The damage to the hood and the replacement of the engine was not covered by the bump shop's insurance. Once again Josh offered no support to Joe.

Joe was becoming overwhelmed by the realization that the adult world was like the jungle, which was the survival of the fittest. He also learned that he could not rely on Josh for any support. No effort was made on Josh's part to try to encourage the gas station owner or the body shop owner to take corrective actions to repair the vehicle. Joe firmly believed that had he been Josh's kid that Josh would have been willing to intercede.

Joe was beyond sick of the car and weary of the lack of support he got from Josh. Joe ended up selling the Healey for $35 to a guy who worked on the assembly line at the factory. It was probably a rash decision to sell the car when he was emotionally down, but Joe just didn't want to keep on throwing good money after bad on a car that was so mechanically flawed.

"Good grief, I lost a lot of money on that car," Joe said to himself. He lay in his bed and thought how much better it could have been if Josh had helped him like Joe thought he should have done. How could Josh have been so quick to recommend someone, then not help when things went bad? Too often, Josh would give high assurances of positive outcomes and then not assist to try to improve or correct a situation when the outcome fell short. Josh had the power and position to help remediate shortfalls, not with a heavy hand, but just with discussion, but he lacked the desire to do it. Joe felt that

Josh had abandoned him in his time of need.

The lesson that Joe learned with these situations is that you need to stand on your own two feet in life. Don't presume that someone will assist you if something goes amiss, even if they say they will. Instead, work hard, save money to have the resources and the wherewithal to be your own backup.

Joe was working very hard during this time of his life. He felt no real attachment to Josh since Josh had shown him where he fit into the family. Joe wrote, "I Give Him My Lonely Hand," which deals with deep sadness.

I Give Him My Lonely Hand

**Sitting on the edge of time,
thinking of this life of mine,
emptiness is coming in,
heartache is coming again.**

**I had watched the children play,
thinking back to happy days.
A chill is now setting in.
Heartache is coming again.**

**Sitting on a bench alone,
the children have all gone home,
even pigeons have all flown,
and I am chilled to the bone.**

**Sitting here, no place to go;
where's the life I used to know?
I see You there tower tall.
It's to me, You give a call.**

**"Take the hand I offer thee.
Hold it close and follow Me."
The wind stirs the leaves and sand.
I give Him my lonely hand.**

Joe read and reread the poem. He thought, "One could make an argument that I am contemplating suicide to rid myself of the sadness and loneliness." Joe laughed to himself, "I do tend to be a little too maudlin and walk on the serious side." The poem was just a poem - not a suicide note. The words of the poem reflected a sadness and frustration that existed in him. Joe was lonely and needed someone or something to fill the void that he felt. In the poem, the answer to his loneliness was getting closer to God. But, he thought, the missing piece of his life just might be the girl who waved to him on his street. The girl who had stolen his heart without saying a word. The girl that he now knew as Kate.

Chapter 44 – Total Betrayal, 1965

Joe had one problem. He had been dating another girl for several years. The girl, Sue, was almost his age, and their relationship had progressed past the kissing phase. After his first date with Kate, Joe called Sue up and said they needed to talk. He picked Sue up and brought her back to his house.

Sue sensed that something was different and told Joe that he could go as far as he wanted to go with her that night. They had never had sex before and while the offer was one that any teenager would desire, Joe was so in love with Kate that he felt guilty even being with Sue. He told Sue that he had found someone else, and that it was over. Then he drove Sue home amid her endless tears.

Somehow Charlie got word of Joe's breakup with Sue and arranged to meet with her under the guise of using his influence to get her and Joe back together again. When Charlie wanted something, he could be very charming. Right now Charlie wanted Sue if for no other reason than to lord it over Joe. He took advantage of the hurt that Sue had felt in being jilted by Joe and what Joe could not bring himself to do, Charlie had no trouble doing.

Charlie called Joe the next day and bragged to him about what had happened between him and Sue and then added, "and all the while we were doing it, Joe, she was calling your name," Charlie laughed. Joe hung up on him.

In shock, Joe drove to Sue's house to confront her. The look on her face said it all. "How could you?" he asked, "With my brother? You know how I feel about Charlie. You know what Charlie has done to me. How in the hell could you have sex with my brother?"

"Joe, I'm sorry," Sue cried out. "I love you. Please believe me."

"If that's love, I don't want any part of it! That's it, Sue, we're done. Joe got in his car and drove off.

As he drove home, Joe got more and more angry at the betrayal. First with Sue and then with Charlie. Sue had tried to use sex as a tool to keep Joe with her. Had she not believed that Joe was leaving her, she never would have offered herself to him. She had never done-so in the past. Sure, they touched and engaged in what some would call foreplay. But it was always understood that it was not going to go any further than that, because Sue had very strong religious beliefs about sex. She was going to wait for sex until she got married. Joe respected that and never pushed her to do something that she did not want to do – especially for religious reasons. But, then to use it to try to keep him made her, in Joe's eyes a hypocrite. And then to allow herself to be lured into such a compromising position with Charlie made Sue worse than a slut in Joe's eyes.

Then there was Charlie, his scumbag, older brother. There was no depth to which he would not sink. As far as Joe was concerned, Charlie ranked right up there with Cain who killed his brother Abel. Something had to be done to put the fear of the Lord into Charlie.

Joe went home and got a baseball bat, got back into the car and drove to Charlie's apartment. He knocked on the door and when Charlie opened it, he pushed the bat straight into Charlie's chest. The force of the blow to his chest knocked him off of his feet and onto the floor on his back. Joe pounced on him and put the baseball bat to his throat.

"I could kill you now, Charlie. But I won't. But you ever pull another stunt like that I am going to throw my Christian restraint into the gutter and come at you like the Devil's hoards from Hell."

Charlie said, "I'm sorry, Joe. It just happened."

"Bullshit, Charlie. Shit like that just doesn't happen. You made it happen. You met her on purpose knowing that she was vulnerable and like the cockroach you are, you were going to take advantage of her sorrow. I'm just telling you, you pull any shit like that ever again, you better find a damn good hiding place. And Charlie, you tell anyone about what you did to her, and you'll be sorry. She doesn't deserve to have her reputation destroyed by an opportunist like you. And don't ever bring it up to me again. In fact, Charlie, I want you the hell out of my life. Understand?"

Charlie nodded to the degree that he could with a Louisville Slugger bat to his neck.

Joe got up went to the door and said, "You are a real piece of shit. You know that?" Joe opened the door and walked out.

Some of the actions that Joe took were a preventive to protect Kate If things did not work between the two of them. The fear of God had to be put into Charlie, and Joe believed he had succeeded in doing that.

Chapter 45 – Crazy In Love, 1965

Joe could only see Kate several times a week. As young as Kate was, her parents did not want her to get too serious with anyone at her age, 15. Also, Kate's mom was a little concerned about the three-year age difference between the two of them and about Joe's past – growing up in a family that had so many divorces and alcoholism. Kate's father on the other hand believed that Joe's background could make him a better person and a better father one day. Not that he wanted to push his oldest daughter into a relationship at her age, he just felt that people who come from bad environments often do not want to return to bad environments. But he too agreed with the restriction on the amount of time the two should spend with each other.

Joe couldn't tolerate being away from Kate. And his heart ached when he had to leave her. The longing that he felt in his heart for her convinced Joe that he had found the girl with whom he wanted to spend the rest of his life.

But the rules were the rules, and where there is an opening in anything other things have the potential of filling the gap. In Joe's case, those other things were toys.

Chapter 46 - The Ford Galaxie XL, 1965

Ray, had a 1964 Ford Galaxie XL with a dual 4 - barrel carburetor, a 427 cubic inch engine with 425 horsepower. It had leather bucket seats, chrome-reverse wheels and was just the coolest car in the neighborhood. It also burned gas like it was going out of style. If Ray didn't race the car often the carburetors would clog up, which would dramatically impede its racing capability. Ray didn't race it often and rather than constantly fight to keep the engine in tune, and engine that sucked down gas like children suck down popsicles, he found someone who would exchange a 390 engine and cash for his 427 engine. It was a little bit like taking the manhood out of Tarzan, but Ray did the exchange and a 390 engine was dropped under the hood. The space under the hood was very full when the 427 engine was there, but there was room to spare with the downsized 390. Not only did Ray lose cubic inches on the size of the engine, he also lost horsepower – going from 425 horsepower to 330. But the car still had a stick shift, bucket seats, chrome reverse wheels and still looked great and commanded a lot of attention on the road. The only thing different was that like an old lion, it was now all roar and no bite. But Ray was ok with that. In the exchange he got a pocket full of money for the mighty 427/425 engine.

After the Healey fiasco, Joe needed a car. Ray had started college and wanted to rid himself of expenses, like the car payment on a late engine Ford Galaxie XL so Joe bought the car from Ray. While it was no longer a good drag-racing car, the 427 flags were still on the front fenders by the engine compartment. The flags fooled a lot of people who believed the car was the muscle car that it used to be and no longer was.

One of the guys that it fooled was a guy who worked with Joe at the factory who had a beefed-up GTO. He was constantly trying to get Joe to race him when they got off work. He thought that Joe had the 427 engine in it, and Joe did to dissuade the belief. Joe skillfully avoided Mr. GTO every day after work, but one day Mr. GTO pulled up to Joe as Joe was leaving the parking lot to go onto Telegraph Road – a main north/south service road adjacent to the plant. The owner of the GTO challenged Joe to a race from a rolling start of 30 miles per hour. Well, from a dead stop, the GTO would have beaten Joe, but from a 30-mile-per-hour roll, the GTO walked away from Joe as if Joe was stuck in tar. After the "race," the owner of the GTO pulled his car up to Joe and said, "What the hell, man, you don't have a 427 engine in that car." A very embarrassed Joe admitted it was a 390 engine.

Mr. GTO said, "Then take off those F-in flags."

For the next few weeks, the owner of the GTO chided Joe about the fact that Joe still had 427 horsepower flags on a car that truly did not have a 427 engine in it. There was a clear suggestion that Joe was being very deceptive, which Joe probably deserved. He was acting like the car had an engine that it didn't have. As Josh said to Joe, "If you're going to be a braggart, you better have the tools to back it up." The upshot was that Joe was exceedingly embarrassed that he had lied about the car and avoided the guy's work area thereafter. Never again did Joe want to be the kind of person who would misrepresent the facts. Joe later had the 427 tags removed from the Galaxie XL. Even though the car was now stripped of all signs of its original heart stopping animal prowess, it was still the coolest car in the neighborhood. Years later people who ask Joe if he had been the owner of that cool 1964 Galaxie XL with the chrome-reverse wheels. Joe would smile and say that he was but with appropriate humility he would say, "I bought it from my step brother, Ray. You should have seen it in its prime."

The whole car thing, and where he was in life, was a humbling experience and a teachable moment for Joe. The time was coming for him to begin to grow up and be truthful in all walks of life. Joe has never walked back from that belief and has adhered to that principle throughout his life – even telling his own kids years later that he could take anything they did and love them unconditionally, but "don't lie to me." When you lie and people know you lie, it is difficult for others to know when you are telling the truth.

Joe's unfaltering allegiance to the truth helped him many times in his life – especially when there were two conflicting stories and who was lying or who was telling the truth was up for debate. With Joe's reputation for honesty, in most questionable circumstances, when it got down to cases of "he said/she said," Joe's representation would be accepted as gospel.

Chapter 47 - Living The Dream, 1965-1966

Between Joe's job at the factory and the bar, he was making more money than he ever dreamed of making. And, while wanting to save money for college was a very worthy and grown-up thing to do, when you have never had money and then you start making what you consider to be very good money, one gets the urge to buy the toys that one has always desired.

Ray had a Norton motorcycle, and Joe got the itch to buy a motorcycle too. So, Joe bought a new BSA Lighting, with a 650 cc engine. He did this without taking a riding lesson or anything else. Joe learned to ride the motorcycle the hard way, by trial and error.

One of the first things he learned was that you didn't turn a corner by turning the handlebars alone. You have to lean left into the bike if you wanted to turn left and lean right if you wanted to turn right. Before getting that concept down, he rode across the lawn at the house on the corner of his street and had to kick at the porch in order to not run into it. After several harrowing experiences like this, he learned the leaning lesson.

While Joe had many very good times on the BSA, there were some events that would scare any parent to the core. Joe was a little too reckless for the motorcycle, and soon it got him in a lot of trouble. One time, he got caught in the medium of a traffic light on Telegraph Road and 6 Mile Road in Redford, Michigan. He was heading westbound. His best friend, Pete, was on the back of the bike. In the intersection, going in the same direction, were a couple of guys in a late model Corvette. The driver of the Corvette nodded and said, "Wanna go?" Well, Joe thought for sure that his bike could take a Corvette, so he smiled and nodded back (not considering the weight distribution with Pete on the back of the BSA.) The driver of the Corvette and Joe both revved their engines, the light turned green, off the Corvette went and up went the BSA with Pete landing on his butt in the middle of Telegraph. Joe's front tire rose from the ground, and Joe and the bike were soon airborne.

Joe held onto the steering wheel of the bike as tightly as he could. He began to slide backwards off of the bike seat. The more he slid down the seat, the more his right hand opened up the throttle. The throttle (gas) was controlled by the grip at the end of the right handle bar. When the grip was pulled back it made the engine run faster. Joe was hanging onto that handle bar and grip with all of his might - pulling it back as he was hanging, making the engine absolutely roar.

The back end of the bike began to come forward through his legs like a Ferris Wheel rising in the sky, and ultimately, he had to let go of the grips – which shut off the gas to the motorcycle engine causing the bike and Joe to drop to the ground. The bike landed with a crash right in front of Joe's sprawling body.

The driver of the Corvette slowed down and asked if Joe was all right. Joe moaned, "Yes." The Corvette driver sneered, "Do you race very often?" Joe heard the guys in the Corvette laughing as they drove away.

Joe and Pete looked at the damage to the bike. Joe had bent the front fork of the motorcycle and scratched the hell out of the bike. The bike could not be ridden, so Pete and Joe had to walk the bike two miles to Joe's home.

After getting the bike fixed, Joe swore he was going to ride more maturely and generally did, but sometimes things just happen.

On July 4th, Joe was riding through Rouge Park, a very popular park that followed the Rouge River flood plain across the western suburbs and western Detroit – ultimately dumping into the Detroit River. Joe came around a bend in the road only to find that the road was lined with cars on both sides and someone was blocking the entire two lanes of the road trying to squeeze into a parking space.

With oncoming traffic blocking Joe from going around the car in the street, and with Joe going a little too fast for the circumstances, Joe hit the impeding car on the driver's side, flew over the roof of the car and landed headfirst on the concrete on the driver's side of the car.

Crumpled on the ground, Joe heard concerned citizens asking him if he was okay. But he couldn't answer back. Fading in and out of consciousness Joe heard, "Don't touch him." "Is he dead?" and other such alarmed comments. Then he heard an ambulance, felt a stretcher, a lift, and a siren. Joe awoke in the back of an ambulance racing him to the hospital.

Miraculously, Joe didn't have any broken bones and didn't sustain any long-term injuries due to a mandatory helmet law for motorcycle riders had been recently passed. The helmet that he wore, the helmet that he hated, had saved his life. When he saw the helmet later, it was split down the middle. Joe fully understood that the helmet could have been his head.

Riding the bike back from the repair shop several weeks later, Joe found himself pulling to the far side of the road each time a car pulled up to enter the road from the left or right. Fear had taken over his riding. Joe knew his motorcycle-riding days were over.

Joe had the bike while dating Kate, but her parents restricted her to riding around the neighborhood with him. Based on Joe's riding experiences, it was a good decision on their part.

Chapter 48 - Viet Nam Came Home 1966

The Viet Nam War was on the mind of everyone and marches and protests against the war were going on all the time. The war was coming home to Joe and to a number of his friends when several childhood friends in the neighborhood came home from Viet Nam in caskets. From a drafted soldier to an officer who graduated from West Point, their position in the military just didn't matter when they came home in a coffin. Families wept for their sons and daughters regardless of what their station was in the military. After going to see the remains of a good friend, Joe wrote:

The Letter From Viet Nam

I didn't really believe it
when the letter came and said,
"You needn't worry, he's been found.

> But, we're sorry, cause he's dead.
> We're sorry, but he's dead."
>
> "We don't know exactly how it happened,"
> the letter went on to say,
> "we found him in a rice pad
> with a bullet through his face."
> There was a bullet through his face.
>
> The writer said, "We're shipping
> his body back to you.
> We're sending along an honor guard
> to do the things we have to do."
>
> Now I can hear him as he says
> my words unto another.
> "All he wrote was, "That's okay,
> the man was only - my brother."

Seeing his childhood friend in the casket propped up on his left side with a pillow to support the parts of his body that were missing (the left side of his back that had been blown off when they found him in the rice fields) was shocking and brought the war right to the doorstep of Joe and many other Americans of military age.

Chapter 49 - Beginning College, Summer 1966

That winter Joe took the entrance exam at Schoolcraft College in Livonia. He couldn't afford to go away to school. Going to Schoolcraft would allow him to save on room and board while living with Josh, who had moved to Livonia, a Detroit suburb. Joe passed the written exam and other tests and was accepted at Schoolcraft College. He quit his job in the factory and entered college in the summer of 1966.

Going to college at Schoolcraft College was so much cheaper than a four-year college, and the funds that Joe had saved, in addition to the money he made from two jobs that he presently had (he still worked cleaning the bar, and he worked 40 hours a week at a grocery store in Detroit) provided him with the necessary income to pay for his classes, books, car and other expenses. Josh allowed Joe to live at home without rent, which was very gracious of him, because Joe was not his kid. Joe reasoned that Josh had to have feelings for him, because Josh didn't have to let him stay there.

Joe kept the BSA but sold the Ford Galaxie XL, and bought a Mercury Comet and tried not to flunk out of school. He had a student deferment at the time, but Uncle Sam was waiting for him if he could not pass his classes.

To cover his expenses, Joe got a job unloading trucks and putting up stock at a Kroger Grocery Store near University of Detroit in Detroit. When he wasn't putting up stock or unloading trucks, he would work the cash registers or bag groceries. He was a very hard worker and very fast. When he was bagging groceries, he raced between three check-out lines and made it a challenge to finish packing the groceries before any of the cashiers collected the money from the customer. He didn't bat 100% in that endeavor but he was a good 85%. Some people called him a whirling dervish. He laughed at the comparison, but never really understood what it meant.

At the store Joe learned about the importance of satisfying customers and providing a good service. The customer may not always be right, but you certainly don't want to treat the customer as if they were wrong. One day an elderly female customer got her dander up when she believed that a new employee of the store was being rude to her.

She said, "Listen young lady, I have been shopping here for 15 years. The money I spend here helps pay you. But you give me that tone of voice makes me say 'I don't have to come here anymore'" and walked out. The woman lived in an apartment complex just north of the store's parking lot. The store was very convenient for her, but she did have her pride, and if they weren't going to treat her with respect, she would find somewhere else to get her groceries.

Vince, the store manager ran after and caught up with the unhappy customer. They talked about the experience and the manager calmed here down. Just the fact that this very important man, who ran a grocery store, would come after her had one the customer over even before he opened his mouth. She just wanted to be shone some respect, which Vince had shown her.

That evening, the manager called his employees into a five-minute meeting to talk about the importance of customer service. He said, "When you anger a customer; when you dismiss a customer; when you talk down to a customer, that customer may never come back. But, it's not just that you may lose that customer, you may lose the business of that customer's circle of contacts. Stories about bad service are more fun to tell than stories of good service, so you may be causing far more damage than you believe. When you feel like you could say something damaging, put a check on your mouth and don't say it. Go get a cup of coffee, take a break, just don't chase a customer away."

Chapter 50 – Charlie Found Guilty Sexual Assault, 1967

The lawless among us seem to always be looking for opportunities to take advantage of unsuspecting victims. This was the case when Charlie, now 22 years old, was driving down Merriman Road in Livonia one October afternoon. Charlie spotted a teenage girl drop her books as she was running to catch the bus at her middle school. As she scurried around to get her books, the bus driver, not seeing her, pulled away. A gallant Charlie stopped his car near the bus stop and got out to help her. Being warned of strangers, the girl said that she did not need help. Charlie backed off and said that he had wanted to get his sister before she left the school on the bus. Now he would have to follow the bus and get his sister at the next stop of the school bus. "You may know my sister, Debbie? Debbie Carlson?"

The flustered girl said she didn't.

"She's in the 8th grade."

The flustered girl thought, "There are a lot of kids in the school that I don't know, and he looks safe. He did mention his sister's name even if I don't know it. He wouldn't do that if he wasn't who he said he was" she reasoned. She decided it would be okay to take a ride with him to the next school bus stop. "Sir," she called out, "I really have to catch that bus to get home. Can I catch a ride with you?"

"Certainly, and it's Mr. Carlson." He took the books from her and put them carefully on the back seat. Then he directed her toward the front passenger seat, and she got in. "Put your seatbelt on. I always have to tell my sister that," he laughed.

She put her seat belt on, and he pulled away from the curb. They were approaching the bus when Charlie pulled into the left lane, sped up and left the bus behind him. "Wait, that's my bus!" the girl called out turning toward him.

"Not today, sweetheart," Charlie said, and roared on down the street.

"But you said your sister was Debbie Gibson. What about your sister?"

"I made it all up. Now shut up."

He drove to a vacant lot and forced himself on the girl. "Don't scream, and I won't hurt you," he whispered into her ear. "Don't fight, and this will soon be over." Just as Charlie was ready to push himself onto the girl, she stabbed him in the thigh with a pair of scissors she had pulled out of her pencil holder. As Charlie grabbed his leg in pain, she opened the door and ran toward the street. Realizing it would be too hard to catch her, Charlie sped away as quickly as he could, with his right hand placed against his wound.

The potential rape victim had the presence of mind to get the color of the car and part of the license number. She had seen a gas station down the street and ran to it. She told the attendant at the gas station that she had been raped and asked him to call 911.

The information that she gave the police enabled them to put out a search for Charlie. Later that evening, the car was seen on a side street of a small rundown motel. Charlie was awakened by the sound of a battering ram knocking the door from its hinges. He was arrested and picked out of a line-up by the victim. He was charged and convicted of third-degree sexual assault and sentenced to two years in Jackson State Penitentiary, in Jackson, Michigan. The judge prohibited any time off for good behavior.

Maggie was shocked by the crime and the conviction. She wept over her foolishness for not believing her first husband when he told her years ago about Charlie's abuse of Joe. At that time, she had thought that Joe could have been stretching the truth. This rape conviction, and other things she knew that Charlie did, convinced Maggie that if she had taken action when Charlie was a child, maybe a therapist or a psychiatrist could have helped Charlie become a normal child. But now, the damage was done.

Joe had taken a job with a grocery store in the City of Detroit. The school year was over, and he had the summer months to make as much money as he could to help pay his college and living expenses when he went back to school in the fall. His job was to fill the store's shelves with groceries during the night. He and two other members of the night crew were locked inside the store from 11:00 PM until 8:00 AM in the morning. He had just gotten to bed one morning when Jayne came into his room and said:

"Joe, wake up, it's your mother."

"My God, I just got to bed. What time is it?"

"It's 11:00 AM, honey, and your mom says it's really important."

Joe stumbled into the house phone in the kitchen and talked to his mother.

"Joe, I just found out that your brother is in Jackson Prison."

"In Jackson Prison? For what?" Joe asked.

"He attempted to rape an underaged girl. She was 16 years old. Charlie is 22. Jesus, I don't know what's with that boy and his infatuation with young girls."

Joe said, "Mom, what is his infatuation with committing criminal acts?" Then he said, "I never heard anything about a trial. How can he be in prison without a trial?" asked Joe.

"I understand that he pled guilty to Third Degree Statutory Rape in front of the judge in the pre-trial hearing."

Joe said, "What does third degree sexual assault mean? Do you know?"

It has something to do with the girl being between 13 and 16 and attempted rape," his mother said. Charlie did not tell his mother that he would have to serve the entire two years. She said, "Maybe he can get out on good behavior."

"And do what, Mom?"

"Well, live."

"Live on what? His good looks? He'll never find a job of any real consequence. If employers know he was in Jackson Prison, who will hire him? He has screwed himself for life, Mom."

"That's a pretty dim view of things."

"Mom, how else can you look at it? I know he's your child and you want to think positively about his future, but he has destroyed any real future he might have had."

There was silence on the phone.

Joe felt sorry for his mother, and all Charlie was her son. He told himself to back off and go easy on her. He broke the silence by saying, "How did you find out about the offense, Mother? And why did they send him to Jackson Prison? That's a maximum-security prison, isn't it? That s for the big-time, dangerous criminals."

"Charlie called me from prison," Maggie said. "The reason he is at Jackson is because your brother is a repeat offender, Joe. Not to the extent that he will never get out of prison, because if he does what he is told and stays clean he may get out early."

Joe shook his head and said, "Well, knowing Charlie like I do know, Mother, I would say that the chances of him obeying the rules and being good are pretty slim. He is more likely to screw up and have his sentence extended"

"That's not very kind, Joe. He is your brother."

"Mom, I know Charlie better than you do. I know the shit that he is capable of. I have experienced what he is capable of first hand. Charlie is one messed up dude. You said yourself, he is a repeat offender. You don't become a repeat offender by learning your lesson and resolving to sin no more. You become a repeat offender because you don't care about people or rules and anyone but yourself. All of that describes Charlie in spades."

"You have lived with Josh too long. He always takes the negative view on things. He always said that one day Charlie would end up In Jackson. I couldn't believe it."

"Mom, to look at things logically and realistically is not being negative, it is being honest. And not to be cruel, Mom, it is hard to be logical when you wander around the house crying with your face in a bottle."

"That was mean, Joe."

"No. it would been mean if it was a lie. You had your head in a bottle most of the time when Charlie was living with us."

"I was going through a lot after getting the staph infection. I was dealing with it the best I could."

"I know you were," said Joe, "but did the booze help the infection go away? Did it help you keep your marriage together? Did it help you protect your children from Josh's belt? Did it help you stop a bullying older brother from beating up on his younger brother?"

Silence.

"You're drinking now aren't you?"

"No."

"No? I can hear it in the slur in your voice."

Maggie took a deep breath. "I am sad about your brother."

"I'm sad too, Mother, but I don't have a drink in my hand, and I won't have one in my hand later."

"He's my son, and I'm sad."

"He's my, brother, and I'm sad too. I'm also really pissed off that he would be so damn stupid and throw his life away."

There was silence on the other end of the receiver. Then Maggie said, "I was hoping that talking to you could make me feel better."

"I don't have a magic wand, Mother. I can't spill fairy dust on it and make it feel better. Everyone has been giving Charlie a pass for years because poor Charlie had to stay at St. Mathews longer than I did. Charlie has been milking the family with that guilt for years and you let, especially you, let him get away with it."

"What was I supposed to you, Joe? Kick him out?"

"No, you and Dad should have said, 'Enough feeling sorry for yourself, Charlie. We did the best that we could do. You've got the rest of your life ahead of you. Now go out and make the best of it.'"

"Well, I need to go. I just called to let you know."

"OK. Before you go, why haven't I heard about Charlie's criminal escapades?"

"Charlie said that you told him to stay out of your life."

"Yes, I did. And I had good reasons for saying that, and I can see now how smart I was. No one can help Charlie, except Charlie. And Charlie doesn't appear to want to help himself."

"Well, he is still my son, and I am going to see him."

"Would you like for me to come with you?"

"Would you?"

"He's still my brother, Mom."

"Yes. I'll call you back and let you know when I am going.

Good-bye, Joe."

The phone went silent.

After Joe got off the phone, Josh came into the room.

'I couldn't help but overhear some of the conversation. So Charlie is in Jackson Prison, eh?"

Joe let out a sign, "Yah. He could have had it all if he hadn't always felt that the world owed him something. He had looks, intelligence." Joe stopped and shook his head. "What a waste. So many people in life have had it so much worse than Charlie. Somehow, they put it behind them and moved forward."

Josh said, "This isn't the time to gloat, but I told your mother years ago that he would end up in prison."

Joe wanted to say that if Josh had talked more and beat less, that Charlie may have had a better chance at dealing with a world where he had to be aggressive to succeed, but not too aggressive to make you do things so that you'll fail. What were beatings but another display of aggression. But he couldn't say that to Josh. Josh was providing Joe with a roof over his head and a family environment, to the degree that there was one, and Joe could not put that at risk. Joe had learned a phrase in an English class about discretion being the better part of valor. He could be a heroic figure here (filled with valor) and tell Josh that his beating fanned the fires of Joe's contempt for the world, but to do that would be to tempt being told to find his own place to live. Given Joe's station in life, it was better to be discreet than be heroic. So, Joe simply got up and said, "You were right, Josh. I am going to go back to bed."

Chapter 51 - Maggie and Joe Visit Charlie in Jackson Prison, May 1967

Several days after Joe's discussion with his mother about going to visit Charlie at Jackson Prison, Maggie called Joe and they arranged for her to pick him up on Sunday to visit Charlie. The visitation was scheduled for 11:00 AM. A guard frisked the visitors before they were taken into the visitation room. Once in the visitation room they were assigned a table and chairs and waited until Charlie was brought in. Several minutes later from another door leading into the room, two guards maneuvered Charlie into the room, sat him down in a chair and cuffed his legs to the table. Charlie was wearing handcuffs as well.

Joe looked at the guard and said, "Is all of this necessary? We're family."

"Do you want to be removed from the room?" asked the guard.

"I'm an American citizen asking a simple question," Joe said.

"And this is a federal prison. All rights are off. You are here at our pleasure."

Charlie said, "Joe, don't make any more trouble for me."

"All right," Joe said, "I just thought you'd be treated like a human."

The guard looked at Joe and said, "One more word and you are out of here."

Joe just looked at the guard, shook his head and looked away. If the guard could have read his mind, Joe probably would have been pistol whipped. As it was, the guard said, "No physical contact with the prisoner" and moved to the corner of the room where he crossed his arms, with his feet spread in case the handcuffed, foot cuffed, prisoner tried to make a run for it. Joe thought, "He is well suited for his job. "

Maggie's eyes were filled with tears at the sight of her eldest child. She wanted to throw her arms around him and tell him everything would be all right, but she couldn't because deep down she knew everything was not going to be all right ever again.

Maggie asked, "How are they treating you?"

"Well, you see it. Three square meals a day, four walls a bed, a place to leave bodily discharges." He shrugged his shoulders. "Not much worse than St. Mathews."

"I'm so sorry, Charlie." Maggie said.

Joe was a little revolted by his mom apologizing to an admitted felon because she and Gregory had to put Charlie and Joe in St. Mathews all those years ago. Certainly, it had to be lonely to be in that home without loved ones around, but many people in the world had it much worse than Charlie did, and went on to live fruitful, productive lives.

Joe said, "The difference between here and St. Mathews, Charlie, is that you put yourself here."

Charlie gave Joe a pained expression. "Why did you bring him, Mom? To torture me?"

"You don't need me for that do you, Charlie? You do enough of that on your own."

"Boys, can't we just have a peaceful visit?" said Maggie.

"Absolutely," said Charlie. "Bring in the cupcakes and Cool-Aid."

Joe said, "Charlie, you may not want me here, but I can offer you this. Once you are out of here, you can vow to never come back and live your life within the law."

"I've tried, Joe. It just doesn't work out for me. "

"This girl you were caught with, did you know she was underaged?"

"I had an inkling."

"Then why did you do it?"

"I don't know," he shrugged, 'I guess I just like the way they look at that age."

"You know it's against the law. Is this an example of how you have tried to live within the law and it just doesn't work out for you?"

Charlie glared at Joe.

Go ahead glare at me. This is what messing

around with that age of girl gets you, Charlie."

"Yah? I thought they brought me here for my good looks." He laughed at his own joke.

"Everything's always a joke, isn't it?"

Charlie said, "Joking helps me handle the bad times."

"If you learned how to handle yourself, Charlie, there wouldn't be so many bad times to handle. That's the kind of impulse you're going to have to learn to control, Charlie, or you'll spend your life behind bars."

Charlie exhaled a large breath. "I know you're right, but I guess that's your path, Joe. Not mine."

Joe countered, "But it can be. You are smart, you're good looking. If you stop feeling sorry for yourself and apply the skills that you have to living within the law and improving yourself, you can still have a good life."

"That correct, Charlie. Start doing that right now," said Maggie.

"That ship has sailed." said Charlie.

"For every ship that sails out of port, Charlie, another ship comes in. It's not too late for anyone who wants to live a full life."

"Where'd you get that shit, Joe, out of a college Psych textbook? The dye is cast for me."

"Only because you have resigned yourself to it. Look what you are doing to Mom. Just give it a chance." Joe got up and said he would give Maggie and Charlie some time alone. "I'll be in the waiting room." A guard took Joe back to the waiting room.

Maggie said, "He's right, Charlie. You should listen to him."

"I'll try, Mom. But Joe can feel that way because he was taken out of St. Mathews early."

Charlie had the old play book out again.

Chapter 52 - The Detroit Riots, 1967

Unrest had been brewing in Detroit for quite some time, but all hell broke loose on the night of July 23, when Detroit police officers raided a bar near downtown Detroit that was open after hours. The mostly black patrons of the bar, fought the police and their standing up to authority spread through the city like a wild fire. Sometimes an action against the police begins for a worthy reason then turns into an opportunity to get stuff for nothing. Such was the case in Detroit. Many retailers had vacated the city because many customers of all stripes and colors were leaving a city that they perceived was heading down the wrong path, if not dying.

When you see anything eroding, it is common sense to protect what you have and cut your losses by selling the item that is in distress and getting out while you still have a shirt on your back. A lot of people who were still financially sound, both black and white were leaving the city in vast numbers. Many quality retailers who needed the demographic that was fleeing, to sustain their businesses left the city with their customers.

Out of naïve curiosity Joe and his best friend, Pete, drove into the city along Grand River in Pete's MG Midget. They got down far enough to see first-hand the rioting, looting, burning and general mayhem. A member of the National Guard came over to them and said, "You guys don't belong down here, it's dangerous. Pull your car in here (pointing at a curb cut) and get out of here." Anyone with a modicum of common sense would have known that that it was dangerous. The boys certainly did, but they were two guys who had a real curiosity of what was going on and why. (The adage of curiosity kills the cat comes to mind.) They had seen what was going on but did not know the why, that would have to be determined, but not from here. It was too dangerous. The boys did a 180 and got back to the safe suburbs where many of the business owners who had been in Detroit before, were also headed.

Rage takes away reason. The rage that was going on in the city of Detroit had dire consequences for the city and the residents of the city in the short and long term. For a city that was trying to stem the outflow of people and businesses, the riots did just the opposite. The people living in the city who could not afford to leave had fewer businesses to satisfy their demands and needs than they had before the riots began. Their lives literally and figuratively became poorer. Yes, rage takes away reason. But it wasn't all rage, many people saw the riots as their cover for getting some free stuff. These opportunists who got a new television or washing machine out of the looting didn't care about the long-term effects of their actions on their neighbors, they were watching television for free or they were pawning the stolen items to get money to buy booze, drugs whatever. It is the same behavior that was perpetrated by Black Lives Matter, Antifa and the opportunists who followed them in the pandemonium that hit the cities of America during the summer of 2020. A break-down of law and order is an indication of a society in extreme distress, which America has become. Too many people close their eyes and minds to what is more and more becoming the reality – America is being overthrown from within. It is purposeful and intentional, but that's for another book.

    The two friends who had witnessed this lawlessness of the 1967 would for years disagree on the causes and who caused it. But, that's also for another time, right now they were just happy as hell to be getting out of the city.

    It was with a great deal of trepidation that Joe went to the grocery store to work night crew that night. The store was located on Plymouth Avenue and Evergreen within the City of Detroit – only a few short miles from where rioters were ripping the city asunder. Joe thought, "What are our freedoms worth if crime is so rampant that we are afraid to use them?" The answer, of course, is "Not much."

    All night long the night crew could hear the sound of gun fire through the city and up and down Plymouth Road. The night crew staff would hear shooting from outside of the building, and several times during the night roving bands of rioters banged on the doors of the grocery store, but no glass was broken and there was no penetration into the building. The crew presumed that the rioters did not try to break into the building because the lights were on and they didn't know the size of crew that might be waiting for them on the other side of the door.

Chapter 53 - Bad Things Can and Do Happen To Good People – or Despite Your Greatest Intentions, Sometimes Shit Happens, June, 1968

Kate graduated from the private high school in June. Joe was invited to the graduation ceremonies like he was part of the family. Kate's grade point average was over 3.4. She could have gone to a number of universities, but seeing how Joe had all of his classes transfer to Eastern induced her to enroll at Schoolcraft College for the fall semester.

Joe had the summer months to maximize the money that he would need for college, books, his car, insurance etc. He would still need to work while going to school, but high pay was critical during the summer months. Joe had applied for a position at The Ford Motor Company assembly plant in Wixom, Michigan and got the job. The starting day was on a Friday afternoon. The hours at Ford were 3:00 PM to 11:00 PM which conflicted with Joe's night crew stock job at the store. Joe called one of his colleagues at the store and asked if he would cover for him that night on the night crew. The colleague agreed.

At the Ford assembly plant, Joe's job was to install interior door panels – including door handles, door openers, air conditioning controls, power locks, etc. into the right front and back doors of the cars as they came down the assembly line.

He would make up the panel in advance based on the specifications of the order for the car. Then he would install them as the car was going past his stations at the speed that experts had determined was at a rate that a prototype worker could complete the tasks at any particular station along the line.

Joe learned the job quickly and had no difficulty keeping up with the speed of the line. As he worked, his mind wandered to a lecture that his Psyche 201 professor gave to his class one day. The lecture was entitled "Why Do Bad Things Happen To Good People?" What Joe had gotten out of the lecture is that if God is a loving God, why does he let bad things happen to good people. Wouldn't a loving God use His Godly powers to protect good people who believe in Him?" was what Joe got from the presentation.

Joe smiled to himself. How strange it was that he was having these thoughts while working on an assembly line at 8:30 PM. Was he having a premonition that something bad was going to happen to him? He didn't know. What he did know, or at least believed, was that the professor was trying to make students question their belief in the goodness of God. Or maybe it was just that the professor wanted to make students think about what they believed in and why they believed in it. In that case, thought Joe as he worked, what do I believe in? He knew that his religious beliefs stemmed from the beliefs of his Grandmother Luci and the historical teachings of the church. She had no question about her faith, at least Joe didn't think so. But what did he know? Maybe she did and kept the questions to herself.

Joe did not believe that God put HIs hand into every aspect of the daily lives of people. And Joe did not believe that a loving God sat on his Heavenly thrown sending good events and bad events to human beings. Joe laughed at the concept. A voice broke his thoughts. "Joe, do you find this work funny?"

It was the line supervisor who was standing in front of Joe's work station. "No, sir. I think this is very serious work."

"Then what were you laughing about?"

"I was just thinking about something a professor was talking about."

"Well, keep focused on your job, Joe. Our customers are relying on the quality of our product. When they are driving our cars, they are putting their lives into our hands." The line supervisor began to walk away, and Joe asked, "Am I messing things up, sir?"

"No, Joe," he said, "it looks like you have it all under control" and he gave Joe a thumbs up. "Just stay focused."

Joe put the completed panels on the car as it was going by. He looked at his assembly sheet for what would go into the next vehicle and began to build the panels out. Thinking back to God, if God sent bad events to only bad people that would only make the bad people more hateful of God. God would be viewed as a vengeful God not a loving God. Joe believed that good events and bad events were part of every person's lives. To Joe, what mattered was how one handled the good and bad events that happened in their lives. That is what separated the good person from the bad person, the mature from the immature and even the smart from the not so smart.

Joe believed that the good person was humble, not arrogant, in the face of good things happening in their lives. And bad events should be handled maturely with a thought as to how the bad event can be rectified or the damage diminished or controlled.

Joe's thoughts were interrupted by a man's yelling up the line. He heard, "The line is moving too damn fast. Slow the line down!"

Joe noticed that the yelling was coming from two stations in front of his station. The worker at the station, Tony, had introduced himself to Joe earlier in the shift. Tony was a nice kid, just out of high school, who had only been on the line for a couple of weeks. Tony seemed to have a job that was either too difficult for him or too difficult for anyone to do. Tony had been adequately trained to do the job, but was totally unprepared for being able to do the required work at the speed of the line. Tony was finding that he could not finish the work during the time when the vehicles were passing through his station on the line. His job consisted of installing several parts under the dashboard and then going to the back of the car to make another installation. Joe had watched Tony several times in the evening as Tony crawled into the car with the parts that he had to install and a power drill. When he was done, Tony somewhat frantically moved to the back of the car to install parts there as well. If the vehicle was in another zone on the line, Tony would have to discontinue his work so the next person on the line could do the work required at that station. Since the vehicle was missing some parts, at the end of the line, the car would be taken to a holding location at the plant until the missing parts were installed.

A report was always done by the installer of missing parts in this area, and many of the parts would be parts that Tony should have installed. That is never a report that workers want to be on. Tony's attitude was that since he had been well trained for the position, the line must be going too fast thereby preventing him from completing the work at his station.

Tony threw down his tools and once more yelled out, "The line is moving too fast. I want my union representative and a time study analyst. I will not do another car until they come here!"

The line was shut down for 20 minutes until the union steward and the time study man came over to check out the problem. The line study expert started up the line and told everyone to work as if nothing had happened. He saw Tony's inability to complete the work. Either the line was too fast or Tony was too slow. A relief man was called to sub for Tony. A relief man is someone who is experienced with the work that is done at every position on an assembly line. If a worker on the line is not able to do the job or is missing for any reason, the relief man fills in so that the assembly line can keep going. The relief man got into the next car coming down the line, made the installation under the dash board then did the installation at the rear of the car. This process continued for 15 cars, and the relief man never fell behind. The line supervisor told the relief man to plan on staying at Tony's position for a while longer. The relief man nodded, and the line kept on churning out Lincolns.

A meeting was convened with the line supervisor, Tony, the union steward, the time study man and a representative from personnel, which was a little disconcerting to Tony. The line supervisor began with a review of what happened that evening. He then asked the time study man to discuss the work that was done at the stage of the assembly. The Time Study representative acknowledged that the position was moderately more challenging than other positions on the line, but not significantly so. He said, "The line speed is fine, because the relief man was able to do it with no difficulty, so the problem is the speed of the worker."

Tony interjected, "I'm going as fast as I can. I am not slouching off!"

The union steward said, "Calm down, son, no one said you were. As you know the job better your speed will increase."

Tony shook his head, "I know that job pretty well, I am going as fast as I can go so as to not screw up. I never will be able to go fast enough to do that job." The time study analyst then said that all jobs on the line are designed to be interchangeable. "If someone is not able to do the work in one position, like Tony here, then that person would likely have difficulty with any other position."

The line supervisor nodded then cocked his head to the personnel man, who brought a security guard to wait outside of the room. The personnel representative said, "Tony, this isn't going to work out."

Tony said, "What, I'm being fired for doing the right thing in asking that a time study be done?"

The personnel representative said, "Tony, you did

nothing wrong. If the time study had shown the line was moving too fast for the positions on the line, then a change in work flow and line speed would have been addressed. The problem was that it wasn't the line speed it was your speed. That was proved by the relief man who had no problem doing your job. And all the jobs call for similar speed which you don't have."

"Well give me a second chance. This isn't fair!"

The security officer came into the room.

The personnel man held up his hand to the security officer as if to say it's ok. Then he said, "Tony, just minutes ago you said to all of us that you could never work fast enough to do that job. Didn't you?"

Tony nodded. "But I didn't think I would be fired."

"Tony, all the jobs are timed to be similar in the length of time they take at a certain speed. You admitted yourself you could not do that speed. So, we'll call this a mistake and move on."

"But my getting fired is really going to look bad on my record." Tony pushed back the chair and the security guard moved forward and restrained Tony."

The personnel man said, "Tony, sit down."

Tony sat. "You know, I have a son about your age. He's a good kid and so are you. I would not want my son to be negatively affected just because a job didn't work out, any more than I would want that for you, believe me."

The personnel man took out a paper and began to write long hand on the paper. After which he gave it to Tony to read. It read: "To whom it may concern, Tony was hired to do a job on the assembly line. Tony is a hard-working, intelligent and dedicated young man. Our parting ways with him does not reflect any dissatisfaction concerning the work ethic, intelligence or character of this fine young man." The letter was signed by the personnel manager of the Ford Wixom Assembly Plant.

Tony nodded and thanked him.

"Also, we will cover your monthly medical insurance for three months. That should give you time to find other employment that will be more suitable to you."

They shook hands and the security guard took Tony's badge and building entry permit and parking pass and walked him to the door.

At the end of the shift, Joe walked out of the plant with the relief man who told him what he knew about the meeting that was held with Tony. "The job isn't for everyone," said the relief man. "That's why they have a three-to-six-month probationary period."

Joe nodded and then said, "But, the guys said that Tony was only here for a month."

"Well, sometimes you just know much sooner than other times. Tony saw that and so did the company. If you see it's not going to work out, it's better to cut your losses and get someone else. It's better for the employee, too. You don't need to gore the ox, as you are going out the door. You can part as friends. As I said, this job isn't for everyone."

As Joe drove home that evening, he thought about Tony. Joe hoped that Tony would find something that worked for him. He was sure that he would. Tony was a good guy, just in the wrong job. Often an event that we construe as a bad thing is really a good thing, because in the case of Tony, he would have gone crazy on the assembly line job. Getting dismissed was a blessing in disguise. It showed Tony what he was not good at working at the speed required for that position, so that he could focus his attention on something other than assembly work. It gave Tony a better chance to try to determine what it was that he was good at. Tony's anger was due to the fact that he thought he was doing the right thing and it came back to bite him. Then it was a matter of a dismissal destroying his future. But, it ended well due to the quality of Tony and the company. God did not have his hand in it. Life happens, thought Joe. What separates us is how we handle what life gives us. Tony will be fine, thought Joe.

The following morning Joe got up early and drove

over to the store to check his work schedule and tell the manager that he no long could work night crew.

As he walked in the door, Joe felt a change in the atmosphere of the store. Everyone seemed to be on edge and seemed to be giving Joe a strange and curious look. He walked into the backroom and the store manager, Al, came up behind him and said, "Where in the hell were you last night?"

Joe turned and gave Al a curious look and said, "What do you mean?"

"What do you think I mean? You were supposed to work night crew last night."

"I called Rob up yesterday morning and asked him to cover for me, and he said he would."

"Well, Rob didn't. I had to ask three guys to stay after to get the stock up. And I had to stay with them to let them out the door."

Joe said, "I'm so sorry, Al, Rob said he was going to cover for me."

Al was too angry to be reasoned with. He said "Your being sorry didn't get the stock put up. I got three hours sleep then had to be back here this morning to open up. Where in the hell were you last night anyway?"

"I was hired by Ford to work the afternoon shift. I got the notice late and Rob said he could cover for me. I can work there and here, but just not the night crew or afternoons."

"Well, that doesn't work for me. I need you on the night crew. I hired you for that, and if you can't do that than just get the hell out of here. You're fired!"

Joe said, "You're making a mistake. I did nothing wrong. Ask Rob."

"I don't have to, you were on the schedule and you missed work, now get out of my store."

"Yes, I was on the schedule, but I couldn't make it and I got someone to cover for me. He agreed. How is that my fault?"

"I'm the manager. It's my store. You're fired, period."

As Joe left the back room of the store, he turned to Al and said, "You're not a manager, Al, you're a dictator." Then he turned to the rest of the crew that had assembled in the back room and said, "This is what you're dealing with guys. You better be perfect in what you do or you're out the door."

"Get out!" Al screamed.

"I'm buying some groceries, first." Joe said. As he was checking out, he walked up to the office and spoke to the assistant manager. Al was not there. Joe said, "This is wrong, Fred."

Fred said, "I talked to Rob. He said he totally forgot to come in."

"And Al knows?"

Fred nodded.

Joe said, "This better not go into my file as a firing, Fred. If it does, I'll hire an attorney'."

Fred nodded. "I'll take care of it. The company understands Al." Fred came out of the office and shook Joe's hand. "You did a great job here, Joe. If you need a reference, just call me."

Joe rode his BSA home and thought, "Tony and I on the same day. Bad things do happen to good people. But it will work out."

Later that day, Rob called and apologized to Joe about not coming in. "I just completely forgot, Joe. I'm sorry."

Joe said, "Let it go, Rob. I don't walk on water either."

A week later, Joe got home from Ford at 11:45 PM. On his dresser was a brief note from Josh that the store had called him and asked him to call. "Some guy by the name of Fred."

After getting up later that day, Joe called the store and asked to speak to Fred, the assistant manager. "You mean Fred, the manager?"

"What? No. He is the assistant manager."

The person at the store said, "He was the assistant manager. Al's gone. Now Fred's the manager."

Fred came to the phone and said, "Hey, Joe, how is it going?" They exchanged pleasantries, then Fred said, "Look, Al was out of line the day you were in here. He's been moved to a smaller store. Less stress and all. I would like you back."

Joe was pleased with the call, but told Fred that he discovered he wouldn't be able to do two jobs after all and respectfully declined reemployment.

Fred understood and finished with "I get it, man, but, again, if you ever need a job or a reference, give me a call." They hung up as friends.

Joe, thought, "Yes, it will work out. And God didn't play a role in this either." Or did He?

Chapter 54 - The Separation, September 1968

At the beginning of his junior year, Joe transferred to Eastern Michigan University for his last two years to get his degree. Again, he would be taking a class load of 16 hours per semester and working in a grocery store. Joe lived near the campus sharing an apartment with three other students who had transferred to Eastern Michigan University from Schoolcraft. Between school, homework, his work schedule, and the distance between Ypsilanti and Detroit, Joe and Kate only saw each other one day on the weekend (if Joe didn't have to work) and, if time permitted, one evening during the week.

Joe was very lonely at Eastern during his junior year. He wrote Kate as often as he could and was disappointed when he did not receive prompt letters back from her. He wrote about his sadness in various poems – some that he would send to her and some that he would simply keep in a binder.

Joe began to think seriously that the three years age difference between him and Kate was too much of a gap, at least at this time when he was 21 and she was 18. He began to convince himself that they had such different backgrounds and family histories, with all the divorces and chaos on his side, that it would never work out. He convinced himself of this to such an extent that he initiated a break up and began dating other girls. It was kind of an ugly break-up with Joe returning to Kate everything that she had ever given him. He was young and foolish and didn't realize what he was throwing away.

Joe began to date, but he found that he was constantly comparing every girl to Kate, and every girl was coming up far short of the love that he had for Kate. He soon found that dating others left him incomplete. This was not what he wanted. He wanted that girl with whom he had so rudely broken up. He missed Kate, but he didn't know how to go back to her after the ugliness of the breakup. Plus, he thought her family hated him for breaking up with her.

Chapter 55 – Kate at Schoolcraft College and the Dance, September 1968

Compared to the demands of the Catholic High School from Kate had graduated, Kate found that she could easily handle her class schedule and mix with students at the school and in the neighborhood. A void is always filled. Sometimes slowly. Sometimes quickly. In the case of Kate. the void that was created with the absence of Joe was filled by several guys in the neighborhood. While she was very hurt about the breakup with Joe, life had to go on, and it did. When the guys began knocking on the door, Kate answered. Getting calls from men other that Joe rebuilt some of the loss of ego that had resulted from Joe's breakup with her. He confidence grew as should be expected from someone as good, sweet, intelligent and beautiful as Kate was (although Kate seemed oblivious to how beautiful and intelligent, she was.) That lack of arrogance was in and of itself an endearing characteristic that separated her from many beautiful women.

Kate began going to dances at Schoolcraft College

and enjoying a coed environment for the first time in four years.

Joey was at Eastern on Friday evening. He did not have to work and he had made no effort to get a date. He sat at the kitchen table looking at pictures of Kate and himself. His heart was broken and he knew he was to blame for it. He had a picture that had been taken with Kate and the entire her entire family at her graduation ceremony. That was only two months ago. He had been accepted and felt like one of the family. This was what he screwed up.

The memory jilted Joe and he tried to call Kate. Kate's brother Jim answered the phone. Joe hesitated for a moment but he and Jim had always gotten along. He tried to make small talk that landed on Jim's very uninterested ear. "You jilt a member of the family and you're persona non grata to the rest of the family," Joe thought. He asked if Kate was home.

"She' not here," Jim said.

"Do you know where she is?"

"What's it to you?" Jim snapped.

"Ah, I just wanted to see if we could talk."

"I think she went to a dance at Schoolcraft College with one of the guys she is dating."

"Hmm, she dating someone?"

"Kate's a beautiful girl, Joe. Did you think she was just going to sit around and wait for you to come back?" The phone went dead.

Joe thought, "That was fun." He got in his car and headed off to Schoolcraft College. At the college, Joe found the correct building, bought a ticket and went inside in search of Kate. It was not difficult to find her, because she was the center of attention as she danced in the middle of the dance floor. She was the most stunning beauty there, and she smiled and danced with hips shaking in a manner that drew every male in the room and half of the females too, out of jealousy.

Joe's heart exploded in the same manner that it did when he saw Kate walking down the street in her bell bottom hip huggers three years ago. There was a slow dance next and Kate folded into the arms of the guy she had just danced with. Joe went up and tapped him on the shoulder and asked if he could cut in. Before the guy could respond Kate said, "Sorry, this dance is taken." She took the lead and steered away from Joe.

After the dance Joe approached her again and asked if they could talk. Kit said, "Everything that we have to say to each other, Joe, has already been said. You hurt me and I don't want to be hurt again."

"Kate, I was a fool. I know that now. Dating others is of no interest to me. You are the only one I want."

"It's too late for that, Joe. I want you to leave. Go back to Eastern where you belong, because you don't belong here and you don't belong with me."

"Kate, please."

"No, you please. Please leave."

Kate's date returned with a couple of Cokes. "Is this guy bothering you, Kate?"

She said, "No, he's just someone I used to know, and he's leaving." She smiled and said, "Come on, dance with me."

Joe took a deep breath and walked out of the room with Kate's eyes on him as he left.

Chapter 56 - The Void, Fall 1968

A somberness began to overcome, Joe. He had his classes, tons of homework, work at a grocery store in Ypsilanti and not much else. He tried dating a couple of times but it always felt like he was playing make believe. Since breaking off with Kate, an emptiness had come into Joe's life that could not filled. You might refer to it as a void. The problem with a void is that something generally slips into it, and often that something is not a good thing and can be destructive.

Joe's phone rang one day. It was Charlie. "Hey, little brother, I am up here in Ypsilanti with a couple of hot girls. Where do you live? We want to stop over."

"When did you get out of Jackson, Charlie?"

"Joe, don't go talking any shit like that. I really do have a couple of cuties with me, and they want to party. Are you interested?"

"What the hell. Sure."

Joe gave them his address and they were there in ten minutes. Joe met them at the front of the apartment.

Charlie said, "What are you doing down here? I thought we would go up."

"That won't happen. My roommates are up there, so let's go somewhere else."

Charlie said, "This is Brenda and her friend, Darlene, is in the back seat. Go on back and make yourself comfortable. Girls, this is my brother, Joe, the good seed in the family and the one with all the brains."

Suzan, who was obviously Charlie's date, said, "If Joe is the good seed, Charlie, what do that make you?"

Charlie pulled her over to him and whispered, "I am the bad seed and damn proud of it."

Brenda nestled very close to Charlie and said, "I like my men bad."

"Well, you have found the baddest of them all, Darlin."

Joe in the meantime was talking to Darlene, who seemed a little shy, much more so that Brenda. Joe asked Darlene where she went to school. Before Darlene could answer Brenda interjected, "We are both sophomores at Schoolcraft." Darlene scooted over closer to Joe and he put his arm around her. Brenda told Charlie that her folks were gone for the weekend. "Why don't we go back to my place? We can order a pizza and watch a movie." Everyone concurred, so Charlie drove to Brenda's house in Livonia. Charlie had a six pack of beer that he brought into the house with him. Brenda got him a bottle opener they threw pillows on the floor, and put on the TV. When the pizza delivery guy came, they sat down on the floor with pizza and beer for Charlie and Brenda and pizza and pop for

Joe and Darlene. Soon Charlie and Brenda moved to the far side of the living room, leaving Joe and Darlene alone. While Joe and Darlene kissed and hugged each other, Darlene said, "I think you are real cute, Joe, and I like you, but I don't want anything to go too far."

Joe had just met her and had no intentions of taking it beyond hugging and kissing and maybe a feel or two and told her so.

Darlene told Joe that she appreciated it because she had a boyfriend who worked at Big Boys, a local restaurant. Joe asked if her if her boyfriend went to Schoolcraft as well.

"No, he's a junior at Stevenson."

Severe moaning and panting was coming from the other side of the living room that was a little distracting to someone who was having a serious conversation, but Joe sat up and said, "The high school?"

"Yes," she said.

"You are sophomore at Schoolcraft, and you're dating a junior in high school?" Joe was incredulous.

"Well about that.."

Joe interrupted her and said, "You don't go to Schoolcraft, do you?"

Darlene shook her head.

'What are you? A junior at Stevenson as well?"

When Darlene nodded that she was, Joes hand immediately came out from under her blouse and he sat up, got his shoes on and said, "I'm leaving."

"Darlene said, "What's wrong? We were having fun."

The sound of sexual release could be heard on the other side of the living room, and then a sigh as the two of them drifted off to sleep.

Joe asked, "Is Brenda a high school student too?"

"Yes, we're both sixteen."

Joe was 21 and Charlie was 23. Joe asked if Charlie knew, and Darlene again nodded her head. Joe said, "I'm gone."

Darlene shook her head and said, "But, why? Was it

something I said?"

"Damn straight. You told me your age." He opened the door and walked onto the porch.

Darlene said, "Don't leave. Charlie doesn't mind our age."

Joe said, "Darlene, I'm not Charlie. Charlie's an ass. You are underage. We're too old for you and Brenda." Then he left.

He was not terribly far from where Josh and Jayne had moved when the Detroit Police Department ruled that officers could live outside of the city limits, so he walked to their house, where he would sleep for the night. As he walked, Joe wondered if Charlie made sure that Brenda was at least 16 or did Charlie just get lucky. At any rate, Charlie at the age of 23 had no business dating a 16-year-old. "What the hell was wrong with Charlie?" Joe asked himself.

Later Charlie called Joe and asked him why he had left. When Joe told him, Charlie said, "You gotta walk on the wild side a little bit, little brother."

"That's your side of the street, Charlie, not mine. I've got to go."

This whole dating thing was Joe's effort to find another Kate. But there was no other Kate. Kate was unique, a one-of-a-kind.

Joe began writing letters and poems to Kate asking for forgiveness. He received nothing back from her. Joe pursued Kate during this period like someone whose life depended on it. In fact, Joe did think that his happiness in this world, his very existence, depended on getting Kate back. Taken to the deepest level, he believed that he could not survive without her.

Joe later wrote letters and poems to Kate asking her to give him another chance. To Joe, at the time, everything he was sending and saying to Kate was falling on deaf ears. He thoroughly thought that what they once had, was over.

In late October 1968 Joe was at a friend's house in the neighborhood (a block away from Kate's street) when Kate's mother happened to see him while she was driving home. She pulled over to the curb, and she and Joe talked for a while. Kate's mom told Joe that he could stop over at their house any time that he wanted and that he would always be welcomed.

This very gracious act on the part of Kate's mother gave Joe hope that maybe there was still a chance to mend the damage that he had done. He called Kate that night and asked her if he could see her. He was shocked when Kate said, "Yes."

Chapter 57 - To Err; to Forgive

When Joe picked Kate up, he wanted to take her somewhere where they could talk without interruption. He knew that this could be his only chance to get Kate back. They drove to the church where they had gone on their first date. At that time a church fair was being held on the church grounds, but today they pulled into an empty parking lot and found a bench near the church to sit down.

"I have been writing, Kate. Have you been receiving my letters?" Joe asked.

Kate answered, "I have received a number of letters from you. I read every one. The poems were a little rambling, but I thought they were very nice."

"Then you know how much I regret breaking up with you. I was lonely and very overwhelmed with school and work, and I lost sight of what was truly important to me – you," Joe said.

Joe moved to hold Kate's hand, but she pulled her hand away. She said, "Joe, I know my mom talked with you, and you may have won her over, but my mom isn't me. You hurt me a great deal, and I don't know if I can ever forgive you or if I even want you back. But I am willing to listen to what you have to say."

Joe sat back and sighed. He said, "Kate, we are all human. I'm just human. To be human is to be inclined to commit errors."

"Well, you sure did, Joe. And your error crushed me. But, I learned I could live life without you, and I have moved on," Kate said.

"You don't really mean that, Kate, or I wouldn't be here with you. "

Well maybe you shouldn't be. Maybe this is a mistake," Kate said.

"Don't say that, Kate. You know that we both loved each other very much. I just lost sight of how important you were to me."

"Joe, even when you came to the dance and I pushed you away, I was still in love with you. The other guys that I dated were just that – other guys. But I don't know that I can trust you."

"Please give me a chance to explain. Just try to let me talk and be open to what I am saying, okay?"

"Okay. Talk."

Joe said, "Sometimes people enter into things, like marriage, in error. To fix the error people make in entering into a bad marriage, society devised divorce. If you are the child from a divorce, like I am," Joe said, "then you were the child of two people who made an error when they entered into marriage. They didn't mean to make that error. No one does. But, I am the result of the error that two people made."

Kate shifted on the bench. She said, "I don't know quite what you are getting at, Joe. Are you saying that you think a marriage to me would be a mistake?"

"No, that's not where I'm going," Joe said. "Where I'm going is that I was absolutely in love with you, Kate. I was ready to be married to you. But I began to think that we were way too young, and I didn't want to make the same mistake my parents made. I don't want to marry and have children, then realize later that it was a mistake and end up getting a divorce and hurting my children the way Charlie and I were hurt."

"Joe, you are not your dad, and I am not your mother. She was an only child, and I am the oldest of five children. I have a pretty good head on my shoulders."

"And a very beautiful one too, Kate."

Kate smiled. "You think so because you love me."

"I do love you," Joe said, "but even if I didn't I would still think you were beautiful."

They were quiet for a while.

Joe then said, "Kate, I was tired and lonely at Eastern. I couldn't see you, and between my school and work I just started overthinking everything. But I have worked it through, and I realized that without you, my life will have a hole in it that I don't believe anyone else could fill. I want you to be the center of my life, and I am ready to commit all of my efforts to build a life together with you."

Kate reached out and touched Joe's hand and said, "I want to believe you, Joe, but what if you slip back into those feelings of loneliness and sadness again? Then what? Will you hurt me all over again?"

"Kate, I can't undo what I did, but I have grown up enough to know that it won't happen again. Now, it's all about forgiveness, because without forgiveness we have no future."

"I am not angry, Joe. I just don't know if I want to let myself care again. Sometimes I see you as a wounded puppy, and I don't know if I want to be your life-long nurse."

Joe's eyes welled up with tears. He breathed deeply and said, "Kate, I am not a wounded puppy. I want to marry you right now, but I am afraid that I would be making the mistake my parents made in getting married too young."

They sat in silence with Kate still holding Joe's hand. Joe looked into Kate's eyes and said, "Kate, I forgave my parents for the divorce, for putting Charlie and I in an orphanage, for not seeing how I was being mistreated by Charlie. I have learned to forgive and not carry anger or hatred in my heart. You are still angry with me, and I get it. But anger is corrosive, a cancer, like rust. Not letting the anger go can destroy your perception of the past, your life today and your future. Even if you don't want to be back with me, at least forgive me – for me and for you."

Joe's hands were trembling now. He thought that he had just given Kate license to forgive him and let him go. But instead, Kate took his trembling hands to her lips and kissed them. She looked into Joe's eyes and said, "Our age difference means nothing, Joe. It is only three years, and as we get older that difference in our ages gets smaller and smaller. You are not your father, and I am not your mother. We are not bound by the mistakes that they made. We can make our own life together."

Joe gripped Kate's hand tighter, and they sat in silence for a while.

Kate then said, "Joe, I fell for you that first day when I saw you hobble out on crutches and look at me. The day you waved at me and I waved and smiled back at you. Remember?"

"Of course, I do," Joe replied.

"Well, I still feel the same about you," Kate said softly. "I never stopped feeling that way about you even when you broke up with me. I just needed to hear your heart, and I believe I just heard it."

He kissed her softly, then passionately, and she returned his kisses.

Chapter 58 – Why Is He Still Here? Fall,1968

What Joe had was an opening in the door. He had his foot in, but there were others who did not have all of his family baggage. As much as Kate said it didn't matter, Joe was not so sure.

One particular guy, Kevin, was someone Joe knew well in the neighborhood. Throughout high school, Joe and Kevin would go to the same parties. The difference between them was, while Joe was at the party, Kevin was one of the cool guys who made the party. Kevin was very much part of the "IN" crowd.

Shortly after Kate and Joe started seeing each other

again, they came home from a date to see a little sports car in front of her house. Kevin was sitting on the porch waiting for her. Kate kissed Joe goodnight, got out of the car and walked up to the porch where Kevin sat.

Intense jealousy and anger overcame Joe, and he sped off down the street with tears in his eyes, he thought, "I'd like to kick his ass in."

Joe drove by Kate's house the next day. Once again Kevin was over, and he and Kate were on the porch talking. Joe didn't know if his relationship with Kate was coming or going. Joe had flowers that he was going to give Kate. He tossed them on the floor of the car and sped on down the street.

Joe went home and began writing a poem to Kate about the state of their relationship. The poem was written in an abstract manner, because that was Joe's state of mind at the time. The poem read:

Four Feet and Four Hands

**I walked on the grass that you walked upon.
Four feet and four hands.
The grass told me what to do about you.
Four feet and four hands.**

**The grass said to run away while I can.
Four feet and four hands.
They say there will be hurt I can't withstand.
Four feet and four hands.**

**I leaned on the tree that you leaned upon.
I looked to the sky.
I listened to the whispers of song birds.
"Leave," as they flew by.**

**"Boy, go away. Leave while you have a chance.
They kissed where you stand.
When you are not looking, there is romance.**

> Four feet and four hands."
>
> The old maple tree then cried out to me.
> "They each wrote their names on the other side.
> Best that you not look. Best that you just leave
> because what you see will just make you cry."
>
> Trusting that you meant every word you spoke,
> Ignoring all of these warnings, did I.
> I went and I saw the words that you wrote.
> Losing composure, I stood there and cried.

Joe put the poem in an envelope and dropped it inside of Kate's front door that afternoon.

The evening, after reading Joe's poem, Kate called Joe and said, "You need to stop overreacting to things that you see or hear, or think you see hear, because sometimes, Joe, your interpretation of what is going on is dead wrong."

Joe interrupted Kate and said, "Kate, my eyes saw what they saw. Kevin was at your house last night when I dropped you off and again today when I was going to stop over."

Kate sighed deeply and said, "I told Kevin last night that I was back with you and told him to go home. He left right away. You would have seen that if you hadn't sped off like a child. Today he came back and asked if I was sure. I told him that I was and that I didn't want him coming over anymore. And that's the end of it, Joe."

Joe was silent.

Kate continued, "If this is going to work, Joe, you are going to have to develop a little more faith in me." Kate was ready to hang up and let Joe stew on what she said. But, being more mature than that, she simply said, "Well?"

"I'm sorry, Kate. I over-reacted again. I'm trying."

Kate said, "Try harder and learn to trust. I love you. See you tomorrow." Then she softly laid the phone down on its cradle.

Chapter 59 - Learning to Trust 1968

Joe had somehow survived the worse decision that he had ever made in his life – breaking up with this woman whom he knew when he met her, was the women who was meant for him. But then he had gotten lost. Joe vowed to himself that he would learn how to trust and vowed to Kate that he would treat her with the greatest respect and love that he was capable of mustering.

The way that Kate had accepted him back made Joe believe that in spite of their differences in backgrounds, they did have the foundation and basis to have a successful relationship. If he was going to marry her, and he wanted to, by God it was going to be until death did them part. Joe was not going to do to another human being – especially his own children – what had been done to him and his brother. By her grace and understanding, Kate moved him to believe that they had as good of chance at making a go of marriage as anyone did. Joe's history was just his history - the past. And the past did not foretell their future. This inner belief that she had in him made Joe believe that he was worthy of having a true love with an opportunity of happiness and family.

Chapter 60 - The New Joe, 1969

This new Joe, who now was before her, had convinced Kate that he was worth taking a chance on and that he was capable of being the man that her father was – a family man. She believed that Joe very well could be a man who would be there for her and for the children that she wanted to have. Given what Kate knew he had been through, it was a special woman who came to those conclusions. But Joe had known how special Kate was that first time on the street and she had waved to him and smiled.

One of his roommates decided to get married to his long-time girlfriend. It was a poorly timed wedding, and the bachelor party was at their apartment during the middle of final exams in mid-December. They got a keg of beer, cigars and picked up a very risqué movie. Each of the four roommates invited friends which guaranteed that their apartment would be packed and loud.

Joe had a final exam in the morning. He had not studied enough for the final but planned to go to bed early and study for the test in the morning. Joe was not much of a drinker, but on this auspicious occasion he had several drinks, which for Joe, were several drinks too many.

One of the last things that he remembered that night was stumbling around the parking lot of the apartment complex and then making a mad dash to the apartment where he emptied out into the toilet all that he had drank and eaten that day.

The toilet overflowed and poor drunken Joe was crawling around on his hands and knees at 2:00 AM cleaning up the mess. He did remember that he had the final exam at 10:00 AM, so he stumbled into the bedroom, set his alarm for 7:00 AM, crawled into bed and fell asleep, oblivious to the partying that went on well past 5:00 AM.

He made it to the final exam on time with leftover vomit still clinging to his shirt. Other students gave him wide berth and held their noses and their breath. He was one of the last students to walk out of the exam room, but somehow, he got through the test and passed the class. His elation about passing the test got dulled by a nasty hangover.

Two weeks later was Christmas. Joe intended to take Kate to midnight Mass on Christmas Eve and propose to Kate. As they walked down Kate's street toward the church, Joe told Kate that he could no longer live without her and asked Kate to marry him before he had to go back to Eastern Michigan in September.

100Kate accepted his proposal. They still had almost nine months before they could be together and both still had work, school, homework and distance keeping them apart. They still only saw each other for brief, abbreviated periods of time. The loneliness, therefore, continued, but they both could see the end of the tunnel to the time when they would be together.

Chapter 61 - Parent Concerns, 1969

Even though it had been the actions of Kate's mom that opened the door for Joe to return to Kate, Nan Jones thought that Kate was too young to get married. Kate was only 19. And then there was Joe's chaotic past. But Jules Jones believed that since Joe had experienced so much chaos in the marriages of his parents, Joe would make doubly sure to try to have a successful and happy marriage.

Nan said, "But he doesn't even know what a happy, successful marriage even looks like, Jules."

"Of course, he does, honey, he has been around ours. Jules pulled Nan close and hugged her tight. "Remember, I had a pretty tough background too, but I married into a good stable family and we're doing fine."

Nan was still hesitant, "I would feel better if they had some kind of a vested interest in their marriage that would help them determine if this is what they really want at this time."

"Well, we could have them pay for the wedding," Jules said. "And we give them a nice honeymoon in, say, the Bahamas.

"Weddings are very expensive." Nan said.

Jules nodded, "But if you wanted something that would test their resolve, that would be a good test. They might decide it just too expensive and hold it off until they saved for it."

"But I wouldn't want to make them so desperate that they elope either. I would like Kate to have a nice wedding like we had."

Jules smiled, "Yes, we had a wonderful wedding. Theirs could be a little smaller than ours so it doesn't break them."

Nan nodded. "Let them plan their wedding with an eye toward paying for it. If he is as smart as he seems to be, they figure out the details that they can afford." They both nodded in agreement.

Nan and Jules talked with Joe and Kate and told them of their concerns about marriage at this time. But if they still wanted to get married, the family would support them and give them their full support,

So, the dye was set. Joe and Kate would pay for the wedding they could afford and her parents would provide a fully paid honeymoon that they would remember. Seeing how much in love Joe and Kate were, neither one of Kate's parents ever voiced their concerns to Joe. They, in fact, were nothing but supportive of the young couple.

When Joe and Kate got engaged, both of them knew that Kate would have to leave college and get a job. This was unfortunate because she was an honor student. But she would have to be the breadwinner, at 19, until Joe graduated and found a teaching job.

Kate had a wonderful resume. She was very intelligent and was soon hired by Ford Motor Company as an assistant to one of the chief engineers in Dearborn, Michigan.

During the time leading up to their wedding day, Kate and Joe diligently squirreled their money away into a marriage account. Kate worked full time at Ford and while Joe was in school, he took on additional hours at the grocery store. During the summer, he worked in the store and six days a week he worked with Josh putting up aluminum siding.

Maggie, Joe's mom, got them a good price on a wedding hall on the lower level of the nightclub where she worked as a bookkeeper. She also agreed to pay for the alcohol that would be served at the wedding. The owners of the nightclub cut some of the profit percentage to help with the cost.

They wanted to have a band. Joe had an acquittance who had a band that played for weddings and in local bars. They called him and met him at his parents' house in Livonia, Michigan and listened to the band play in the garage. The band leader and his younger sister were the lead singers in the band. The band could play everything from waltzes, to rumbas and fox trots to rock and roll. They negotiated a price that Joe and Kate thought was fair.

When money did run short, they found that a good source of income was to return some of the bridal shower and wedding gifts and use the cash to pay bills. They rationalized that many of the people attending the wedding would never be seen again after the wedding, and, after all, the show must go on.

Now there were a few hiccups in the process. Nothing as complicated and involved as a wedding and a reception ever comes off without a few test moments on the way.

One such hiccup involved pots and pans. You read correctly – pots and pans. Kate had a company come to the house that sold a top-of-the-line stainless steel pot and pan set with a lifetime warranty. When the pitch was made and the schmooze was in, and the dust cleared from the air, $200 had been spent on pots and pans, an eight-setting complete china set was thrown in for good measure. This was a deal that would make world class negotiators proud.

Kate proudly showed Joe their new possessions, and Joe damn near went into cardiac arrest. His head swirled with the thought that out of their hard-earned money to pay for a wedding and reception, $200 had been spent on pots and pans and dishes. Joe went on and on so much that Kate seriously considered calling off the wedding off. .Little would Joe know that 53 years after their marriage, while almost everything having to do with the wedding being a distant memory, the pots and pans and plates would still have a prominent place in their kitchen.

By the time the wedding day came, Joe and Kate had scrimped and saved so much, that every expense was paid for, and they were debt free.

Chapter 62 - Kate and Joe's Wedding, 1969

Joe and Kate got married in the summer of 1969 in a chapel that was part of a monastery that was at the end of Joe's street and three blocks away from Kate's street. The monastery had not been open for masses in years, but Kate and all of her siblings had gone through the parish school, and the family was very active in the church, so when they asked the priest if they could have the wedding in the monastery chapel, the question drew and immediate "Yes!" The chapel did not have air conditioning, though, so it was very hot. Several of the groomsmen and the best man looked like they were going to faint during the wedding service. But the bride could not have been more beautiful as she came down the aisle on the arm of Joe's future father-in-law – a man who had already become Joe's friend and tennis partner.

Kate was indeed the embodiment of the finest words that the greatest poets could ever write about a bride. Kate was not only lovely enough to be in a bridal magazine, she would have been on the cover. The marriage, of course, resulted in the poem "Into Your Palm."

Into Your Palm

Into your palm, my palm it went.
Into your hand, my hand I placed.
Fingers carried the love we sent.
Our hearts mirrored the hands embrace.

Spoken words fell deaf on the floor.
Only words of the heart were heard.
"Do you take her?" his words implored.

My heart drank deep - lips barely stirred.

My dreams carried my heart that day.
His words my mind sang to my bride.
They came ever gently my way,
fell on my ear and slipped inside.

"You're one now, you may kiss your bride."
We're one now, I may kiss my bride.

As their wedding gift to Joe and Kate, Kate's parents paid for their honeymoon in Freeport, in the Grand Bahamas. The trip included the hotel and meals. This was a very precious gift to Joe and Kate, because it was paid for from the pocket change that dad put in the cookie jar when he got home from work every day. This change provided the funds that were usually spent on the family's annual vacation. This year, though, the money went for the honeymoon of their first-born and her husband. There are no greater gifts given than those gifts that come from want.

Several romances began at the wedding reception. Pete, his best friend, and now the best man found the bride's maid of honor especially attractive. The wedding dance brought the entire wedding party together. Once Pete and Jennifer walked on the dance floor being introduced as the best man and maid of honor, they remained close to each other for the remainder of the evening. He was a city boy and she was a small-town girl, but there was no question that there was an attraction between them.

Though Charlie was not in the wedding party, he was at the wedding. As previously mentioned, the band leader was a good friend of Joe's. As the band set up, Charlie noticed Denise, the sister of the band leader. Denise did vocals with the band and helped in the setup and takedown of equipment. Denise was very attractive and her being a singer in the band gave her star quality, especially in Charlie's eyes. Charlie was like a red hawk that circles the cute little bunny then swoops in for the kill. For the remainder of the night, when Denise wasn't singing, she was on Charlie's arm on the dance floor.

The only thing that went wrong at the reception is that Maggie got drunk and told the bar tender to stop serving alcohol at 11:00 PM. Many of the guests left early when the flow of alcohol was shut off. It was things like that that made Joe always hold his breath when he was dealing with his mother. When she drank proper decorum and self-respect were qualities that were hard to find.

The married couple left the wedding after going around and presenting all of the guests with a rose that had a thank you note attached to it. Then they drove to a rather inexpensive motel on Grand River Avenue just off of I-96. They weren't being cheap, the motel held special significance for Joe, because whenever Joe had gone up North and was anxious to get home – especially once he met Kate, he would recognize that the trip was almost over when he saw the motel's sign. Having married Kate, Joe was now home and intended to stay home always with Kate.

The couple had been true to the ideals of the church, their parents' wishes and their own sense of propriety and had never had sex until that night in the motel. While many feel you should try it on a couple of times before the wedding day to make sure you really like it, Joe and Kate believed and believe that liking it is a matter of loving the person that your have sex with. With them the term was not having sex, it was making love. And making love they did, often, and they liked it a lot. It was the coming together of two people sharing a very intimate moment and sharing it out of the love that they felt for each other.

Chapter 63 - The Honeymoon

After having breakfast with Kate's family, the following morning, they were driven by her parents to

Metropolitan Airport where they flew to Miami and then took a much smaller plane to Freeport. The hotel was lovely, the food was wonderful, the room was beautiful, the bed was soft and beckoning and Kate and Joe fell into each other's arms at the slightest glance.

They also enjoyed the outdoor mall around the hotel, got too much sun laying on the beach and had a lovely afternoon on a glass bottomed boat. Everywhere they went heads would turn at the ravishing beautify who was now Joe's wife.

One day on their honeymoon, Kate and Joe rented a car and drove out to find conch shells lying on the beach. They had no idea how badly the shells would smell as they were finding the shells and putting them into plastic bags. They found a dozen or so and brought them back to the hotel to clean them in the bathtub. What better way could a newly-wed couple spend their abbreviated time on their honeymoon?

When the honeymoon was over, they brought their luggage, containing the conch shells, through customs. The custom's officer opened the suitcase, and then shut the suitcase as quickly as possible. He looked at the young couple and said, "This is what you did on your honeymoon?" Joe smiled and said, "Well, that wasn't the only thing."

Kate simply blushed.

The suitcases did air out in time, and Joe and Kate had a prominent display of conch shells in their new apartment at Eastern Michigan University.

Chapter 64 - Married Life, Fall 1969

Their lives were once again back in the real world. Kate had arranged to car pool into Dearborn each day with some Ford employees who lived in Ypsilanti. Joe was taking classes, doing student teaching and working at a grocery store in Ypsilanti. Their days were long, but both of them were very happy in this young marriage. Then across the country came the riots against the Viet

Nam War. The Eastern Michigan campus was hit very hard as were college campuses across the United States. Burning pillows and throwing furniture from dorm room windows, riots on the campus and campus shutdowns became the norm.

The city of Ypsilanti, Michigan was put on a dawn to dusk curfew. Unless you had a permit for being out between dusk and dawn, you ran the risk of being arrested and put in jail. Even the married housing units at Eastern Michigan were put on lockdown when an ROTC (Reserved Officers Training Corp) car was overturned and burned on campus.

Married housing was significantly apart from the main campus. Some of the married students came out of their apartments and watched the red glow and smoke coming from student housing on campus. A city helicopter flew overhead with flood lights aimed at the students below. The police obviously thought that the students, some with children by their side and in their arms, presented an eminent threat to the life and safety of the community. A bull horn came from the chopper warning the students that they had to return to their apartments or they would be arrested. The married students complied, except one poor married student who was caught out after curfew walking her screaming baby. She and the baby were arrested and thrown in jail for the night. The Ypsilanti police said rules were rules, and she broke the law walking her baby after the curfew. The woman had to nurse her baby in front of strangers in her holding cell. You couldn't put this idiocy in a movie or a book, because no one would believe that police officers could be so stupid, but, I just did. It was real, it happened and the police were that stupid. The woman was considering suing the police department for what she and her child were put through. One could either laugh or cry about the absurdity of the situation. Ultimately the situation cooled and the curfew was lifted.

Chapter 65 - Joe Held at Gun Point, February 1970

Joe and Kate had a very scary occurrence one evening while Joe was working at an Ypsilanti grocery store. It was around 9:00 PM, and the store was closing for the day. Joe and several other employees were going through the store to make sure that everything was ready for the next day's opening. A man came into the aisle that Joe was working in and asked for help in the baked goods aisle. As Joe walked to the front of the store with the man, the man grabbed Joe by the arm and put a pistol to his head. "Don't look at me," the man said. "If you don't look at me, I won't kill you." Joe closed his eyes and looked away from the gunman. "I'm just a poor college student, man," Joe said. "I'm just working to pay my way through school." As Joe was being held at the front of the bakery aisle, the gunman's partner was going from cash register to cash register and pouring money into a cloth bag. Next the two gunmen went into the manager's office, with the gun still at Joe's head, and emptied out the store safe.

Joe was then taken outside of the building and around a corner. With eyes closed all he could think about was being shot in the head and Kate being left a widow and going back with her family. He felt the gun being taken away from his temple and expected to hear the squeeze of the trigger and the hammer coming down on the bullet. Silent prayer was all he could muster. But no bullet was fired. The voice said, "Keep your eyes closed. Count to 200, slowly, then go back into the store. If you treasure your life, do not look back." Joe did exactly as he was told and lived to talk about it.

Kate and Joe later agreed that if that robbery had occurred at the present time, the gunman likely would have killed Joe just for the hell of it. We live in such dangerous times. So many people have so little regard for their fellow human beings.

This guy could have taken Joe out at any time. He did not have to spare Joe's life. Joe was later asked to come to the Ypsilanti police station to look at mug shots, but he had only briefly seen the gunman's face, so he was not able to identify the men who had robbed the store.

Chapter 66 – Joe and Kate's Early Years

In 1970, after Joe graduated from Eastern Michigan with a Bachelor's of Science Degree and a certificate in secondary education, he and Kate moved to the east side of Dearborn Heights, Michigan, to be close to where Kate worked in Dearborn. Teaching jobs across Michigan were very scarce, and Joe received letters of rejection from school districts across the State on a regular basis.

One Sunday they drove to Kate's parents' house for dinner and noticed a sign posted on Telegraph Road that a Catholic high school in the area was looking for English teachers who had the appropriate State certifications. Joe's major was English and he was certified by the state of Michigan, so the following day he went to the school to apply for one of the jobs as an English teacher. After a rigorous interview, Joe was hired into his first professional position that required a college degree. He began teaching high school English that fall.

Joe taught school during day and worked at a Dearborn grocery store several evenings during the week and one day each weekend. Kate was doing well at Ford. They were making decent money, were saving for a house, and their life together was everything that they had hoped it would be.

He primarily taught ninth grade students who came from various parishes around the school. One exception was a boy named Billy. Billy was in Joe's ninth grade class. He was a shy boy and a little on the quiet side, but he seemed like a nice kid. One day Billy stayed after class and asked Joe if he could talk to him. Billy said that his parents were driving him to school every day and things were going poorly at home and his mother had to go back to work. Unless Billy could find another way to get to school, he would have to drop out and go to school in a fairly rough school system.

Billy lived just north and west of Joe and Kate's apartment so the young couple talked about having Billy's parents drop the boy off in the morning just before Joe left for school and they would ride to school together. Billy had after-school activities, so the car pool was only in the morning.

Neither Joe or Kate wanted Billy to be sitting in their small apartment while they were getting dressed for work, so they arranged for Billy's mom to arrive at Joe's apartment at the same time as Joe would leave the apartment building and go to his car.

Everything started out fine, and Billy never had to enter Joe and Kate's apartment. But then Billy's mother said that she had to go into work earlier which meant that Billy would have to wait outside or come into the apartment while Joe and Kate got dressed. The apartment consisted of the living room, walk in kitchen, one bedroom and the bathroom. The bathroom was visible from the living room.

One day the phone rang in the apartment. Kate picked up the phone and someone said, "I want to screw you." The caller then hung up. Several days later it happened again. Kate was afraid, and Joe was very pissed off. The next day as he drove Billy to school Joe casually asked if Billy had accidently called their apartment by mistake. Billy said he hadn't. Joe did not pursue it further and Billy did not ask why the question was asked.

At school that day Joe met with one of the school's counsellors and talked about the phone calls. The counsellor was very disturbed.

"Do you think it was Billy?" the counsellor asked.

Joe answered, "I thought it could be, but I asked him casually if he had accidently called me and he said he hadn't without even a hint of guilt or surprise or anything. What do you recommend I do to get it to stop?"

"Well, most of the time these callers are getting sexually turned on by your anger, so don't get mad. Just be very calm."

"I can do that even though I'd like to wring his throat."

The counsellor smiled, "That's what they want. A lot of times they are playing with themselves and a violent reaction is a stimulation. Keep that in mind."

That weekend on Saturday morning Kate answered the phone to a similar call. Joe was standing by, and she handed the phone to him.

Joe asked, "Hello, how can I help you?"

"I'd like to screw your wife, man."

Joe wanted to reach through the phone and pull the son of a bitch into the room with him and beat him senseless. Instead, he calmly said, "I've heard about people like you. Are you having a hard time getting it up?" Before the pervert could answer, Joe added. "I bet you've got your little dick in your hand right now hoping that I'll get angry. But, because I am calm, your poor little dick is getting softer and softer, isn't it. Well, you might as well put the little thing back in your pants, because it not going to be of any use to you on this call."

What came on the other side was something that sent a chill up Joes spine. The caller said,

"You are disgusting. I'll bet you didn't talk like that in front of Luci."

Joe was stunned. "Charlie? Is that you?" The phone went dead.

All thoughts that it could be Billy died with the mention of his grandmother's name.

Kate was in the bathroom putting on her makeup. Joe got out the phonebook, found Charlie's phone number and dialed it. On the third ring Charlie answered it very timidly with a "Hello?"

Joe said, "Charlie, how are you?"

"Ok, Joe, how are you?"

"Charlie, I couldn't be better."

"That's great. What's going on?"

"Did I tell you that I bought a shotgun?"

Silence.

Joe continued. "Probably not, but I did. We had a scare at Eastern, and I shot someone trying to break into our apartment."

Silence.

"Shot him in the legs." (He paused.) "Next time I will go for the head."

Silence.

"Charlie? Are you there?"

"Yes, just wondering why you are telling me?"

"Oh, it was just something that Grandma Luci said. Do you know what she said, Charlie? She said it was OK to shoot the Devil. She said if I ever met the devil, I should shoot it in the head."

"Well, I've got to go," Charlie said.

Joe said, "Ok. Give me a call if you want to chat."

The threatening calls came to an end.

Chapter 67 – Bliss Surrounded By Chaos, 1970

Joe often wrote to Kate of his love for her. It was

nothing that he planned to do; the words just flowed out of his head and landed on paper. Sometimes the most mundane events would fill Joe with overwhelming joy and lines of poetry would start coming into his mind.

One Saturday morning Joe woke up with entire stanza's of a poem bouncing around in his head. He grabbed paper and pencil and wrote the following poem while sitting in a chair in the bedroom watching Kate as she slept.

<u>The Lonely Fisherman</u>

*The lonely fisherman awakes before dawn
so that he may be alone to hear
the silent song
of the sea.*

*Looking silently into the waters near,
unblemished, unscarred, delightfully clear,
the fisherman listens to the ocean's sound,
alone on the deck; no one around.*

*Peacefully hearing the waves as they lap
against the boat and slowly go back,
and softly return in rhythmic score
bobbing the vessel, lapping the shore.*

*The waves, which can be tyrannically mean,
do little more now then add to the scene -
to the blue of the ocean, the blue of the sky
the fish in the water, the gulls that fly by.*

*Awaking in the queen before the song,
the song that awakes us to the dawn,
I arise before the one I had wed
who peacefully sleeps at dawn in our bed.*

I think, never before had I had such dreams

that awoke me in comfort before the streams
of light and life carried me away
from the silence and calm
of the new-born day.

Only since I was able to wed
the woman who lies beside me in bed.
And I wonder how such transitions could be
from nightmares to dreams,
from disquiet to sleep.

Then my hands along with my eyes
and my mind
softly caress the arms and the rest.
The eyes slowly rise to the brown of her eyes
and silently say at the dawn of the day,
"Good morning, darling."

Joe and Kate were truly kindred spirits and similar in many ways. They finished each other's sentences. They both could be moved to tears when watching something on television or watching a movie, listening to a song, whatever.

The Viet Nam War was bringing the United States to the point of anarchy. Marching in the streets against the U.S. Government and the war was perpetual. The war was causing some breakdown in extended family units as fathers and mothers, who supported the government during World War II, were pitted against some of their children who thought the government was corrupt and evil.

But, because of the love they had for each other, even with everything swirling around them, Joe was happier than he had ever been in his life or ever dreamed he would be. This happiness was attributable to Kate.

Chapter 68 - Kate's Dad, Jules, May 1971

Joe and Kate moved into their first home, a 950

square foot ranch-style home near West Chicago and Middlebelt in Livonia, Michigan. Kate's entire family helped them move, just as they had helped them move into Eastern Michigan's married housing when they first got married. On the day they moved in, they noticed that Kate's dad was having a lot of difficulty with directions on how to find the new home. The family became very concerned when he began having a difficult time doing things he had previously been very proficient at doing.

Kate's dad was a highly accomplished man who worked for, and retired from one of the Big Three car companies. He could design and build things in his sleep and measure distances to the nth degree. He was a proficient and fierce skier and tennis player. He had a built-in GPS unit in his head and never would need any kind of GPS system to help him find his way around. Now, all of a sudden, he couldn't do these things anymore. He was diagnosed as having Alzheimer's disease. It was the first time that anyone in the family had heard about this disease that has become much more prevalent in our society since then. In addition, he later developed stomach cancer and was in severe pain much of the time.

This man who had sat on the porch in his bare shirt to send a message to Joe not to mess with his daughter had not only become Joe's father-in-law but also had become Joe's friend. They often played tennis together – each of them striving to win each set. Kate's dad helped Joe learn how to ski. They would play two-handed pinochle together almost every time that Kate and Joe went to her parents' home, was losing his capabilities at an alarming rate.

Jules had days that were peaceful and removed from pain, but he also had other days that were not so. His illness had a deep and exceedingly sad effect on this wonderful family into which Joe had married.

Chapter 69 - Charlie Plans to Wed, Summer 1970

For the first time in his life Charlie found a woman who meant more to him than he meant to himself. Ever since Joe and Kate's wedding, Charlie and Denise had been a couple. The angry side of Charlie's personality seemed to have been put to sleep, at least for the time being. Charlie seemed to have finally turned the corner to putting his childhood behind him. When it had become evident after Ron and Kate's wedding, that Charlie and Denise cared for each other, everyone who knew Charlie hoped that they would get married, because Denise was so good for Charlie. It was hoped that Denise could be a counter-balance to his mood swings. She may be able to keep him calm, it was believed, when he started feeling sorry for himself because of his childhood. Hopes for changes in one's behavior are often misguided, but one can hope.

Charlie wanted Joe to be his best man, but he hadn't talked to Joe since the whole telephone incident. As he thought about the last conversation with Joe, Charlie knew for sure that Joe believed that he had made obscene calls to Kate. Charlie didn't think that he made the calls, but when he got drinking who knows what he may have done? Charlie did find Kate very attractive. He remembered back to when he had sex with Joe's old girlfriend years ago. If he could do it to her, why not Kate? Just because she had a wedding ring on and was his brother's wife, what did that matter?

He sat back in his chair and inhaled deeply on his cigarette. "That little prick owes me anyway, he was taken out of the damn orphanage before I was. Long before. He owes me. "

Charlie shook himself, "Shit, I've got to stop thinking that way he said to himself, but, I can't be held responsible for what I do when I'm drunk. That's not fair. But when has life been fair to me?"

Charlie would drift In and out of these neurotic thoughts and conversations with himself all of the time. He just couldn't stop himself. "Yes, I may have done that," but he wasn't absolutely sure. He tended to drink more than he should, and he did find Kate very attractive.

As for Joe, he was as sure as he could be that it was Charlie who made the obscene calls to their house and had so cruelly talked to Kate. Joe didn't want to have a damn thing to do with Charlie. He certainly didn't want him too close to his wife. Charlie was capable of anything and had done damn near everything. He had no conscience.

Months after their last phone call, Charlie sent Joe a long hand letter begging Joe to forgive anything he may have done and asking him to be his best man in his marriage to Denise. The letter read:

"Joe, you got it wrong when you thawt that I called Kate. Kate is a beutyful girl, and you have to no that sum people might want to date her, but I know she's marred and even tho I sometimes think about what it might be like, I woud never do anything to hurt you as long as you were alive. Im just joking about that. But yer my brother and I really woud like you to be my best man. And you do owe me a favor for not including me in yur wedding party. Not that im holding that agenst you. You mentioned you had a shotgun. Do you?

**Yer Brother,
Charlie"**

Joe showed Kate the letter, and she found it frightening. "His mind rambles like he is talking to himself, " Kate said. "He also needs a dictionary or a spelling book."

Joe knew that Charlie was intelligent, but he sure didn't know how to spell. He spelled phonetically, by the sound of the word. Charlie's ramblings and admissions worried Joe as well.

The plea from Charlie fell on deaf ears. No one was going to do what Charlie did to Kate and remain in Joe's good graces, but when Charlie had Maggie call Joe to ask him to at least forgive Charlie long enough to stand up in the wedding for him, Joe reluctantly agreed.

The wedding and reception were held at the bride's family home. Her brother's band played for her wedding, and Denise joined the band for some of the songs. Charlie drank and checked out the girls.

Chapter 70 – Charlie and Denise, Post Marriage

Denise and Charlie moved into an apartment complex on Plymouth Road, on the border between the city of Livonia and the town of Plymouth. Denise had very good taste in furniture design and layout, and the apartment looked good. Denise worked in the furniture department of J.L. Hudson's, a local department store, and Charlie worked in a small machine shop where the management gave second chances to people whose lives had taken a bad direction, whether it was self-inflicted or not. Between the two of them they made enough money so they could afford some of the niceties that comes with a decent income.

It appeared that Charlie's life had turned a corner. But what is seen on the surface often does not reflect what is going on internally. Such was the case with Charlie. He was always just moments away from a frightful thought or action.

An example of this was with the fish tanks. Charlie loved fish tanks, and Denise allowed him to put a large fresh water tank in their living room. Charlie put several large piranhas in the tank. He enjoyed feeding them meat and watching them rip apart their food with their exceedingly sharp teeth.

One evening, when Denise was not home, Charlie was watching the fish and playing the stereo very loud. The neighbor next door banged on the wall and screamed for Charlie to turn down the music.

Charlie didn't.

Next a banging/rapping was heard on the door of

Charlie's apartment. Charlie ignored it at first, but when it continued, he strolled to the door, opened it calmly and said, "Can I help you?"

The neighbor responded that it would be a big help if Charlie could turn the music down. Charlie said he was so sorry about the music, that he had gotten preoccupied with his fish.

"Won't you come in?" Charlie asked. The neighbor, seeing that Charlie seemed like a nice guy said, "Well, okay, but only for a moment. Just to be neighborly. Nice place," the neighbor said.

Charlie responded, graciously, "Well, thank you so much. I have been doing a lot of work on my fish tank. Would you like to see it?"

The neighbor, again, wanting to be neighborly, said, "Sure."

Charlie smiled and said, "Come here, let me show you."

The neighbor came up to the tank and looked in. "Pretty cool," he said. "What kind of fish are those?"

Charlie ignored the question. "Do you want to see them eat? It's kind of cool." Charlie then opened the tank and threw bloody chicken in. At the same time, with snake-like speed and a vice grip, Charlie grabbed his neighbor's arm and hand and stuck them into the tank. "They are piranha's you damn moron. And if you ever knock on my wall and door again, I'll pick your ass up and feed you to them!"

Withdrawing his neighbor's hand from the tank, Charlie pushed him across the room and screamed, "Get out! You're trespassing! I'm gonna call the cops!"

The man, much smaller than Charlie, almost peed his pants and said, "Man, you're crazy. I'm going to get you thrown out of here."

Charlie said, "My word against your word, you asshole, and who would believe I would do such a thing to you?" Charlie then added, "And remember, if I'm crazy, do you want to mess with someone so crazy? Of course not," he answered his own question. "So, get the

Hell out of here and never come back, or I'll really show you what crazy is."

The neighbor hurriedly left the room and had a moving truck there the next day. A bad neighbor is one thing, but Charlie was more than what the neighbor wanted to deal with.

Another situation came up when Charlie was sitting on his deck one afternoon. The upstairs neighbor let his dog out on the deck to go to the bathroom. This was very much against the apartment rules, but he did it anyway. The urine came through the deck and trickled onto Charlie's deck. Charlie bounded up the stairs and knocked on the door of the owner of the dog.

When the man came to the door, Charlie said, "Your dog just peed on my deck. If it happens again, I'll beat the crap out of you." Charlie then turned on his heel and went back to his apartment.

Several days later, the upper door wall opened, the dog came out and peed on the deck once again. Charlie was sitting on his deck at this inopportune moment. He had a cup of coffee in his hand, which he poured out and put the cup where it would catch the urine when it came through the upper deck. Cup in hand, he went up the stairs and knocked on the door. When the dog's owner came to the door, Charlie grabbed him by his collar and literally lifted him off the ground. Charlie took the cup of dog pee and poured it on the man's head and then kneed him in the balls for good measure.

"I warned you the last time that if your dog peed on the balcony again, I'd kick your ass in," Charlie roared. "I wasn't shitin' you. I want you out of this building," Charlie said calmly. "Either you leave the building, or I'll kill your dog." The next day the movers were there, and the man and his dog were gone. Charlie had a knack for getting his way.

Denise heard of these exploits but was never a witness to them. But then Denise had her own issues with Charlie. Charlie had signed up for Tae Kwon Do lessons, and he liked to practice his kicks at home. He would put a pillow in the corner of a room and see how close he could kick without making contact with the pillow.

One day, Charlie asked Denise if she would stand in the corner and give him something other than a pillow to kick at.

"It will make my practice more realistic. I promise that I won't kick you. I have enough control of my kicks that I won't come near you."

Denise reluctantly agreed. Anything to keep him happy," she thought to herself.

Charlie's first few kicks were a foot away, but he wanted to do better than that. The next kick only missed Denise because she moved to get out of the way. Charlie screamed, "Dammit, Denise, you are really screwing up my practice."

Denise said, "Charlie, I can't do this. You're scaring me." He glared and said, "Helping me practice isn't too much to ask, Denise. I help you with things."

Denise tried to reason with him saying, "My things can't hurt you, Charlie. Your kicks could kill me."

He kicked again while she was talking. The kick landed on her chest and knocked her off her feet into the corner of the room.

Charlie, only said, "I guess that was too close. But, it's your fault for distracting me."

"You're nuts, Charlie. I can't do this anymore," Denise said and she left the apartment. Denise retained an attorney and filed for divorce. She got a restraining order on Charlie, and only came back to get her things when she knew he was gone and she had her two older brothers and three of their friends to accompany her.

Denise said, "How could I have been so stupid to marry an asshole like him?"

Joe and Kate continued their relationship with Denise for a while after the divorce. Six months after the divorce, Denise married again. Several times Joe and Kate went out with Denise and her new husband, but it was uncomfortable because each meeting turned into discussion about Charlie. While Charlie was an ass, he was the Lane family ass. It was also uncomfortable for the new husband to be out with the Charlie's brother, so ultimately the families stopped seeing each other.

Chapter 71 - Joe and Kate's First Home 1971 - 1973

Soon after Kate and Joe moved into their first home, they started their family. The first member of the family was a puppy that they named Mona. Mona was a mix between a poodle and a cocker spaniel.

Mona was their baby, and they almost treated her as if she were a human – even putting her in a basket that Kate had on the handlebars of her bike and taking her for rides around the neighborhood. This worked well until one day a dog ran into the street chasing them. Mona panicked and jumped out of the basket. She rolled along the ground and shook herself off when the rolling was done. She wasn't hurt, but she resisted their future efforts to try to put her in the basket. Joe and Kate eventually stopped trying.

During the next three years Joe and Kate lived the carefree life of a young married couple. They had a ton of friends and family, went out every Friday and Saturday night, danced until the wee hours of the morning, took skiing trips, played tennis and enjoyed the life that they had carved-out together.

Chapter 72 – Going After an MBA, 1973

Joe was in his third year of teaching at the Detroit Catholic school. A school that paid significantly less than public school teaching positions. Joe had promised that if Kate wanted to, and they could afford it, she could stay home and raise their children as her mom had done. The prospects of Joe being able to honor that promise looked rather dim given his income, so Joe sat for the test that, if he passed it, would allow him to go to graduate school to get a Master's Degree in Business Administration (MBA.). Joe did pass the test and was admitted into Wayne State University's MBA program. He would teach all day, go to classes at night and study and sleep when he had the chance. It was not a way of life that he would recommend to anyone, but it is shocking how many people do exactly that, especially it they are not from rich, supportive families – which Joe was not. But these situations often produce the best workers for company's when the degree is accomplished because the students have to learn to budget their time. And the struggle to budget and balance time was about to get more difficult.

Chapter 73 - Charlie's Car Theft, 1973

Charlie wanted a change in venue. He decided to hitch hike his way west. On a rural Missouri road, one car after another passed him by, and 29-year-old Charlie Lane was getting pissed. His right hand was in the air trying to flag down anybody willing to pick up a stranger on this cold and blustery November night. "What the Hell, doesn't anyone have compassion for the poor of the world?" Charlie said out loud. No one answered, because no one was there. Only Charlie. "I'll bet they would stop if I was some broad with my dress hiked up to my panty-line." He laughed at what he thought was a cute comparison between what men would do for their fellow man and what they would do for a woman.

Charlie was halfway out in the street trying to get drivers to slow down long enough to see him. A car honked and swerved to the left to avoid him. After the driver passed, he slowed down, rolled down his passenger window and screamed out, "Get out of the road you asshole!" The man sped off. Charlie screamed, "You better hope I don't catch up with you, you jackass!"

Another 15 minutes went by when an older man slowed down and asked Charlie if he was in trouble.

Charlie, said, in his most innocent, sweet voice, "Yes, sir. I had a flat tire, and I don't have a spare. Just need a lift to a gas station."

"Well, get yourself in," the driver said.

Charlie opened the door and stuck a knife close to the driver's ribs. "Pull your ass over, before I cut you." The driver started to speed up, but before he could get the car moving too fast, Charlie hit him across the head, grabbed the steering wheel and pulled the car to the side of the road.

"I wasn't shittin' you, man!" Charlie screamed. "Now give me the keys, and get away from my car."

"Your car? It's my car.! Why are you doin' this? I stopped to help you out."

With disdain, Charlie punched the older man in the face and said, "Well, aren't you the good Samaritan. It's my car now. You shouldn't have stopped!" Charlie grabbed the man by the neck and pulled him out of the car. The older man did not go down easy, but several kicks to the belly took the fight out of him.

"I didn't want to have this end this way," Charlie screamed, as he punched the man several more times while he was lying in the street. The man's head bounced off the asphalt street with each punch. Charlie then got in the car and sped away – leaving the man bleeding from the head on the side of the road.

Another car, filled with teenagers, came by a few minutes later and saw the beaten man lying on the side of the road. The old man was virtually incoherent and bleeding badly. The kids helped him in the car and drove him to the hospital in town.

In the emergency room at the hospital, the old man came to and mumbled something about some hitchhiker beating him up and taking his car. The emergency room nurse urged him to calm down, and they gave him a sedative that induced sleep. Their diagnosis was that the old man was suffering from a severe concussion.

The emergency room doctor called hospital security to come to the ER and relayed what the old man had told the ER team. The hospital's security officer called the local police who put out an all-points bulletin about the stolen car and the driver that covered a 100-mile radius from the scene of crime.

At the hospital the old man slipped into a coma and was taken to a private room where he was put on life support and watched around the clock.

Charlie was found by the police at an all-night diner forty miles from the scene of the crime. The police saw the car in the diner parking lot. The car door was unlocked and the keys were on the floor. Except for some older couples, Charlie was the only person in the diner.

One officer asked the waitress when Charlie had walked in. She said, "Just a few minutes ago."

The two police officers approached Charlie and asked him about the car in the parking lot. Charlie said he didn't know anything about the car. The officer turned to the others in the diner and asked if the car belonged to any of them. Everyone shook their heads. Turning to Charlie, one officer said, "The engine is still warm, and you haven't been served yet, are you sure you don't know anything about that car?"

"No, sir. I had been hitchhiking and was dropped off at this café."

"Please stand up, sir."

"Why?" asked Charlie.

"Sir, we have good reason to believe that you stole that car, beat up an old man and left him for dead."

"You're wrong. I know nothing about what you are talking about. This is a false arrest."

The officer grabbed Charlie by the arm and dragged him to his feet. "Cuff him," he said to his partner.

Charlie tried to fight having the cuffs put on and screamed "Police brutality!"

"Shut your mouth or we'll take you in for resisting arrest." He pushed Charlie against the wall and said, "The car was stolen by knife point. Search him." The second officer patted Charlie down and found the knife.

180

The other officer said, "What's the knife for?"

"Protection. It's a dangerous world," said Charlie.

The police talked to other patrons and employees of the diner, but no one could connect Charlie with the car. This concerned the police but based on the description of the victim in the hospital, and the fact that Charlie and the car were in the same place at the same time, the police thought they had sufficient grounds for arrest, and Charlie was taken to the town jail.

When Charlie went before Judge George Prichard at the pre-trial, Charlie said it was all a mistake and pled not guilty. He did not beat anyone, and he did not steal the car. He was an innocent person hitchhiking west who was just at the wrong place at the wrong time when the police picked him up. He asked the judge to just let him go so he could get on with his life.

Judge Prichard smiled at Charlie and scoffed, "Son, this isn't Ohio. We know about the deal that you worked out with that Ohio judge in that underage rape case a few years back."

Charlie thought that when he worked out the deal with the judge in Ohio that the whole incident would be expunged from the record. He was wrong.

"Because the girl had fake ID, boy, that Ohio judge gave you a break. But I looked at the pictures of that girl, and fake ID or no fake ID there is no way someone as smart as you would believe that she was 18 years old." The judge stared down at Charlie, and Charlie, nervously, began shifting his feet back and forth. "You knew that girl was underage, didn't you, boy?" Charlie looked at the ground then lifted his head and stared back at the judge.

"Whether I did or I didn't doesn't matter, sir. That case was thrown out."

"Don't tell me about the law, boy! And don't think you can tell me what I can or can't do in my own courtroom. I'm the law around these parts!"

The judge then added, "I'm seeing a pretty ugly person here, boy. A person who needs to be taken off the streets of this country as soon as possible." Charlie was charged with assault and battery and car theft and bound over for trial.

At the hospital, lights were going off everywhere. A loud speaker crackled, "Code Blue! Code Blue! Room 209." The old man who had been beaten up by Charlie succumbed to his injuries and was pronounced dead.

With the death of the victim, the police increased their scrutiny of the car for any evidence that Charlie had been in it, and found none. The town's prosecutor, along with several policemen, one a detective, sat down with Judge Prichard and reported that the victim in Charlie's case had died. They also reported to the judge that they were not able to connect Charlie to the scene of the crime or the car.

The prosecutor told the judge that prosecution could not prove the case and said that they would have to withdraw charges.

"Damn!" roared Judge Prichard. He thoroughly believed that Charlie was guilty of rape in Ohio, and everything for which he had been arrested here in Missouri, and he needed to be removed from the streets.

Prichard looked at the team in front of him and said, "If we let him go, he will break the law again. I want him followed and arrested if he so much as spits on the sidewalk. Understood?"

They all nodded that they understood.

Charlie was taken before a very pissed off Judge George Prichard, who said, "Boy, you are one lucky son-of-a- bitch. I am not buying at all your story about hitchhiking to the diner. I believe that you beat that old man, resulting in his death, and you stole his car." He paused. "But prosecution tells me they don't have the evidence to place you at the scene of the crime."

"Because, I wasn't there, Judge."

"Bull!" The judge roared.

"Am I free to go, sir?"

"Yah, you're free to go, but I want you out of my State. We don't want you here. Get back to whatever hole you crawled out of." To the uniformed police officers he said, "Get'em out of here."

As Charlie was leaving the courtroom, he looked back at the judge, smiled and said, "It's a wonderful thing, isn't it judge?"

"What are you talking about, boy? That you can get away with murder?"

"Nah, that you're innocent until proven guilty."

"Get out of my courtroom! "

The judge gave a nod of "follow him" to the detective standing by the courtroom door. The nod was understood. Then Judge Prichard raised two fingers to the detective. That gesture was understood too. The judge wanted two counts against Charlie.

When Charlie walked out of the courthouse and breathed the fresh air of freedom, the detective was not far behind.

Charlie walked a couple of blocks down the street and went into a local tavern. He took a seat at the bar with his back to the door. After what he had just been through, Charlie was in the mood for a burger, some fries, and a cold beer. As he talked to the bartender, Charlie did not notice the plain-clothes officer who slipped into the bar and took a seat in a booth.

Charlie finished off the food and beer and asked the bartender to get him another beer. As the bartender was going to get the second beer, without paying, Charlie walked out of the tavern, turned a corner and was gone.

None of his actions, though, were lost on the detective who slipped out of the door behind him.

Charlie's next stop was a nearby small downtown grocery store. While the clerk in the store was busy at the register, Charlie stuffed several items into his pants. He stopped at the register and paid for a package of Little Debbie's wafers, then left the store and stepped into the waiting hands of two uniformed policemen and a detective. They spread-eagled Charlie against the wall and retrieved the stolen items from his pocket. Charlie was cuffed and taken into the store with the stolen items.

The clerk thanked the officers and said he would press charges.

The three cops and Charlie walked over to the tavern where the bartender said that he would press charges, as well.

The next day, Charlie, with a court-appointed lawyer, was before Judge George Prichard once again. At the trial's end Charlie was found guilty of two Class A misdemeanors, each carrying a sentence of no more than one year in prison. As a smiling Judge Prichard read the verdict and the sentence, he looked at Charlie and said, "That's two years, boy. And don't expect to be let out early on good behavior. Now get him out of my courtroom."

As Charlie was being taken out of the courtroom, the judge called out, "Oh, Charlie?"

Charlie turned and said, "Yes, sir?"

"Isn't it a wonderful thing, Charlie?"

"Isn't what a wonderful thing, judge?"

"That scumbags like you are so predictable that they can walk out of a courtroom free but will soon put themselves in harm's way." The judge smiled then laughed as Charlie was taken from the courtroom.

Chapter 74 – Kate's First Pregnancy, 1974

Kate and Joe had been married for four years when Kate got pregnant with their first child. They were ecstatic and set out to prepare the baby's room. They didn't know if Kate was carrying a boy or girl, and it didn't matter. All that mattered was that the child would be born healthy. The anticipation prompted Joe to write "Upon the News of Our Child," which Joe gave to Kate on Mother's Day.

Upon the News of Our Child
Happy Mother's Day

Her voice cracked while a smile creased her

face,
and down her cheeks her tears could be traced.
She spoke her thoughts through a joyful smile.
"Dearest Joe, we're expecting a child."

She came near me and then took my hand-
whispered the words to me once again.
I saw the warmth and glow in her eyes.
My heart overflowed with love inside.

Your pure joy from that moment I took.
I'm at your side to catch my first look.
Ideas we've had, and plans set down
on living life with our child around.

Today, many months before his birth,
we celebrate his coming to earth.
Your gift's not here, but he's to be seen,
as you carry, the child of our dreams.

You care for him, so mother you are.
Our child lives in, and through you, thus far.
Though he is not born, he's on the way,
so I wish you Happy Mother's Day.

Kate loved the poem but protested that she was not a mother yet. Joe said that he disagreed because the fetus is a child that needs to be cared for even though it is unborn – making Kate a mother already.

"Well, women's groups would disagree with you," said Kate. Joe said, "Women groups aren't carrying our child. You are." He then added, "Listen, if one of the roles of a mother is to protect her child, then Kate, you're already taking steps to protect our child. In my opinion, that makes you a mother."

Joe would always say "our child, not Kate's child," because Kate and Joe together created this new life. "In fact," Joe would say, "the whole position of women having the right to control their body and doing what they wish to do to the child – even abort it, is based on a false premise – that the child is only the mother's child. That's not correct, Kate. That's not just your child, that's my child too. My sperm and your egg created that child. So, I, and all fathers, should have a legal and moral right to say what happens to the child that they, along with the mother, conceived."

"I agree with you, but you would get an argument from women's lib groups," replied Kate.

"Well, their arguments are based on emotion not science," said Joe. "The father and the mother, in union together, created that child. It's plain and simple. Taking religious beliefs completely out of it and strictly looking at it from a scientific standpoint, from a sheer biological point of view, before the fetus is removed from the woman, the father should be given a say in the matter, because the seed was fertilized by the father. Unfertilized, the seed never would have grown to any life form. So, why should the woman alone have the right to dictate the future of the fetus that both the father and mother brought to life?"

All of the arguments about when life begins, when life is viable, were mute points to Kate and Joe when they found out they were having a child. Instead, they felt what parents have generally felt since the time that man and woman became father and mother - absolute elation over the coming of their child.

Chapter 75 - Birth of the First, November 1974

Joe was sweeping the garage when Kate called out that he better get in the house and get her to the hospital, because their child could not be kept waiting much longer. They were already packed, and had been for a month, so they threw everything into the car and headed for Mt. Sinai Hospital in Detroit. Man, were they ever prepared. They had taken Lamaze child-birthing classes. Kate knew how to puff, pant, pant, and Joe knew how to coach her, so this was going to be a slam-dunk!

Things were going pretty smoothly, when Kate had a contraction that wasn't terribly high on the scale, but it caused Kate enormous pain. Joe caressed Kate's shoulder and, trying to be comforting, he softly said that Kate needed to practice her breathing more because later contractions would be more severe than what she was experiencing at this time. The voice of Satan welled up in Kate's throat. She said something that sounded a lot like, "Get him the hell out of here!" It may not have been those exact words, but the meaning was well understood, and a nurse quickly ushered Joe out of the room.

Joe spent the rest of the evening watching television until he had learned his lesson that Kate was the one trying to push out this child, and dealing with the pain – not him. And while Joe could try to encourage her, comfort her, and help her, it was Joe who needed to be a more supportive coach and not be so judgmental. Joe got it. Actually, this was something that Joe thought he understood pretty well, but in real life situations often what you are dealing with is not what was planned for.

There is a first time for everything – including having a baby. God certainly could have given Kate an easier task, because a 10 pounds 4-ounce boy would be hard for anyone to deliver. Plus, the baby was 23 inches long with big feet that were pushing directly into Kate's spine. Hello!!!! How does one plan for that?

Chapter 76 - The First Meal, November 1974

The new family had their first meal together after their son was born and placed in Kate's arms at 4:20 AM the morning after Kate had been taken to the hospital. Kate held her son close to her lips and kissed him gently. The baby was named James after Joe's middle name. The words of a poem that wanted to be written down virtually jumped from Joe's mind to his hand. The poem was called "A Mutual Gift."

A Mutual Gift

*Smiling as we look down at him
as he gives us a little grin.
Holding him close, so very tight,
checking on him throughout the night.*

*This child dispels all of my doubts
of what our lives are all about.
To give, to share, to provide love.
Sacrifice, place others above.*

*My life's no longer just for me,
or yours for you, we both agree.
We had a choice; let go or save.
God smiled on the choice that we made.*

*As we sit down this Christmas Eve,
James is the only gift we need.*

Parenthood fit the couple like a glove. They had enjoyed life as a twosome and when their child came into their life, both Joe and Kate just kind of moved over and made room for the new member of the family. Unlike so many things in life, there really is no textbook on how to be a parent or how to raise a child, but love and nurturing were the center of the endeavor for Kate and Joe.

Chapter 77 - Maggie's Death, April 1, 1975

Joe, Kate and James were down in Florida with Kate's family when Florida State Police came to their camp site and told Joe that his mother had been killed in Florida by a hit and run driver. Maggie, her husband Bill, and their son Kurk, were in Florida on vacation. They came upon a home that they looked at for the possibility of purchase. The owner was a widow who recently lost her husband and wanted to return to her family home. She was not using a real estate broker and said that she wanted X price but was willing to take Y if she could sell it soon. Maggie, the negotiator in the family, said that they could only afford Y less $3,000. The seller said she would sell the house at that price but the offer would have to be presented that day. Maggie said they wanted to review things as she walked out of the home.

As they drove away, Maggie started going over all the features in the home and became convinced that this was the home she wanted. Bill said, "If you are sure that's what you want, call her and tell her before someone else comes along." They pulled onto the side of the road when they saw a pay phone across the street. Maggie took a quick look at the traffic, determined she could make it to the phone easily enough, then got out and stepped in front of a speeding car that came around the curve they were parked on. She was thrown by the speeding car, and if the impact of the car didn't kill her instantly, the fall to the ground did. The body was being shipped back to Michigan for burial.

Shortly after getting the details from the state troopers, Joe, Kate and James returned home to Michigan. The tragedy was compounded by an April snowfall of 20 inches and all 20 inches plus drifting were waiting for them when they got to their Livonia home.

A true piece of humanity was shown by Josh to Bill at the funeral. Bill was not in a position that he could afford a suit for the funeral, so Josh took Bill to a men's clothing store where he had him fitted for a suit for the funeral. All the two men had in common was the love they had and once had for a woman, but that was enough to make the love of God work through them. Bill's son, saw the kindness and one day would also become a policeman.

Joe had several visitations to her gravesite. The most meaningful one was when he went to her grave, sank to his knees and forgave her for the divorce and the problems that it had caused him in his life. He forgave her for any shortcomings she had as a mother and asked for forgiveness for any shortcomings he may have had as her son.

Chapter 78 - Joe Leaves Education, October 1975

Joe was about 70% completed with his MBA when he saw two opportunities to get a job as a manufacturer's representative with Fortune 500 companies that had local offices in the Detroit area. The first company sold baby products like diapers and such, which didn't really interest Joe but he would take it if the other company didn't offer a job.

The second company was a Wisconsin-based international, privately held conglomerate that dealt with household products and sundry other lines. Joe would be separately interviewing with two of their representatives. One, Ed Soder, would be his boss if Joe were to get hired. Ed was a jive and shuck, self-made man who had gotten as far as he likely would go in this company given that he did not have a college degree. Don't get me wrong, a college degree is not the be all and end all in getting a job. To the truly gifted, a degree is not a necessary passage to the higher rungs of a corporation, but Ed fell far short of being gifted.

The company was looking to hire someone who could get the job done at the store level that a sales person at the corporate level may not have been able to accomplish. In addition, the company sought someone who could improve their shelf position in stores that carried the company's products. Ed felt that Joe was the guy he was looking for, and set up an appointment for Joe to meet with Ed's boss at the district management level.

A meeting was set up between Joe and Jim Wallace, the district manager. Jim was so smooth that he made 10W40 oil feel rough. Had he gone into the acting profession he could have likely been given the lead in a James Bond movie. Joe never asked and never knew if Jim had been to college, because in Jim's case it didn't matter - Jim was very gifted. Joe met Jim in the field one day and went to a half dozen stores that were in the region the company was trying to fill.

During the day, Jim sold several large displays of products that were knew in the market and worked with a stock man on resetting a portion of the household products aisle where the company had a number of products. Every question and objection put forth by the stock person was professionally and knowledgeably addressed by Jim, and he gained Joe's instant respect.

In a follow-up meeting with Ed and Jim, Joe made it clear that he was working on his MBA in marketing and would like to relocate to the company's product development department. Jim said that most of the product development positions were filled by recent MBA graduates. Therefore, most of them would be six years younger than Joe. But, if Joe did well in his position, the region would help Joe set up interviews with corporate for any product development job that needed to be filled. Jim's representation of what the company could do was satisfactory to Joe, and Joe was hired in as an area sales manager in this major market.

Chapter 79 – Working in Corporate Sales, 1975 - 76

Learning a new job of a marketing representative with a young son at home was not for the feint hearted, but Joe had handled difficult tasks before and tore into this new task with zeal. He no longer had to prep for teaching and there were no papers to correct or compositions to read at night, so he felt that the workload kind of evened out.

Right from the beginning Joe found that he had no difficulty dealing with his customers. After all, he had worked in retail stores himself and knew the lay of the land. He spoke their language and understood their personalities because that was a part of his background.

Success came and Joe began receiving very positive messages from high-ranking people at corporate. Ed seemed less than enthused about Joe's successes.

Joe made a call on a K-Mart store at Telegraph and Twelve Mile Roads – a very busy intersection in Southfield, Michigan. The store was one of the biggest stores in his sales area and was called on by Joe every two weeks. On this particular day, Joe was selling a new line of solid air freshener that the company had just manufactured and wanted to get high distribution into retail outlets because they were spending a ton of money on advertising the product.

Joe met with the buyer responsible for the household goods section of the store and pitched her the new air freshener. Joe's company was offering one case free with the purchase of four cases – a 20% savings. The buyer loved the deal and bought 1,000 cases of the air freshener, with 12 packs in each case. It was the biggest sale of its kind that the company had ever sold to one store at one time. Joe received letters of commendation from the vice president of the company and from the company's product manager.

But the next time Joe was out with Ed, his boss told him that Joe had oversold the store on the 1,000-case order and had gotten the region in trouble at the buyer's corporate level.

This didn't make sense to Joe. If that was the case, why did he receive the letters of commendation from headquarters? During his next visit to that K-Mart, Joe asked the department buyer if the order had caused him any trouble or was their any fallout at the corporate level over the size of the order. The buyer assured him there were no problems except K-mart would have liked to have bought the deal at the corporate level for all the stores. Apparently there had been a miscommunication between the K-Mart corporate and the company corporate seller.

Chapter 80 - Charlie and Grandpa, 1975

Charlie was released from the Missouri prison when his two years were up, and not a day before. Charlie was now 30 years old. He was looking for a friendlier environment, so he drove up to Roscommon, Michigan to see his grandfather, Benjamin.

Benjamin welcomed Charlie somewhat tentatively because he knew of the car theft and the prison sentence in Missouri. Benjamin did not feel comfortable with this grandson, but he was Charlie's grandfather, and maybe he could help him. Charlie spoke of prison life and how he was in the best shape that he had ever been in because of all the exercise he got in prison. Benjamin tried to get Charlie to talk about the reason he went to prison.

"It was all a set-up, Grandpa. I served two years in prison for not paying for a beer and for taking $5 of crap from a grocery store."

"Well, why did they make the punishment so harsh?" asked Benjamin.

Charlie stalled, but then said, "The judge thought I beat up some old man and stole his car. When the old man died, and they couldn't find any proof that I took the car, the charges were dropped. The judge got all pissy about it and said he knew I did it."

While Benjamin knew that Charlie had been in prison in Missouri, the details had never been shared with him. He asked, "Why did the judge feel that you had anything to do with the car theft or the beating?"

Deep down Charlie was proud of what he had pulled off that day. He looked at his feet, then smiled and said, "Well, let's just say I was hitchhiking on my way to Texas, and I wanted a faster ride. I was cold and wearing gloves. People should have seen that and helped me, but no one was picking me up. So, along comes this older guy who stops and picks me up. He seems like a nice guy, but I'm not looking for a friend. I had a small knife and showed it to him and asked him nicely to get out of the car. I figured if he's out of the car, and I'm in the car, the car is mine. It would be my car now.

Benjamin was going to comment that what Charlie was doing was armed robbery, but he held his tongue and let Charlie continue.

Charlie, enjoying the stage that he had, continued. "Well, the old man gets all angry about me asking him to get out, so I hit him a couple of times and dragged him out of the car. And the asshole is still fighting me, Benjamin! So, to calm him down and make him see things my way, I kept on lifting him up by the shoulders and slamming him down on the street. Not too hard. I didn't want to hurt him. I just wanted his car. I needed it more than he did. He was okay when I left, just not talking very much and a little bloody – but not too much. I then left. My gloves had a little blood on them, so I pulled off the road and got my tire iron out and dug a hole for the gloves. I wiped the dirt off of the tire iron and put it back the way I found it. I learned that at the orphanage, always put your stuff back where it belongs. I didn't want to leave any fingerprints in the car, so I pulled the arms of my shirt down over my hands, started the car and drove off. I was hungry and saw a place to eat, so I left the keys in the car and went to get a hamburger. That's when the police came and all hell broke loose."

Benjamin stared at Charlie. He told the story so calmly. "Do you feel remorse, Charlie?" he asked.

Charlie said, "Feel remorse, Grandpa? Hell, I don't feel any remorse. He had a car and I didn't. I needed the car. With the life I've had, Grandpa, I deserved the car. I've never felt remorse. Hell, no!"

"But, Charlie, the Bible says Thou Shalt Not Steal, and what were you doing? You were stealing,"

Charlie glowered at his grandfather, "Is that the way you see it? I thought I could count on you to see it my way. I didn't steal anything, Grandpa, I needed the car, and I took it. If I didn't need it, then it would have been stealing. Now, let's watch TV. Is wrestling on?"

"I don't watch wrestling, Charlie."

"Well, I'm your guest, and guests are always right, Grandpa! Or should I just call you Benjamin, because you're not acting like my grandpa." Charlie said as he stared at his grandfather.

"Charlie, what you are referring to are customers - not guests. If a customer wants something in a store or from a sales person then if the store management or salesperson is smart, they will try to satisfy the customer's desires. You are a guest in my house as long as I choose to have you as my guest. When I no longer want you as my guest, I will ask you to leave. And, Charlie, I am Grandpa to you – not Benjamin. You'll show respect for me, especially in my own home."

"Benjamin, I'm not a boy anymore. I'm an adult. You call me Charlie, so I can call you, Benjamin." Charlie laid back on the couch and lit a cigarette. "And don't try to make me feel stupid with all that customer/guest crap."

"No smoking in the house, Charlie. If you want to smoke go out on the porch."

Charlie turned on his side and said, "When in the hell, Benjamin, did you become such a little ole' lady? Rules, rules, rules. You're just filled with your damn rules. Well, here's a new rule – when I am your guest, I make the rules."

Benjamin, stood up. All 6' 3" of him and said, "Charlie, I think I want you to stay somewhere else for the night. I'm not comfortable with you here."

Charlie rose to his feet and approached his grandpa. He was an inch taller than his grandfather, "You know, Benjamin, in prison I worked out all the time - lots of weights; lots of crunches. I'll bet if I wanted to, I could kick your ass in right here, right now. What do you think?"

Benjamin had been a tough builder in his prime, but his prime was 30 years ago. He just looked at his grandson and said, "Grandson or no grandson, Charlie, 30 years ago you would have been on the floor by now."

Charlie laughed, "Well, Grandpa, this ain't 30 years ago. Do you want to try your luck now?"

Benjamin looked Charlie in the eye and said, "If it would make you feel like a big man to beat up your 70-year-old grandpa, go ahead. But then you better run like hell because the cop who lives next door will hunt you down and you'll be back in jail before you know it."

Charlie, looked Benjamin over, up and down, and said, "Ah, gee, Grandpa, can't you take a joke? I guess I will head out. This place stinks anyway."

"Don't come back, Charlie."

"Benjamin, I wouldn't come back to this pisshole if my life depended on it."

With that, Charlie sauntered out the door, got in the car, stared at his grandfather, flicked his cigarette at his grandfather's feet and drove away.

Benjamin took a deep breath then waved to the elderly widow who lived alone next door.

Chapter 81 - Grandpa and Joe, 1975

Several weeks after Charlie had been to see their grandfather, Joe, Kate and James spent the weekend at Joe's grandfather's home. Pictures were taken with Grandpa holding James, his first great grandson. Joe took pictures of all four of them with the camera on a tripod. It was a pleasant visit with his grandfather.

As they were leaving, his grandfather told Joe about the incident with Charlie. "I just don't know how Charlie could turn on me like that. I never did anything to hurt him, and I was always supportive of him whenever I spoke with your mom."

"He had kind of a tough childhood Grandpa."

"Hell, Joe, many people have had bad childhoods, and they become stronger from it. Charlie uses his tough childhood as an excuse for his weakness. He's just a bad seed."

Chapter 82 - The MBA, A Giant Leap Away, 1976

Having a child and working full time made life full enough for anyone. Add two classes in a Master's program and you'll see someone who is burning candles at both ends and in the middle. In fact, you could be describing Joe. Making it even worse was that one class that he needed to obtain the MBA degree, a marketing class, was not being offered until the following winter semester - six months from the present time. Joe did not want to wait that long to finish the degree, so he approached a professor in the marketing department who was teaching an undergraduate marketing statistics course that spring. Joe asked the professor if he could take the undergraduate course for graduate credit. The professor said that he could with a few extra assignments, and Joe registered for the classes. In anticipation of completing the MBA degree at the end of June, Joe and Kate bought plane tickets to Phoenix, Arizona to visit an old friend who had moved there a few years back after going through a bitter divorce with his wife. The couple had been best friends of Joe and Kate.

On the first day of his final semester, Joe was asked by the marketing professor to remain after class. He told Joe that the additional work that he wanted Joe to do for graduate credit of this undergraduate class was to recreate the computer output that the professor had obtained that went into his doctoral thesis.

Joe protested that he only had one computer programming class and that had been written in Basic. The professor said that if Joe wanted this class to qualify for graduate credit, that is what he, the professor, was requiring. He then handed Joe his doctoral thesis which contained all of the programming data and a thick book on how to write an SPSS program.

Joe looked at the material and said, "Professor, with all due respect, I have a full-time job, a wife, a child and I am taking a second class. This is way beyond what I can accomplish. Can't I do some other analytical paper or make my tests more challenging than everyone else's tests?"

"Mr. Lane, if it is too much for you, then drop the class and wait and take the regular class next winter."

Joe had already paid for the class and did not want to admit defeat before he was defeated, so he stayed in the class and tried to get a handle on how to do what the professor was demanding that he do to pass the class.

The phrase totally and absolutely overwhelmed cannot get close to what Joe felt when he drove home that evening. He had felt that college professors often operated outside of the real world. They could take an often almost dictatorial position because they were dealing with students that were virtually powerless in opposing them. The professor could say, "You want this, I demand that." The student is left with few alternatives. The German Philosopher Fredrich Nietzsche's quote "Power corrupts; absolute power corrupts absolutely," came to mind.

Two months later, Joe received an A in the statistics class and an Incomplete in the marketing class. He had gotten A's on all of the assignments but could not get the program to run to duplicate the professor's doctoral output.

Joe and Kate prepared for their vacation to Phoenix, which would also include Disneyland for James while Kate packed away clothes and shoes, most of Joe's suitcase was filled with notes and other papers having to do with the incomplete marketing class.

Joe would not be part of Wayne State's graduation ceremonies that summer.

They stayed with Larry, at his house in Phoenix. Larry worked in a field that required a lot of statistical analysis and he knew people in the computer programming department of the University of Arizona. Joe and Larry met with one of the professors to review the requirements Joe's professor demanded. The University of Arizona professor was very aware of the

SPSS program. He asked Joe how many computer classes he had taken. Joe told him one class – Basic. The professor looked at Larry and Joe and laughed. "With the background that you have in programming, this was an impossible demand by your professor." Joe could not agree more. The professor took pity on Joe and helped him write the program that duplicated the professor's doctoral thesis.

With the output in hand, Joe was able to write the paper that the professor required. When Joe and Kate got back to Michigan a week later, the paper was well on its way to being completed. When finished, it was submitted for credit, and Joe's Incomplete was turned into an A. Joe had completed the work for his MBA degree.

Joe was able to juggle school, family and work fairly well, but there was no question that life was happier now that the demands of school were off of him.

Chapter 83 - Use the Book, Lose the Sale, November 1976

Several months later, Ed wanted to go with Joe on his calls again. They called on a grocery store in Troy, Michigan that had never bought anything from Joe. Joe asked for the assistant manager and was directed to an aisle where they were doing a reset of part of the aisle.

Joe, with the sales book in hand asked the assistant manager if he could talk to him about the items that were on sale that month. The assistant manager said that he did not have time because he had to block out the aisle.

Joe had reset aisles when he worked in the grocery store in college. He knew how to block out an aisle. He asked the assistant manager if he helped to block out the aisle, could he tell him about the month's offerings without using the sales book. The manager said yes. Joe put down the book and began to work with the manager. As he worked Joe told the assistant manager everything that was in the book without using the book.

He told him about the amount of advertising that being done on television and what television stations and shows the advertising was going to be on.

The assistant manager so thoroughly appreciated the efforts that Joe was giving him, that he told Joe to go up to the office and have the purchasing manager order 20 cases of the product that he would display on the endcap of the household goods aisle. Joe worked with him for another few minutes, they shook hands and Joe and Ed went to the store's office where the purchasing manager wrote 20 into the ordering book.

Joe and Ed went out to the car and were ready to leave when his boss told Joe to shut off the engine. Then Ed said, "What the hell just happened in there?"

Joe had been astatic about getting his first display in the store, but his Ed's question took the smile off his face. He looked at his Ed and said, "I truly don't understand the question."

"Do you have any idea how much money is spent on putting together those presentation books?" Ed asked.

"Not really, but do you know what those presentation books are for?" Joe answered with a question.

"My question first. A tremendous amount of time and effort is spent by the marketing staff in putting together those books to tell the story about the product."

Joe said, "With all due respect, boss, that is not totally true. The purpose of the presentation book, as you know, isn't just to tell the story about the product, the purpose is to help get the sale. Our job is to sell. And that is what the hell just happened in there."

"But you didn't use the material that you were given. You didn't do your job."

"Ed, I did do my job, I got the sale. The presentation book is a tool to help get the sale. In this case the presentation book was an obstacle that prevented making the pitch, so II put the book down, because it stood in the way of giving the pitch. But I used the data in the book to present the product while I was assisting him with a task that he had to do. I was building a relationship with someone who has never thrown me a bone. Because of the that assistance and the data that I presented, I gained the appreciation of the assistant manager and got my first display sale in that store."

Ed would not be deterred. "I call you guys into the office each month to put together this material and practice the pitch to help get the sale."

"Yes," said Joe, "and I used the data in the book, but I put aside the book that was impeding me from even being able to present the material. Don't you understand that I was only given the opportunity to make the pitch was to put the book aside? Only then did I get to use all the material that marketing provided to help close the sale, which I did."

Ed refused to listen. "I'm going to write you up. This is not going to look good on your record."

Joe said, "I would like to see how you explain to the vice president of sales that it was a bad thing to get the sale without using the book, when I used the data in the book, just not the book itself to close the deal."

"Drive me home. We're done here. I have a report to write." They drove to the boss's house in silence. When they got there, Joe said,

"Boss, you do what you feel you need to do, but if you write that report presenting the facts as they were, you are going to hurt yourself more than you'll hurt me."

"We'll see."

"Yes, we will," Joe thought.

Chapter 84 - Joe's Graduation, December 1976

Joe's graduation from Wayne State University was scheduled for December 2, 1976. Joe told the company long in advance that he needed to leave early that day to get to his graduation exercises in downtown Detroit, Ed decided to work with him that day. Joe would have to first drive to his boss's house in Novi then head north to his territory. At the end of the day, he would have to leave earlier than he otherwise would have to take the boss home before going to the graduation exercises.

When he picked his boss up at 7:30 AM, Joe told him that the graduation exercises downtown were at 6:00 PM. They would be working in Pontiac and Joe had planned to go straight down I-75 to Detroit from Pontiac. If he left at 3:30 PM, given rush hour, he could get to the arena, change into his cap and gown and be ready for the graduation. Now that he had to drive Ed home, he would need an extra hour to make it.

His boss nodded when Joe said that he needed to leave the territory at 2:30 PM.

"You are more than welcome to join me today, but are you sure you want to, given I need to leave at 2:30 PM?"

"What? You don't want me to go?" his boss asked.

"Well, since you asked, it would be better if you joined me another day. If I was alone, I could work until 3:30 PM and take I-75 to Detroit. I will be losing an hour of work having you along, because I will have to drive you home before I go down town."

Ed laughed. "I'll help you along. We'll make more calls and you'll still get there on time."

Making more calls because there were two of them didn't make any sense. Only one person was needed to make the sales pitch, but Joe wasn't going to push the matter further, so he remained silent, except to say that his wife, son and step parents were going to be there, and he didn't want to be late.

"Got it," his boss said.

At 2:20 PM they finished what Joe thought was their last call, and he started heading back to Novi.

His boss said, "There's a hardware store right on the way, we'll stop there and make a pitch."

"But…"

"Don't worry, Joe. You won't be late."

They got to the store at 2:45 PM. The manager was tied up in a meeting, so they checked the aisle and made some adjustments to the location of their products.

At 3:15 PM, the store manager came out and met with them. Ed chose this time to go into a discussion about how the store would make more money if they moved the company's products elsewhere.

The manager, a little annoyed, said. "Joe and I have already talked about the location of your products, and I told him we would consider it in the spring when we reset the store."

"Well, look," his boss said, "this is what we could do now," and he started blocking out a section for their line of product.

The manager said, "Please stop. This is my store, and I will change the product as I see fit."

"Well, we have the number one products in this market," his boss replied.

The manager retorted, "I sell so little of this stuff, you are lucky to have any shelf space at all. This meeting is over." The manager left and went back to his office and shut the door.

The whole exercise took 50 minutes. Joe was steaming. He said, "I'll never get there on time."

"Oh, you'll be fine. It's just a graduation. It's not life and death."

By the time he drove Ed home, Joe knew he likely would never make it on time.

He raced through Novi, got on the expressway and got to the assembly as the graduates were heading for the stage to get their diploma's. Joe got his cap and gown on one minute before his name was called and he went up and received his MBA.

Everyone gathered afterward, and Josh said, "I wish you had gotten here earlier so we could have had some time to talk."

Joe explained what had happened and Josh said, "You work for a prick."

Joe nodded. He couldn't agree more."

Chapter 85 - A Request Denied and Shattered,

1977

After Joe finished the MBA requirements, he called a meeting with Ed and requested that his name be put in for an available opening in marketing and product development department in Wisconsin. His boss told him that the only way that he could go from sales to marketing was to become a manager in a small market, then relocate to a larger market and be a successful manager there. After doing that, the company might consider moving him to marketing.

Joe said to himself, "That process could take years." Then he looked at his boss and said, "I told you on my first interview with you that I was interested in transferring to marketing once I got my MBA. Why didn't you tell me then about these restrictions?"

Ed just shrugged his shoulders. "We needed people in sales."

Joe thought, "That's the game. Just say whatever it takes to close the deal." From that point forward Joe began to look at other job opportunities.

Chapter 86 – A Career, December 1976

After the altercation with his boss regarding the use of presentation materials, and the whole graduation fiasco, Joe believed that who he was and what he was doing was not a good fit. Joe was looking at the professional help wanted section of the paper one day and saw an ad for a real estate sales position in downtown Detroit. The ad was unique in that it was advertising for people who were not trained in real estate sales. The ad said the person had to have a degree, have sales experience (but not real estate) and be a self-starter. Joe had all of those attributes. He sent in his resume and hoped for the best.

Shortly thereafter Joe received a call from a personnel representative from the company. They were on the phone for fifteen minutes with the personnel manager trying to determine who the person was behind the resume. The personnel manager said, "I think we have covered enough information for now. I would like to set up an interview with you and the manager of the department."

Joe called into his office and told them he would be taking a personal business day that day, then he got in the car and headed to downtown Detroit. When he got to the facility, he parked where he had been told to park and made his way to the designated floor.

He was led back to the personnel managers office who took him to a corner office where he met the Real Estate Manager, Mark Martin. Mark told him to sit down and the interview began.

Mark said, "Well you made it past the personnel manager, that's not an easy thing to do, so you passed step 1. I want to hear about you. Tell me about yourself." Joe did. Without going into too much detail he explained his background, his marriage, his child, who was the love of his life. He talked about teaching and his job as a manufacturer's representative.

"That's a big company and it sounds like it's going pretty well for you, why did you send us your resume?" Mark asked.

Joe explained the incident with the presentation book and Mark listened intently. The conversation had been serious and guarded friendly, but Mark stopped him when Joe explained how he put down the presentation book and worked with the assistant manager and closed the sale.

"Wait a second," Mark said as he leaned forward at the table, "you get the sale by making the pitch without the presentation book and you get written up for it? Are you kidding me?" Mark began to laugh. He was incredulous that anyone in a sales supervisorial position could ever be so stupid. He said, "Look, Joe, I want people who are good on their feet. Who can improvise and go with the flow – people like you." Mark stood up and said, "I want to show you around the place, but you need to talk to a couple of other people first."

He called the personnel manager down and said, "Dick, would you take Joe down to see Arthur?"

Dick came down to get Joe and took him to the office of the President of the company, Arthur. After a few pleasantries Arthur asked several questions that Joe felt that he handled fairly well. Arthur picked up the phone, called Dick and said "I'm fine here. Take him to Branch. "

Dick and Joe were walking down the hall and Dick asked, "How do you think it is going so far?" Joe said, "I never try to get too comfortable until the final vote is in."

Dick said, "Well you are heading there right now." Joe said, "I figured that was the case. What is the chairman's name?"

"Branch Durban," Dick said, "hand-picked by the chairman of board of the parent company and heading for a vice presidency with the parent company one day. Don't let that intimidate you though. He puts his pants on one leg at a time, just like the rest of us. I think you'll like him."

Dick stuck his head into the chairman's office and said, "Branch, do you have time to see the office leasing candidate?"

"Absolutely! Send him right in."

Joe went into the chairman's office with a smile on his face and a hand extended. "So nice to meet you Mr. Durban. Joe Lane."

Shaking hands, Branch Durbin said, "It's Branch, Joe, unless someone outside of the company is here. Have a seat." They sat at a conference table in Branch's office. Branch was not a big man. Muscular, fit, but not big. But he carried himself like he was the biggest man in the room. He exuded a confidence like Joe had never witnessed before. Branch had a smile and graciousness that was even bigger than his confidence. Joe knew that he was in the presence of a great man, and felt honored to be there.

"Well, Joe, what do you think?"

"Think?" Joe asked.

"Are you interested in the position or do we keep on looking?"

"Are you offering me the job, Mr. Durbin?"

"No, I am just concurring with the decision to hire you. We have a different way of doing business here, Joe. The company calls it participative management; I call it bottoms up. You would be working for Mark, so by Mark sending you to meet with the president, Arthur, Mark was saying that you are the person he wants to hire. If Arthur or I find a reason to overrule that decision, we can do that, but it better be a darn good reason. Obviously, Arthur was fine with you and that is why he sent you to me. I'm fine with you, so if you want to join our team, we would love to have you with us. So, what do you think?"

"I think I will fit in very well here," Joe said. "And I think you will be pleased with your decision."

"All right, then. Let's get this place filled up! Sue, tell Dick to get the agreements drawn up."

It was decided that since they were so close to the end of the year that Joe would start right after the first of the year.

Chapter 87 - Coming to Grip With Incompetence, December 1976

Joe went back to work the following day as if he had not signed the agreement to start working at the McNamara Towers in January. December 15 rolled around and at 4:45 PM he drove into Dearborn and hand delivered a letter of resignation to his boss. The letter said that he was giving his two week notice and would be terminating his employment at the end of the year.

Ed showed neither shock nor disappointment. If he showed anything at all it was relief. Ed sat back in his chair and said, "We always want to know why someone is leaving our employment. Could you share with me why you are leaving?"

Joe looked at Ed and thought, "Always the same old smarmily prick. The deceitful prick with a smiley face." Then Joe said, "This is not the correct venue for me to say all that I have to say. I will reveal my reasons for leaving at the right time, the right place and to the right people for me." What Joe didn't say is that he intended to write a very thorough letter to senior management in Wisconsin on what he had experienced in the southeastern Michigan market of this world-wide corporation.

Ed could see that he likely would not get any more from Joe, but he asked him if he would meet with Jim. Ed was actually hoping that Joe would reveal something to Jim that he would not say to Ed.

"Why don't you wait in the conference room? Jim will be right in. Several minutes later Jim entered the room sporting a friendly smile. "I must be honest with you, Joe, I didn't see this coming."

They shook hands. "Are you sure this is what you want to do?" Wallace asked sincerely.

"It's a good opportunity that keeps my family here," said Joe. "Michigan is home and always will be."

Jim said, "I hope there was no dissatisfaction with us. I hope we did everything you expected from us."

"Well, I told you right from the start I wanted something more in marketing than sales. That apparently couldn't happen because of the structure of the company."

"Ohh?" Jim questioned.

"You know, the process of a person in sales needing to become a successful manager of a large market, then a small market and then possibly the person could be considered for a marketing position. That process could take years," Joe said.

"Hmm." Jim uttered, "I don't know that we have a policy like that. Who told you that?"

"Ed did. When I got my MBA I asked him about a marketing position that was open at corporate, and he took me through the process."

"I see," said Jim. "Frankly, Joe you are only the second MBA that we have had, and he didn't want to go into marketing. He just quit."

"Was he in this district?" asked Joe.

"Oh, he worked for Ed, too," Wallace said.

"You're a smart guy, Jim, you should see a pattern here. I've enjoyed working with you, but I am meeting my wife for dinner tonight. I've got to go." Joe got to his feet and shook hands with Wallace then left.

Chapter 88 – Clearing The Air, Late December, 1976

After Kate and Joe had the entire family in for Christmas and their son had been put to bed after a very busy day of church and Santa Claus, Joe sat down at his typewriter and wrote about the true reasons he had left the position of manufacturer's representative. He talked about the successes and the letters of congratulations from senior management. He talked about being forced to work late and almost missing his graduation commencement. But most of all he wrote about how he had gotten his first display at a major store by putting the presentation book down while presenting the data and helping the assistant manager block out the household goods section of the store. He finished that paragraph with the following:

"And do you know what I got for thinking on my feet and getting the sale? I got a lecture about the importance of using the company sales presentation material and a warning letter was put into my employment file by my boss. My boss took my success as something that could be used to build a file against me. When I saw that, I immediately decided that I did not want to work for a company that promoted such short sighted, ignorant people." Joe's letter was sent Ed, Jim Wallace, the vice president of household products, and the chairman of the board of the company.

Several months later Joe came into contact with one

of his old colleagues at the household products company and learned that his boss had been called to corporate right after the holidays and came home unemployed. He had moved back to California where he was from. Joe truly felt that he did a good thing for the company.

For a sales staff to be successful you have to give the staff the flexibility to close the sale by making modifications to the desired terms of the sale so long as the modification does not put the company into jeopardy. To do otherwise is to not have a sales staff, but expensive order takers.

Chapter 89 - Joe and Kate's Second Child – 1977-1979

With the new position, Joe found that while the hours were long and what he had to learn was monumental and challenging, because he had management and co-workers whom he could trust, he did not come home mentally and physically exhausted as he had before. James was a beautiful, intelligent child and Joe and Kate wanted to add to their family. Joe and Kate were having a difficult time bringing another child to term. Twice Kate had miscarried, and she was having problems with her latest pregnancy. Kate and Joe had taken James to an amusement park, and Kate had been doing a lot of walking. Kate was past the point where she had twice-previously miscarried, and she thought she was safe to travel and lead a normal life. But her body was showing signs of rejecting this child as well.

Kate called her doctor who told her what she already knew – rest and take it easy until she could get to the doctor's office.

When she saw the doctor, the problem was discovered. The doctor put Kate on special medication and told her to take it easy. Kate followed her doctor's orders and five months later Kate gave birth to a lovely, redheaded girl. Joe and Kate named their daughter April.

Kate, Joe and James were all ecstatic. Kate joked that now she had a daughter to go shopping with all day. The four of them were a picture-perfect family and happiness prevailed. Joe wrote many poems to April, as he also did to James and Kate.

A favorite poem to April was called "Irish Lace," which Joe wrote while watching April as she slept.

Irish Lace

**Like Irish lace, her hair so fine
wrapped around her angelic face.
The pillow carried her profile,
and in its place her image traced.**

**Deep in her blanket as a bird
nestles close against mother's breast,
my tiny bird in peace she sleeps.
With sweet dreams she lays in her nest.**

**In silence I crept to her side
and share the cheek which Burt has kissed.
My hand alights her Irish lace.
I share the thoughts I can't resist.**

**"I love you, April, babe so fair.
I love you my sweet baby girl."
My feet retreat, "I love you too."
And everything's good in my world.**

Chapter 90 - Another Scam, June 1979

It was a long day. Kate had just gotten James to bed and was sitting down with Joe to watch some television. The doorbell rang, and they raced to get it before it woke James up. At the door was Charlie with a young woman wrapped around his waist.

"Hey, Joe...Kate. We just happened to be in the neighborhood and decided to stop in to see you. Joe, can we talk for a second?" Charlie asked.

Seeing Charlie was never a good thing because he always wanted something – usually money - but Joe and Charlie went into a back room and Joe said, "What horrible event brings you around, Charlie? You never just stop in."

"Nice place, Joe. I knew you would end up okay."

"We work our asses off for it. But, come on, Charlie, I've heard all your crap before, what do you want?"

"Well, to be honest with you, I knocked her up – the girl I'm with, and I need money to take care of it."

"Good grief, Charlie, haven't you heard of protection? Rubbers?"

"Well, you know how it is, Joe, you get excited and…"

"Yah, yah, yah. I know how it is. How much?"

"I don't know. Probably take a thousand."

"A thousand! Charlie, we just had a baby. Kate's not working, we don't have that kind of money."

"Well, what can you do, little brother?"

Joe pulled out his wallet. He had $150 in cash. He said, "I can go $140 tops, but I need to ask Kate."

Charlie sighed and said, "Oh, God. Not Kate. It's only $140, Joe. I don't even know what I can do with $140. I'll have to borrow more money elsewhere. It's just a loan. I'm good for it. I'll pay you back next week when I get paid."

"You're working?" Joe asked.

"Yep, at a gas station in the city. Good money. I'm just a little short right now, because she just sprung it on me today."

"Here's $140, Charlie, but don't say a word to Kate. I will talk to her after you leave."

Charlie put the bills in his pocket, got the girl and was out the door in minutes. He didn't care about seeing Joe or Kate; he just cared about the money.

After Charlie and his girlfriend left, Kate looked at Joe and said, "How much money did he want?"

Joe laughed. She knew Charlie too well.

"And how much did you give him?" Kate asked.

Kate knew Joe too well, too.

"He got the girl pregnant and needed a $1,000 to make the problem go away. I gave him $140," Joe said.

"Joe!" said Kate, "She was just telling me how she fell from a horse when she was a girl, and she can't get pregnant. She said they were on their way to buy a stereo."

Twenty minutes later, Charlie and the girl walked through the door of an electronics store.

"Where'd you get the money?" she asked.

"From my brother," Charlie laughed out loud. "I get him every time."

Chapter 91 - Joe's Promise to Kate's Dad, 1983

The last time Joe saw Kate's dad they were alone in the hospital. Joe and Kate's Dad both knew that the end was near. Joe looked at his father-in-law and tried to make conversation. But, how do you do that when you both know that you are really saying "Good-bye?"

The tears in his father in law's eyes told Joe that his father-in-law knew the end was near. Joe knew at this moment that he had to give this man some peace of mind.

Joe knew that a major concern of all fathers, of all parents, was what would happen to their loved ones if anything were to happen to them, the parent. Joe took the dying man's hand and leaned close to his ear and whispered, "I love you, Dad. I promise you that I will take good care of your daughter and grandchildren. You have made this family strong. Get better." Joe kissed him on the cheek and felt his father-in-law's hand squeeze his own. They separated, both with tears in their eyes.

As heartbreaking as Kate's dad's illness was, Joe

was moved to try to capture his thoughts of Kate's dad's struggle with cancer in the poem "Rippling Waters and Churning Sands." It was Joe's way of dealing with his own grief.

Rippling Waters and Churning Sands

Rippling waters and churning sands;
violent crosswinds, turbulent lands;
rolling thunder, limbs that are breaking;
torrential rains leave creatures quacking;

At times like this when dangers abound
it's good to bow low and kiss the ground.
It's good to think as lonely men wail
of those you love as dangers prevail.

Dangers need not be perilous storms,
needn't be engines from airplanes torn;
they need not be catastrophic size,
when you rise and thank God you're alive.

The dread can be a fight with one's self,
where punching won't help return your health.
The duel is fought with villains within
who've witnessed your pain, know where you've been.

We think of you now, near battle's end
and ask God to send strength He could send.
We send to you this wish that you may
be with us to share many a day.

If this is for you God's chosen time,
we hope that with you God will be kind –
lifting you with the least bit of pain,
allowing us to meet you again.

Chapter 92 - Death of Kate's Dad, 1983

Two days after Joe had said good-bye to Kate's dad in the hospital, the head of the family passed. He had long suffered with Alzheimer's Syndrome and cancer. His loss left a huge hole in the family that did not soon go away.

Through the years of illnesses that led to her husband's premature death, Kate's mom had stayed by her husband and had given him the love and care that he would have given her had their roles been reversed. Though Dad had passed, life still had to go on and did go on. God was still loved, albeit His actions and purposes may have been questioned, but the family still held together – leaning on each other for strength. At the funeral, Joe and the family listened closely to the priest who talked about how one might question God in times of sorrow.

The priest said, "To question God's actions or inactions does not mean you have condemned or turned from God. Questioning is a human condition. To not question and not try to seek a rationale for a tragedy would be out of sync with the human brain and the emotional make-up of man. It would make us less than we are – intelligent, analytical and truth-seeking beings. We are, with all of our flaws and blemishes, in compliance with what God planned for us to be, and knew that we would be, because it was God who gave us our ability to think, analyze, and feel, and it would be a sacrilege not to use these gifts from God."

Before taps were played, the priest took out a poem that Joe had written about Jules. Nan had given the poem to the priest and asked him to read it at the grave site.

Jules Jones - A Family Man

**All who are here will pick and choose
memories we wish not to lose.**

The special times we seek to hold
will be our stories oft' retold.

This moment will be set in time,
but I choose not to underline.
I won't recall this resting place
when thoughts of Dad are retraced.

For Dad, dear friend, I'd rather see
fond moments in my memory.
The good times that we often shared;
the special ways you showed you cared.

I remember when first we met.
Your stare was firm, your eyes were set.
For daughter Kate, I'd come to call,
but felt like running most of all.

From your eyes a dad's message came.
It crystallized and could be named.
She's my baby, treat her with care.
A father's message in your stare.

At Ponce De Leon, time we spent
vacations wrapped in camping tents.
Feeding peacocks- high in hanging trees,
Snorkeling in springs with shaking knees.

From boards came the diving display.
"Hey Jimmy, I'm better," you'd say.
Jimmy would climb without delay.
In loving encounter you'd play.

So good were you at all you tried.
Adept on skis, down hills you'd glide
Slicing serves, pinochle made fun,
early morning runs under the sun.

A lap for Gabriel and Ron,

a knee to set Terri upon.
Always the center of your life
were your five children and your wife.

This love which began with your own,
like yeast expanded as seeds were sown.
Grandchildren were your heart's delight.
Love sent, received, in hands held tight.

These and more, I'll remember, Dad.
My thoughts will be of joy - not sad.
For you made a mark when you came.
Your mark's on us - who love your name.

Chapter 93 - A Third Born, May 1984

After Kate had almost lost their daughter in pregnancy, she and Joe had decided not to have any more children. But four years after their daughter was born, Kate and Joe decided to try to have another child. The stars came together, and nine months later a beautiful baby boy came into their life. They named the boy Erin.

With the help of two older siblings showing Erin the guidelines and constantly bringing around friends, Erin grew into a child who had a smile and personality that turned a gathering into a party, just by his entering the room. Whenever Joe came home from work, it seemed like Erin was waiting at the door.

Joe and Kate were the parents of the type of family that Joe never had as he was growing up. The three children all loved and were supportive of each other. The house was filled with cheer. They were all good in school. They all were very athletic and joined baseball, soccer, basketball and swimming teams all of which Kate and Joe supported with their time and attendance.

While work was important and provided the income needed to live a happy and secure life, work was not the most important part of life. The most important part of their life was living it and sharing it with their three children, and the days whirred past amidst the most joyous of times that Kate and Joe could ever imagine. They would look back on all of the activities that they were engaged in – both at work, at play, at their children's' activities as the happiest years of their lives.

Chapter 94 - *From Missouri to Nebraska, 1986*

With Charlie's record it was difficult for him to find good jobs. It wasn't that he intellectually couldn't do the work, it was that no one trusted him or wanted him as an employee. He found that the best way to handle this was to change his name, which he did. He got fake ID made up that was in the name of Calvin Leonard.

In going through the help wanted ads Charlie noticed that a company in Omaha, Nebraska was advertising for truck drivers. The company was opening up a chain of steak houses throughout the Midwest and down into the Southwest, as far down as Houston, Texas. The company had purchased a number of refrigerated trucks and was looking for people with chauffer's licenses to drive them. Charlie was living in St. Louis, Missouri tending bar. He met with the party who had done his fake driver's license and insurance card and had him make up a chauffer's license that would allow him to drive commercial vehicles from state to state.

Charlie figured that it would really show initiative if he drove to Omaha and applied at the company headquarters, but he wasn't sure if his 1962 Chevy Nova was up for the trip, because it did have over 120,000 miles on it. He decided to give it a shot and before he left for work on the afternoon shift of the gas station, he loaded his few belongings into the back seat and trunk of the Nova, left his room key on the night stand with $5 and a note for the landlady that he was moving out and this should settle what he owes. It was just a little short of the $50 that he paid for rent per week. On the way to work he thought $5, $50 what's the difference? Zero's equal zero, which is nothing he smiled to himself. Looking at his stuff, he was always so pleased with the Navy for teaching him how to pack his bags so efficiently.

The gas station was a full-service station, and the manager of the station had brought in his 1980 Ford Explorer for service on the brake pads. The work was done and the manager told Charlie that he would be coming up in the morning with his wife to pick up the Explorer. All evening long Charlie thought about how the Nova couldn't be trusted to get all the way to Omaha, but the Explorer would certainly have no trouble making the trip. Before he locked up for the night, he moved his belongings from Nova into the Explorer. He left a note for the manager that said, "I left you my Nova and my weakly pay for your Explorer and a tank of gas. I think that's a fair trade. The gas station keys are under the driver's seat." Charlie was off for Nebraska.

Chapter 95 – First In Line

Charlie arrived in Omaha seven hours later. It was 7:00 AM when he checked into a motel under the name of Calvin Leonard. He caught a couple of hours sleep and then got dressed and was at the corporate headquarters of Nebraska Steaks, Inc. by 10:00 AM.

Rain was coming down fairly heavily as Charlie pulled into the employment office parking lot. There was only one other car in the lot, a late model blue, mid-sized car. When he got to the line outside of the employment office, one person was in front of him. Charlie wanted to be first.

He tapped the shoulder of the guy in front of him and said, "Are you driving a blue, mid-sized vehicle?"

The guy turned and said, "Who wants to know?'

"A security guard who said you were parked in the wrong place, and they'd have to tow you."

"Are you shittin' me, man?"

"That's what he said."

"Hold my spot will ya?" Without waiting for a response from Charlie, which Charlie wasn't about to give, the man ran back to the lot in the pouring rain. His car was where he left it. He saw a security officer and asked, "Did you say my car would have to be towed away because I parked it in the wrong place?"

The security officer said, "I said no such thing."

"Well is there someone else here who may be planning on moving the car?"

"I am the only security officer here, and I said nothing about your car. It is fine where it's at."

"Well, someone must have said it, because a guy in line told me. Now look at me! Here for an interview, and I'm soaked to the bone. This is bullshit!"

The officer said, "Sir, you better calm down or I will have to call the city police, and they will tow your car away."

The outraged man ran back to the employment line, where the job applicants had been brought inside of the building due to the rain. There were now twelve people in line all wanting to see personnel for various job postings. The man went to the front of the line and faced off against Charlie. "You lied to me, man. My car wasn't illegally parked."

"No?" Charlie responded innocently. "I thought for sure that is what he said. I was just trying to do the right thing."

"That's bullshit, man!! You lied to me on purpose. I was here first. I'm going in front of you."

Some big shouldered men with forearms the size of a horse's thigh, began to tell the guy to get to the back of the line. "No cuts, asshole." "Get to the back of the line where you belong."

Two security officers were called from the security office to the employment center and asked what was going on.

The enraged man began screaming about Charlie, and security told him to slow down. "What's your name?" they asked. He answered, "Bob Collins, sir"

"Mr. Collins, why don't you just calm down and get to the back of the line? There's time enough to see all of you."

"But I was in line first. This son of a bitch said I was parked illegally so I went to move my car. He said He would hold my place in line."

Charlie seeing his opening said, "I said no such thing, officer. I never said anything about holding his place. He ran off to the parking lot, mumbling something that I couldn't understand and was gone."

The officer said, "Mr. Collins, personnel will see everyone today who was here by noon. You're here. Just go to the back of the line and calm down."

Charlie smiled and winked at Bob Collins, and said, "Just a big mistake, Bob, take it like a man and go to the back of the line." Charlie knew his words and actions would be like rubbing sand into an open would. That's why he did it.

Bob lunged at Charlie. Charlie just sidestepped Bob and pushed him to the floor.

The security officer turned to the enraged man and said, "Sir, I am going to have to ask you to leave." The two security officers walked Collins back to his car with him bitching and complaining all the way and escorted him out of the parking lot.

Chapter 96 - The Job Interview with Calvin Leonard (Charlie)

Being first in line coming all the way in from St. Louis, Missouri really impressed the personnel representative. "Mr. Leonard, when did you leave St. Louis to make sure that you were first in line this morning?"

"Well, I closed up the gas station at midnight and drove straight through to Omaha," Calvin said.

"Quite frankly, Calvin, you seem to be very bright. How come you aren't applying for one of our office jobs?

Can you explain that to me?"

"Well, my folks got divorced when I was six years old. They placed me into St. Mathews Home For Children, in Michigan even before they got divorced because they both had to work and there was no family to take me in. I have been forced to work hard my whole life, and I am certain that I could do this job."

'I am absolutely certain that you can do the job too, Calvin. With the life that you have had, you need a break, and I'm going to give you one. You are hired. When can you start?"

"Immediately sir, and I promise not to let you down."

"All right, Calvin, be back here at 10:00 PM this evening. Report to the distribution docks and see the Distribution Manager. Most of our shipping is at night when it is cooler. We don't freeze our meat products because we have found that it effects the richness of the taste of the meat. We send them in refrigerated cars instead."

As Calvin was leaving, he asked, "I hate to ask this but do you know if there is a soup kitchen around?"

The personnel manager said, "Soup Kitchen? You mean, like, for people in need?"

Calvin nodded.

"Why do you need a soup kitchen, Calvin?"

"Well, I traded my car and my week's pay for the Ford Explorer I drove here. What little money I had I spent on gas and my motel room."

The personnel manager said, "I have the authority to give two weeks' pay in advance. I usually don't do that for someone just hiring in, but yours is a special situation, Calvin." He wrote out a pay order and gave it to Calvin. "Take this to payroll Calvin and they'll give you cash for two weeks pay. Don't spend it all, because it needs to last you for two weeks."

Chapter 97 – Post Interview Excitement

As Charlie was driving out of parking lot of Nebraska

Steaks, Bob Collins roared up next to Charlie and gave Charlie the middle finger. Collins was screaming obscenities at Charlie that Charlie couldn't hear because his windows were up. Charlie made a gesture with his forefinger going around his ear meaning to say he couldn't hear which enraged the driver even more because the driver took the signal as if Charlie was saying he was crazy. Now the enraged driver was past being reasoned with. Collins swerved his car to the left and quickly brought it back to the right into Charlie's driver's side door. The collision of the two cars was so great that Charlie's car left the road and sideswiped a tree before Charlie was able to get it to stop.

The enraged driver got out of his car and was coming at Charlie with a tire iron. Charlie always kept a chain in his vehicle. He grabbed the chain and began swinging it in the air, which neutralized Collins. Bob stood outside of the circumference of the savage chain and yelled, "You cost me a job today with that bullshit stunt you pulled"

Charlie answered back, "Collins, you cost yourself the job. If you are going to be an asshole you have to do it with poise and grace. You can't be yelling and screaming like a common fool. Now get in your car and drive away before I let this chain accidentally slip out of my fingers."

Bob Collins got back into his car and vowed to get even with Charlie come hell or high water.

Chapter 98 - First Day on the Job, 1986

That night Calvin (Charlie) showed up at the docks at 10:00 PM, Sunday evening. He met with the distribution manager and introduced himself.

The manager said, "We've got you almost loaded up, Calvin. Take a look at your delivery sites."

"These files here?" asked Calvin.

"Yes, we have mapped out the best roads to take and a time schedule for you so that you will know whether or not you are on schedule."

"How, do I know which packages go to which restaurants?"

The manager said, "All of the meat is separately labelled and is on the truck last in, first out. Your last stop is at a company restaurant in Houston, Texas. You should be finished in Houston around noon tomorrow."

"What do I do when they unload the truck in Houston?" Charlie asked. "Just leave it in the parking lot. They have sleeping quarters in the restaurant, so you can sleep there and then drive the truck back here when you wake up. This will be considered four day's work, so after you deliver the truck back here, you will be off until Friday at 10:00 PM."

"Ok, anything else I should know?" asked Charlie.

"Watch yourself on the roads. You are carrying about $200,000 in steaks, so be smart and avoid areas that you think could be troublesome."

When Charlie heard $200,000 his eyes rolled back, and he began to count dollars like a slot machine in a casino. He headed out on the road proceeding to his stops in Oklahoma and down into Texas.

Fifteen minutes into his drive, that little glitch inside of Charlie's brain that caused him to be erratic and deceitful, went off, and instead of continuing south/southwest Charlie turned east towards St. Louis, Missouri at 70 miles per hour. Thoughts like "slaughterhouse special sales program selling steaks at 30% normal wholesale - cash only" went through his mind.

A hundred miles east of Omaha, Charlie pulled into an all-night restaurant. He went into the restaurant and asked to speak with the manager. He told the manager that he was with a Nebraska slaughterhouse that was on the road selling freshly cut steaks at 30% normal wholesale prices. The manager grabbed his chef and went out to look at the product in the refrigerated truck. They loved what they saw, and at 30% normal wholesale, they would gladly pay cash. The chief cook asked, "But, why so cheap?"

Charlie said, "For two reasons, they are trying to expose their steaks to as many places in the midwest and south as they can get into. They are sure that once you experience their steaks, you will come back again and again. Second, has to do with Uncle Sam, and I won't go any further." Both the cook and the manager nodded understandingly. That was the line that Charlie used at every restaurant that he went to that evening and morning.

At 3:00 AM on a St. Louis television station that reached into Nebraska, there was a news report about "a unique car theft because the thief, a Charlie Lane, (they showed a picture of Charlie) thought that a good exchange was his 1962 Chevy Nova for his boss's 1982 Ford Explorer." That got a few laughs from the late-night news crew.

One of the Nebraska viewers of the news show that morning was none other than Bob Collins. He bolted upright when he saw the picture of Charlie. He immediately called the local police station and told them what he saw on the news.

The dispatcher at the police station said, "But, that was in Missouri, sir. "

Collins said, "I had a run-in with a guy at the headquarters of Nebraska Steaks in Omaha.

The dispatcher at the station sent a squad car to Nebraska Steaks. The officer walked into the employment office of the slaughterhouse. He was escorted into the manager's office and met with the Employment Manager.

The police officer said they were looking to find Charlie Lane and showed the picture of Charlie to the Employment Manager.

The manager almost spit out his coffee when he saw the picture. "That's Calvin Leonard. I just hired him yesterday."

"Hired him? He's got a criminal record as long as your arm. What was the position?"

225

"Truck driver. He should be arriving in Houston, Texas in about four hours with a load of steaks"

"How much are the steaks worth?"

"A typical truckload is between $180,000 to $250,000."

"I hate to say this, sir. Given his record of armed robbery and car theft, he may never reach Houston. He may not even be heading for Houston."

"Oh, God help me." The manager said. "In addition to the steaks, we have the refrigeration truck in the hands of a car thief."

"We'll notify the state police departments in a 500-mile radius to look out for him and the truck – including specifically Texas. But I think Texas is a long shot. I doubt if he went east to St. Louis having just stole his boss's car, but you never know with these criminal minds. They're bold as hell."

"Officer, how did you know to come here?"

"Some guy by the name of Bob Collins saw the story on a late-night TV show. He said he had a run-in with Charlie in this office."

"He did," said the manager. "He claimed Calvin Leonard (Charlie) lied to him about his car being illegally parked and being towed away. Charlie denied any wrong doing. Collins got upset, and we had to remove him from the property."

The officer laughed. "Sounds like something this Charlie would do. It looks like you hired the wrong guy."

"And I gave him two weeks advance pay too," said the manager.

"Oh, Oh. You may be the one driving trucks soon," he laughed as he left the manager's office.

Chapter 99 - Another Inexpensive Car

At 9:00 AM Charlie had sold the last of the steaks. Now he had to get rid of the truck. He was on the western outskirts of St. Louis heading east when he noticed a closed bar on the right side of the road. A car was in the parking lot. Charlie figured that it was either a drunk who had fallen asleep in the car or a college kid cleaning the restaurant. He pulled into the parking lot and pulled up next to the car. The key to the car was in the door and the man inside looked like he would be sleeping for hours. Charlie picked the drunk up and placed him in the driver's seat of the truck. He took the money out of his wallet and checked the man's name - Jim Peterson. In the glove box of the car Charlie found some paper. He ripped a sheet of paper in half and wrote up two agreements. On the first agreement, which he would keep, he wrote "Received from Calvin Leonard, $100 for the purchase of my 1981 Chevrolet Impala. Jim Peterson."

On the agreement he would leave with Peterson, he wrote "Sold to John Smith for $100 a 1981 Chevrolet Impala." He signed it in Peterson's name in the worst scrawl he could do. After all the guy was drunk. Charlie thought that the fake name of John Smith was ingenious. It made it look like a real sale and there are so many John Smith's that no one would know where to look.

He put $100 and second agreement on the floor of the truck, closed the truck door and drove away.

Charlie had a cousin, Clint, who lived several miles outside of St. Louis. He would rent a room from Clint until he was ready to push on. Clint wasn't a fan of Charlie but money makes friends.

Forty minutes after Charlie had moved Jim Peterson into the truck, a Missouri state trooper pulled up on the driver's side of the truck. With gun drawn he opened the door of the truck and saw poor drunken Jim Peterson laying across the front bench seat of the truck. The trooper knew Jim well. Often Peterson slept off his drinking in his Chevy Impala. The officer saw the $100 on the floor and the bill of sale for the car and said, "Oh, Jim, what the hell did you do now?" The officer stirred Jim awake. "Wha?...wha?" "Jim, where is your car?"

Jim said, "My car?"

Officer, "Yes, it's gone, and you have this bill of sale on the floor with $100."

The officer held out the bill of sale and asked, "Jim, did you write this?"

Jim read, "Sold to John Smith for $100 a 1981 Chevrolet Impala. Jim Peterson."

The officer said, "Jim, is that your signature?"

Jim said, "I was drunk. I could have signed this." He began to cry, "I sold my car for $100? It was worth more than $2,000."

The officer pressed, "Is that your handwriting?"

"I guess it could be," I was drunk."

The officer said, "Well, my friend, maybe it's time you really gave Alcoholics Anonymous a shot because your drinking just cost you your car."

In a small town on the outskirts of St. Louis, Charlie showed up at his cousin's house with his newly acquired Chevrolet Impala and $73,000 in his pocket.

Clint came out and said, "What brings you to town, Charlie?"

"Clint, I figured I would give the Midwest a shot. Do you have an extra room I could rent? I like staying with family."

"Charlie, the house is pretty well filled up."

Charlie took $5,000 out of his pocket and said, "I have $5,000 here. Do you suppose you could find a spare room for me?"

Clint, smiled and said, "I suppose I could free up a spare bedroom upstairs. Where did you get that kind of money Charlie."

"Oh, I've worked here and there for some time."

He put the $5,000 in Clint 's hand, and Clint showed Charlie his room. Charlie figured that if he laid low all of this would go away.

Chapter 100 – The Center of Their Lives, 1987

As much as the children were the center of Joe and Kate's world, the nucleus of the center for both Kate and

Joe were each other. Joe tried to get the point across to Kate that there was far more about Kate than the raw physical attraction that he had for her when they met. All of the physical attractions were still there, but Kate's inner goodness, intelligence, character and kindness were as important to Joe as her beauty.

Joe went through periods of time when he had to travel more often than he wanted – which was none at all, because when he was away, Joe was not able to protect Kate and their three children. He was that family man that Kate's dad had been, and he enjoyed being with his family. When he couldn't avoid traveling, Joe would make it a point to call Kate each night and tell her about his day and find out what was going on at home. If something interesting had been done, he would always reflect on how much Kate would have enjoyed doing what he was doing.

Joe and Kate and their three children were vacationing in Florida one year and watched people on the beach making wonderful sand castles. Later in the day the waves crept up the beach and washed away all remnants of the sand castles that had been built there. Joe thought of the importance of laying a good foundation in everything that is done – whether it be building a house, learning a language, getting a degree, building any kind of a relationship, including a marriage. Joe said to a colleague at work, "The strength of anything that any of us do in life is only as strong as the foundation on which it is built." Joe's thoughts of this evolved into a poem.

Some Draw Memories In the Sand

Some draw memories in the sand
only to see them washed away.
Some carve memories in granite,
so in the rock, they'll ever stay.

Some build tall castles for their love

*out of cards stacked on each other.
Move a card, the whole thing crumbles -
like their love for one another.*

*Others build a firm foundation
on a hill to see distant lands,
at the edge of greening valleys,
of bricks and mortar - with strong hands.*

*We have carved our dreams in granite.
In the granite, we pledged our love.
We have built a firm foundation;
its cornerstone is endless love.*

*Respect and honor sent to you
as you send the same back to me.
We vowed to each that we'd be true,
to bind into eternity.*

*Awake we not to dawn's first light
with evening's rancor on our lips.
We put an end to all our fights
and slip to sleep in fellowship.*

Writing his poems to Kate was not just done on holidays and special occasions. Joe's writing was like someone with a camera who has the camera ready at all times to catch that perfect picture. Something would strike Joe at any given time, and he would write down the lines that were coming to him. Sometimes it would be a phrase, a sentence, a stanza and sometimes an entire poem, needing fine-tuning, but essentially done.

Joe reflected that married couples after a certain number of years share so many highs and lows, ups and downs, deaths and births, laughs and tears that he couldn't fathom how that all could be cast aside by parties who divorce and move on.

He thought, "Kate and I have held hands and stood at the gravesite of grandparents, parents, siblings and dear friends. We have lost loved ones and friends together. There are memories and feelings, the good and the bad, that we have had with only each other that no one in this world has with me." All married couples have the same connections. Joe couldn't understand how people could just throw all that away as if those events had never occurred. Whatever he faced in life, he wanted to face it with Kate.

Chapter 101 – Charlie Laying Low, 1988

Charlie's cousin, Clint, and his family lived in rural St. Louis – on the outskirts of the city, but Charlie was forever looking over his shoulder for the police to show up – possibly even the FBI. He had taken two vehicles across the state lines – the car that he traded with his boss, and the truck with the steaks. The company had gotten their refrigeration truck back so if the FBI was fair, that should not be construed as a theft, it was more like he borrowed it, but he doubted if the feds would see it that way. The steaks were another. He knew that taking the steaks and selling them for his own benefit was a felony. He kind of figured that he did the slaughterhouse a favor by exposing their steaks to a broad circle of retailers who likely returned for more steaks, but he knew the company probably didn't see it that way. "Shortsightedness is such a curse," he thought.

Chapter 102 - Buried, But Not Dead, 1988

Charlie's case was not a high priority for the FBI, but new agents were often put on the case as a training exercise. The FBI believed that Charlie could have hunkered down in the St. Louis area. The FBI office in St. Louis had hired a new recruit, Agent Darla Jackson. She was handed the case and told to see what she could find. Agent Jackson saw that the rural area of St. Louis had been heavily ignored. She presumed that after Charlie had "bought" the car and left the truck at the restaurant, he would likely want to go into hiding because the police were on his trail. So, Agent Jackson began to go through villages to see if anyone had either seen him or the car. She had been through two towns and found nothing. She drove to the next town and stopped for breakfast at a local diner. She asked her waitress if she had seen this guy (showing a picture of Charlie.) The waitress looked at the picture and said, "I know this guy. He comes in here a couple of times a week. Always for breakfast."

"Has he been in here lately?"

"Not long ago," said the waitress. "Why are you looking for him?"

"We think that he may have witnessed a robbery just over the state line. How does he generally pay his bill?"

"Always cash." Said the waitress. He sees himself as a real player. Always trying to pick up the girls. Likes the young ones – you know, jail bait."

Darla Jackson eyes lit up, "Bingo," she said in her mind. "That's my guy."

She asked the waitress, "What about family in the area? Does he ever talk about family at all?"

The waitress thought, "I only remember one time he came in with a boy about ten or twelve. He referred to him as his cousin. He was getting breakfast with him before he took him to school."

"And where is the closest school?"

"Wilson Elementary, just a few blocks from here."

"You've been so much help. And the pancakes were great."

Agent Jackson was on her way to Wilson School. The school had a list of people who had authority to drop off and pick up children. The list contained pictures and contact information of people dropping off and picking up children. The agent went through the list and found the picture of Charlie that she hoped she would find.

Pulling into the driveway of a rather reclusive home, Agent Jackson made sure that her gun was ready, then she approached the house. Clint answered the door.

"He looks innocent enough but you never know," thought the FBI agent. With her right hand on the gun, which Clint noticed, she held out her badge and a picture of Charlie and said, "I am looking for this man."

Clint said, "Whoa, whoa, whoa, easy officer. I'm not involved in anything that Charlie is up to. "

She relaxed her hand from the gun. "Is he here?"

"No, I don't know where he's off to this morning."

"Does he live here?"

"Well, yes, he does. He rents part of the upstairs."

"You know you are harboring a fugitive, and that makes you an accomplice."

"Look officer. I don't know anything about what Charlie does. He is my cousin and he lives here, but I am not involved in his activities in any way, shape or form. I just rent him a room."

"You know he has a criminal record?"

"Well, yes, but that doesn't make me complicit just because he rents a room from me. I thought that he had done his time for what he did, and he came here to get a new start."

"When do you expect him back?"

"Officer, Charlie's not my kid. He's a grown man who can come and go as he sees fit."

"You'll let me know when you hear from him. It will go easier if he comes in peacefully."

Clint said, "Tell me, is he dangerous?"

"Probably not, but watch your stuff."

"What did he do?"

The agent said, "Remember that steak truck story a couple of years back?"

"Yah, I do."

"That was Charlie."

Agent Darla Jackson gave Clint her business card, and he promised to call her when he heard from Charlie. Then she left.

When she exited the property, she did not notice the Chevrolet Impala that was parked in an opening in the woods. Charlie had seen her car in front of the house.

If Charlie knew anything, he knew what an unmarked police car looked like and he quietly pulled the Impala deep into the recess that he was in.

He waited for ten minutes to be sure that she was gone then drove up to the house.

Clint came out with a shotgun in his hand. "What the hell have you been up to Charlie? The FBI was just here looking for you."

"I know, I saw the car when I was pulling up. Was she cute?"

"Good grief, Charlie, it that all you think about? You get your shit out of my house and don't come back."

"Do I get a chance to explain?"

"They are viewing me as an accomplice. I am going to have to call her to let you know you were here."

"You would do that to a blood relative?"

"To protect my family, I sure as hell would."

Charlie glared at Clint and said, "I could take that gun from you and turn it on back on you in a heartbeat."

"I don't want to kill you, Charlie. Don't make me. It would be self-defense."

"I never should have stayed here. Go west young man. Like a Phoenix I shall rise again."

In five minutes, Charlie was out the door and heading for the interstate where he would go west and hopefully keep on going until he reached Arizona.

Clint dialed the St. Louis FBI office and asked for Agent Darla Jackson.

She wasn't in. Clint said, "Please tell her that Clint called and Charlie was here and gone. Please tell her that he had seen her car and decided to move on."

"Ok, I'll tell her."

"Tell her I did not warn him to leave, he left on his own."

"Ok, sir, I'll tell her. Any idea where he might be heading?"

"Oh, he implied he was going west. Maybe Phoenix, Arizona."

"Thanks for the tip, sir. That narrows it down."

Clint turned to his wife and said, "I never want to have anything to do with that family again."

Chapter 103 - Charlie's On The Run, 1988

Charlie was driving west on Interstate 20 through Texas. He figured it was a less traveled road and shouldn't draw as much attention as major roads. Even if the police and FBI were following him, which he doubted, they would likely stick to the bigger roads.

What Charlie did not know is that FBI Agent Jackson was only 20 minutes behind him on the same highway heading west. When she had reached her St. Louis office, she saw the message from Clint that Charlie had seen her car, grabbed his stuff and was heading west. The note said that he would be like the Phoenix and rise again. "Cute," she thought. "So Charlie is heading for Phoenix, Arizona."

She went to her manager's office, "That Charlie Lane is spooked and on the run. I'm giving chase. She looked at the various routes to Phoenix and selected Interstate102, as Charlie had, as her route. She figured that she was 35 miles or so behind him, and hoped that he would leave signs along the way.

Charlie's engine began to smoke. He had been laying on the gas, and a great black cloud of smoke came from the hood of the Impala, and Charlie coasted to the side of the road.

He gathered his few belongings and began walking west.

A man in a pick-up truck slowed down and asked if Charlie needed a ride.

Charlie said, "Sure do." He opened the door with a gun leveled at the man's head. "And now I've got one. Get out of the truck."

"You're in Texas boy, and we don't take kindly to any kind of theft. You might want to forget about this and let it go," the man said. "It's not too late."

"It will be too late for you if you don't get out now,"

Charlie warned the man.

Unable to save the sinner from himself, the driver got out of the truck.

"Adios, asshole!" Charlie called out as he pulled away.

A mistake is made when you rob someone and don't know anything about the person that you are robbing. Another mistake is when you rob someone and you don't know the lay of the land. The road ran through a cattle ranch - a big cattle ranch, The Judge Ranch. The owner of the ranch was Frank Judge, the man who just had a gun stuck in his face.

Judge reached into his coat and pulled out a new Motorola invention called a cell-phone. It was big and bulky but it was perfect if you were in the middle of nowhere (even if it was your ranch.) Watching his pick-up truck vanish in a cloud of dust, Frank Judge called his foreman who was down the road.

"Hello, boss," the foreman said.

Judge said, "I've just been robbed by a man who is now driving my truck in your direction. He should be there in 15 minutes or so. Round up some boys and bring a couple hundred cattle across the road."

"Sure, Mr. Judge, but won't he try to run through the cattle?"

Judge said, "Nah, not if there are enough cows in the road. Cover the entire road, ten cows deep. Act nonchalant like you're just pushing cattle. And Pete, send someone to pick me up. Oh, be careful, this piss-ant's got a gun."

"Well, hell, Mr. Judge, so do we." Pete set out to follow his boss' instructions.

As FBI Agent Darla Jackson barreled west down Highway 102, she came upon the smoking Chevy Impala sitting the on the side of the road. As the engine was still hot, she knew that she was not too far behind him.

Up the road Charlie had a big-ass grin on his face. It was all just too easy. He was going to like dealing with people in these Western states; they were very trusting.

Ahead of him Charlie saw a lot of dust. So much so that he slowed down and edged the truck forward slowly. He saw cattle by the hundreds and cowboys by the dozens. While Charlie was slowing down, a cowboy came up to his passenger window and said, "Sorry, stranger. We'll get these cows out of your way in a couple of minutes." Charlie smiled his appreciation for the words of comfort and waited while watching the cowboys push the cattle across the road. Some time went by when the driver's door opened and Charlie was dragged out of the truck by several big, muscular cowboys. They took Charlie's gun, slid a rope around his neck and dragged him over to Mr. Judge.

"Is this him, boss?" Pete asked.

Judge said, "You damn well know it's him. He was driving my truck, wasn't he?"

Judge got in Charlie's face and said, "I told you to let it go, didn't I?"

In dismay, Charlie answered, "Yes, sir."

"You're damn right I did. And didn't I tell you we don't take kindly to any kind of theft here in Texas?" he said.

Charlie nodded, yes.

"Are you a God-fearin' man, son?"

"Yes, sir. I sure enough am," said Charlie trying to pick up the man's dialect.

"Well, I am too, boy. And I never hang anyone without first letting them ask God for forgiveness. Now, get on your knees and pray."

Charlie was shoved down on his knees where he mumbled, "God, don't let them hang me."

"Bad prayer, boy. String him up!" Judge said to his men.

Charlie was dragged to a large cottonwood tree. The rope was thrown over a limb, and he was lifted up until only his toes touched the dirt.

He gagged out, "Please, please."

Judge came up to Charlie and said, "What kind of

worthless piece of garbage robs a man who stops on the road to help him?"

Agent Jackson came upon the crowd of cowboys stringing someone up to a Cottonwood Tree. She presumed the man was Charlie.

She got out of her car and fired a shot into the air yelling, "FBI, loosen the rope and let him down slowly."

Twenty cowboys drew their guns and had them trained on the agent. She yelled out "Who's in charge here?"

Frank Judge's voice was heard loud and clear. "Holster the guns, boys!" He asked to see the agent's ID. Confirming who she said she was, he called out "Lower the thief and let the agent through to do her job."

Charlie was lowered from the tree. He had peed his pants in the process of the hanging. The FBI agent took a handkerchief out of her back pocket and told him to clean himself up.

Charlie, being Charlie, said, "Do you want to see what made this mess?"

She thought, "Oh, he is so full of himself." Then she retorted, "Do you want to see how fast they can hang you up there again?"

Charlie didn't see even the remotest indication of humor on the agent's face, and decided to be quiet.

Jackson got a full report from Frank Judge on what had transpired that resulted in what the agent had seen. Judge said, "Sorry that you had to see that. Texan's hang horse thieves, and to us a truck is just a big artificial horse. Old habits die slowly."

He then jerked his thumb toward Charlie and said, "I want this piece of crap off my land."

Charlie was put into the back seat of the agent's unmarked car and handcuffed to the passenger-side front seat. For good measure one of the cowboys tied Charlie up with a rope that went around the two rear doors of the Agent's car. Charlie was secure for the hour trip to Abilene, Texas.

After a fair and speedy trial, which all people

deserve, the federal judge in Abilene ruled that Charlie posed a perpetual threat to society, and he was sentenced to life in prison – with no parole. Charlie would be serving hard time for the rest of his life.

Chapter 104 - An Unexpected Call, 1988

Several weeks later a message was on Joe's desk when he got back from lunch. The message was from a Jenni Lane. Joe returned the call. Jenni answered the call and told Joe that she was Charlie's wife. She told Joe that Charlie had been arrested in Texas for multiple crimes and was sentenced to life in prison with no parole. She went on to say how bad Charlie's life had been. Charlie had obviously tutored Jenni well.

Jenni said that Charlie had been diagnosed as being dyslexic and that is what caused him to have trouble in school. She added that they had a son who was dyslexic as well. Charlie being dyslexic totally flew in the face of the facts as Joe knew them. He remembered clearly Charlie sitting behind the garage rapidly wading through book after book after book, with almost total recall.

"Jenni, I have been estranged from my brother for years. What is it that you want?"

"Joey, I thought we be part of the family. Charlie always said that you were the "Good Seed.""

Joe said, "Jenni, to show you how estranged I am from Charlie, I haven't gone by Joey in 25 years."

"Well, that's what Charlie always called you."

Joe sighed, "Jenni, Charlie always called me that because he never could get past his past. He could never accept that however bad his past was, it was his personal choice to remain there and blame his past and others for everything that he has done wrong in his life. My past was bad as well, but I was not bound by my past as Charlie has let his past bind him."

"Charlie always said that everyone loved you more. That you were the chosen one."

"Jenni, please give me the contact information of the prison in case I ever need to call or write Charlie" She gave it to him.

Joe was being called into a meeting and said he had to go.

"Can we keep in touch?" Jenni asked.

Joe asked innocently, "Why would we want to do that?"

"Well, I am your sister-in-law. I am Charlie's wife."

"Based on the conversation we have just had, Jenni, I don't think I want that. Charlie and I were never close, and I don't believe we could ever be close either. You see, Charlie and I are brothers in name only. We're like two cotton-wood seeds flying helter skelter from the same tree. One seed took, and grew, and one didn't. I have to go now. Good-bye."

Joe did write Charlie several times over the next few months, but he did not receive anything from Charlie.

Chapter 105 - The Stroke That Killed, June 1989

The phone rang, and Kate answered it. Joe could hear her voice go from upbeat to sad. She thanked the caller for calling then told Joe that his dad had just had a severe stroke and was in the hospital.

Joe got the information and drove to Cottage Hospital on the east side of the city. His dad, Gregory, was hooked to life support. The doctor on call came in and offered little hope. "His entire system has shut down. All of his organs. He is only being kept alive by life support."

Joe sat there holding his father's hand. His dad was handed some pretty big challenges when he was young – many of which were out of his control. His dad's father had left the family when his children were small. The family was very poor, and barely got by. But Grandma Harriett, (the one who had intervened to get Joe out of the orphanage) and her children were strong of heart and mind and most of them brought themselves up from their humble beginnings.

World War II was devastating to Joe's parents. It resulted in the break-up of their marriage, because his parents had grown apart during the war. Coming out of his mental trip back in time, Joe said to himself, "Pretty big challenges for one so young."

Joe thought back on how disappointed his father had been when Joe and Kate had moved away from Livonia to Plymouth because his dad knew his way to the old house. His dad never did learn his way to their new house in Plymouth, Michigan. So, his father would drive on Eight Mile Road from his home on the east side of the city to meet up with Joe at Eight Mile Road and Beck. He would then follow Joe to Joe's home. At the end of the day, Joe would have his dad follow him back to Eight Mile Road where his dad could find his way back to the east side of the city. As daunting as the drive was for his dad, he would not miss a special day that was held for his grandchildren.

When Joe was ready to leave Cottage Hospital, he sought out the doctor and asked once again if there was any chance that his father could live off of life support. The doctor said there was no chance. "Joe, all of your father's organs have stopped functioning. We don't know the extent of his mental damage, but it is severe. We shut the machine down, your father dies. I think you should talk this over with your family and make a decision on what you want us to do." There was no cruelty in the doctor's tone. He was just laying out the facts.

So, there it was. His dad's life had run its course, and Joe would likely have to be the one to decide to unplug his life support.

That night and the following day Joe called all of his siblings, even Charlie in the Texas prison, and told them what the doctor said and asked for their opinion on whether or not to stop life support for their father. Each of them said that it was Joe's call. If Joe didn't believe there was any hope that their father could become the person they knew, then the siblings would accept Joe's decision.

Joe left work at noon the next day. As he was driving to the hospital, he was still wrestling with the decision. Ending someone's life is a big thing. What if? His mind was filled with "what if's." When Joe got to the hospital, nature/God/his dad, whatever, had made the decision on when and how his dad would die, and his dad had taken his last breath 15 minutes before Joe got to the hospital.

Joe was relieved that a higher power had made the decision to take his dad's life before Joe had to tell the doctor what he had decided.

Funeral arrangements were made. An Honor Guard from the United States Navy came and played "Taps" and gave Joe an American Flag for his father's service in the Navy in World War II.

Several days later, Joe wrote Charlie a letter describing the funeral arrangements and who attended. He then went on to say,

"Charlie, the two people who you have blamed all of your life for the condition that your life is in are both dead. There is no one left to blame now. You need to forgive them for what they did and realize that you are hurting your loved ones, as you believe that Mom and Dad hurt you. Charlie, if you don't stop hurting others, when you die one day, there will be no one there to weep for you. You now need to take personal responsibility for your own actions and forgive those who you feel have hurt you throughout your life. It is not too late for you to have a life of honor."

Joe mailed the letter to the prison and never heard from Charlie again.

Chapter 106 - Endless Love, From Then To Now

Joe's love for Kate continued to grow as life went on. After a few years of marriage, many married couples will, partly in jest and partly because they mean it, refer to their spouse as the "old nag" or "the chain around their neck" and yearn to be away from their spouse so that they can breathe. Joe never felt that way about Kate. Oh, he enjoyed getting out with buddies to play golf and tennis, but he was not, and never had been, the kind of guy who liked to go on multi-day trips away from Kate. He had wanted to marry her because he wanted to share in her life. All of it. He had never considered himself trapped in marriage. Marriage to Kate was always something he sought. He wrote the following poem to express how he felt:

Some Say, You Know, Yet I Deny

Some say, you know, yet I deny
that love's transfixed within the eye.
Some say that love cannot transcend
one's lust in which in love's the end.

Some say beyond one day's a bore,
so brief the time to spread amour.
Some say when gripped by loving swoon
one's trapped to spend a life in ruin.

If trapped is recognized in smiles
and tender words through savage trials;
if trapped is felt in soothing hands,
by looks that say she understands-

then trapped I am by one who's rare
and say, "My love, hold tight the snare."

Chapter 107 - Joe's Reflections

One day at a family gathering for his mother - in - law's birthday, Joe mentioned that when he was young he sold greeting cards throughout Kate's neighborhood and that he believed Kate's mom had bought greeting cards from him. Joe said that he remembered that when he walked up to the house, the Magnolia tree was in bloom. Joe was ten or eleven years old at the time and said that he remembered a little girl wrapped around her mother's legs as her mother was listening to his "pitch" to buy boxes of greeting cards.

Kate's Mom said, "I do remember a cute, freckled little boy who came around with greeting cards. He had carried the cards in a newspaper bag. I felt so sorry for him that I bought three or four boxes of cards."

She looked at Joe and said, "Was that little boy you?"

"It could have been. I carried the boxes of cards around in my newspaper bag, and I had a face full of freckles."

Nan then said, "Well your marrying Kate was destiny – arranged by God."

Joe wasn't going to argue that on her birthday, so he just smiled and wondered about what degree God's force may be entering our lives when we just think events and coincidences are just that. Perhaps there is more to them than we choose to acknowledge.

Chapter 108 – The Viet Nam Memorial

Kate and Joe had the opportunity to visit the Viet Nam memorial in Washington, DC. The Viet Nam War was their generation's World War I or II. They looked up three names on the Viet Nam Memorial in Washington D.C. With Kate holding Joe's hand, they sought out the location of Joe's friends who died in Viet Nam. They found each name, stood by their names on the wall, held each other's hand and cried for the lives so shortened.

Joe and Kate would never take away from what their friends, and all soldiers, had sacrificed by disparaging the war, but they have asked a question of God. "God, why can't you intervene to help make human beings just a little less inhuman? Joe had heard many answers to this question, no answer to the question ever satisfied either Joe or Kate. They reached a point where they simply accepted that the world was flawed, and God wasn't likely to take an active role in controlling evil on earth. It is up to us humans to deal with evil. Despite the fact that the World is flawed, and evil is a fact of life, and always has been, each of us can carve out a wonderful life filled with wondrous moments. Their life had so many different segments – some alone, some with children – one, two and three, some with grandchildren from each of the three sets of parents, some with the greater family.

One day Joe sat down and within an hour composed a poem for Kate entitled "This Moment." The poem speaks of the compilation of all of the moments that Kate and Joe spent together. They had their share of lows and a multitude of highs in their life together. All of those moments in their life had created a fabric of what is their life. The removal of any particular moment may result in the undoing of the life they had together. Joe would never want to risk what he and Kate had by amending any moment in the past that was painful, because it's possible that any such removal, and the changing of any such events, could result in a change to what they shared today.

"This Moment" is also a reminder that no one knows if there will be a next moment. In such case, we should live for the moment we are in. That is not to say we shouldn't plan for tomorrow's moments. We should, but just not at the expense of enjoying the moment in which we are living.

This Moment

This moment came into my life
and swept my heart away.
This moment showed me how to live;
when to go; when to stay.

This moment clothed me all in white.
It painted so my soul.
This moment took away my fright
to some enchanted knoll.

This moment raised my spirits up
and brought my sorrows down.
This moment filled my empty cup,
filled me with happy sounds.

I measure moments as they come.
This moment's been the best.
Against this one they're all outdone.
This better than the rest.

This moment brought me happiness
from where there was lament.
To wondrous joy, from deep sadness,
in this special moment.

This moment came, but now it's gone.
There may come another.
But, if no other comes along,
this I'll hold forever.

If my essence had been taken
by my age or by strife,
If I had just one moment left –
one moment in my life,

how would I choose to spend the time
before my life was through?

**I think I'd take that last moment
to be alone with you.**

**I know whose hands I'd like to hold
when I depart someday.
I'd hold Kate's hands with all my might.
In peace I'd slip away.**

Joe didn't put a lot of stock in the concept of a marriage made in Heaven and God intervening in life to orchestrate events in accordance to a master plan. Joe preferred to think that life's forces came together which enabled two people to fall incredibly in love, live their lives respecting and devoted to each other, and working to appreciate and enhance the opportunities that life has afforded them.

With every beat of his heart, Joe was thankful that he was not looking down when he and his stepbrother drove past that beautiful, young woman walking down Hazelton on that summer day in 1966. All of Joe and Kate's following moments were dependent on that moment.

Chapter 109 - A Call From Prison, 2008

Joe was working at home when the phone rang and a woman's voice asked, "Are you Charlie's brother, Joe?"

"Yes, I am. Who's asking?"

"I am Chaplain Irene O'Connor with the Texas Penal System. I am sorry to bring you this news, but your brother is very sick and dying."

Joe sat down by the phone, "Dying? What does he have?"

"He has Lou Gehrig's Syndrome and Alzheimer's. He does not have long to live, and we need to know if the family or Charlie may have had any special death provisions such as a grave site."

"I am not aware of any such death provisions, but

Charlie and I have been estranged for a long time. Is there any chance that I could come to see him?" Joe asked.

"I'm sorry, but you are not on his visitation list. So, no you can't."

Chaplain O'Connor asked, "Does your brother have any closer family? A wife? Children?"

Joe remembered Jenni, but Jenni should be on the visitation list. He asked the Chaplain if Jenni was on the list. "No," was the Chaplain's reply.

Joe shuttered to think this but asked, "Does Charlie have anyone on his visitation list?"

"We aren't supposed to say, but I'll make an exception here and say, 'No.' No one is on the list."

Joe shook his head. No one was on the visitation list. He said, "Charlie was a Christian, and I think he should have a Christian burial. I would be happy to send you money for that."

"That won't be necessary. I just wanted to see if he already had a burial plot somewhere."

Joe interjected, "You may want to check with the U.S. Navy. Charlie was in Navy during the Cuban Missile Crisis. He signed up for four years but only served less than two. He never said why, but it would be worth looking into."

The chaplain said, "I will check with the U.S. Navy.

"Chaplain, Charlie was baptized a Christian. As I said before, Charlie deserves to have a Christian burial. I will pay for it if the Navy doesn't."

"Charlie is a little irrational right now," the Chaplain, said, "but he told me long ago that he does not want you to have anything to do with how he is buried. I have to respect his dying wishes."

"Of course," Joe said.

If the Navy doesn't cover the burial, he'll be buried here. We have a cemetery at the prison. I will keep you in touch."

Well, she didn't keep in touch. Joe learned of Charlie's death through an obituary that a relative living in Texas had seen. The obituary did not say where Charlie had been buried.

After seeing the obituary, Joe wrote to Chaplain O'Connor and asked if she could send Joe anything that might have belonged to Charlie. Joe would not have asked this if Charlie had kept contact with anyone else.

Chapter 110- A Package From Prison, 2008

A month after Joe sent his letter to Chaplain O'Connor, Joe received a package from the Texas Penal System. A note in the package said that Chaplain O'Connor had left the prison.. The package contained Charlie's personal belongings. There were personal hygiene items, a couple of books and some personal letters.

Joe sifted through the letters. The letter that Joe had sent Charlie describing their father's death had "Piss Off" written on it in what Joe recognized was Charlie's handwriting. Apparently, Charlie hadn't taken very seriously Joe's suggestion to forgive others.

Joe found a letter dated 1950 from his great grandmother Luci addressed to Charlie at the orphanage. Charlie would have been five years old at the time. The letter was handwritten. It was yellowed and smudged at the edges like it had been read and re-read many times over. Joe unfolded the letter and read it.

Dear Charlie, I am so sorry that I could not take you with me when we came to get Joe. You may be too young to understand this but your mother, my granddaughter, has given me the right to make decisions for Joe. I do not have that same right for you, because your father did not give it to me.

Your mother asked me to take Joe because he was getting very sick. You were bigger and stronger than Joe and your dad thought that you were doing fine.

I asked your dad if I could take you with me as

well, but he said he wanted to keep you close to Detroit where he lived, so he could visit you more often than if you were living up here with me.

I am sorry, Charlie. I hope one day you will be able to come up north to visit me, and we can spend some time together. You be a good boy and listen to your father.

Love, Grandma Luci.

Printed at the bottom of the page, in Charlie's neatest printing was "You're a liar, Grandma. My daddy would have let you take me. Liar, Liar, Liar."

"Hmmm," thought Joe, "I never knew that Grandma Luci wrote to Charlie in the orphanage." He put all of the letters and other keepsakes together, then went downstairs where he had a storage cabinet labeled "Family." Joe pulled out the Luci box, which held, among other things her jewelry box. Joe had gotten all of Luci's personal items when Joe's grandfather (Grandma Luci's son) died.

Joe had never looked real close at the items in the box, especially Luci's personal letters that were bound together with a ribbon. But now Joe was curious if Charlie ever wrote Luci back. He sifted through the letters and found old newspaper articles about Charlie's criminal offenses that Maggie had sent to Luci. Paper clipped to one such newspaper article was a folded yellow piece of paper with blue lines on it. Joe opened the letter. It was from Charlie to Luci. In large print, the letter read,

"Grandma Luci, I got your letter. You could have taken me up north if you wanted to. You are a liar. You just didn't want to. I am a big boy, and I don't need you or anyone. Leave me alone. I hate you." The letter was signed, **"The grandson you didn't want, Charlie."**

On one of the newspaper articles in Great Grandma Luci's longhand was written, "I never thought there were good seeds and bad seeds in this world, but maybe there are good and bad seeds after all."

Chapter 111 - Bad Seeds and Good Seeds

Joe was in a Kiwanis meeting one day talking with two good friends. One friend, Jim, was a criminal attorney; the other friend, Lee, was a nature lover and would-be horticulturist.

The three of them got into a conversation comparing good and bad seeds with good and bad people. After the formal meeting was over, the three stayed behind and continued their conversation. Jim, said, "I believe that most people are mostly good but are capable of doing bad things."

Lee interjected, "I do too and I call them "good seeds." "Yes," Jim said. "Can I continue?"

Lee said, "Sure."

Jim said, "I also believe that some people are average seeds that can do bad or good things. Using your vernacular, Lee, I would call these average seeds."

Both Lee and Joe nodded and concurred.

"Then there are some people (and I see them all the time in my business) who are just plain bad. They are capable of doing worse than bad and often do, and are capable of some good, but usually for conniving, destructive reasons."

Joe thought for a moment, then said, "Well, I believe that all people have within them seeds of goodness, if not greatness. I don't believe there are good or bad seeds per se as much as there are soil conditions and other stimuli or events that enable the seed to either flourish or wither."

Lee said, "The seed that lands in a hostile environment has a greater chance of dying than does the seed that lands in rich soil."

Jim pointed out that "not all seeds that land in a hostile environment wither and die. Some of them even flourish. The seed that flourishes in a hostile environment is undeniably a good seed. It has to be. Through all that bad soil, the bad conditions, that seed adapted to its environment and overcame its environment, where a lesser seed (an average or bad seed) would have withered and died."

Lee added, "The good seed that can overcame all those obstacles may produce even better fruit, because it has grown even heartier than other seeds because of the struggle that the seed had to exert to exist in that hostile environment."

Jim said, "Well said, Lee. Good people, like good seeds, may even do better in a less than comfortable environment. The struggle to survive and thrive makes the good person, like the good seed, even stronger than it otherwise may have been. In people, more alert, malleable, adaptable, creative."

Joe asked, "Is it possible for a good seed to do poorly in a good environment?"

Lee jumped in and said, "There are studies that show that an environment that is too rich can have an adverse effect on producing good plants, whether the seeds are good, average or bad."

"Why would that be?" asked Jim.

"In that rich soil," Lee said, "the seed, good, average or bad, does not have to send in deep roots or establish a strong foundation. It doesn't have to fight to survive, therefore, when inclement weather comes in, as it invariably does, the seed or plant languishes."

Jim said, "Much like a child who has never had to work hard because the family is well to do. If the family falls upon hard times (dad or mom die or the stock market tanks and they lose everything) the unprepared child could do very poorly and may even turn to crime. "

Joe said, "In that case the child would be a bad seed."

"Or certainly an unfortunate seed," Lee commented.

Joe added, "But unfortunate or not, shouldn't the desire to live, its self-respect, ego, instinct, whatever, induce that child to try to throw off the bad event and seek to succeed?"

"If it were a good seed," said both Jim and Lee.

Lee, "But the bad seed will either just die, physically or spiritually or blame others and either go on the attack or wither."

Joe said, "I think that even in the case of a helping hand, some seeds (people) will either condemn the helper.."

Jim interrupted, "or take advantage of the helper."

Lee said, "But in all cases, other people, society, groups like Kiwanis need to try to assist the bad seed or person to try to get it to reach its highest level of its ability."

Jim nodded and added, "That's true, but in some cases, with the really bad seeds, no amount of help will make a difference."

Joe said, "but how do you know if something you have said or done didn't make a difference?"

Frank, a retired, marine captain came into the room. Can I join in on this conversation?"

"Sure, Captain" they all said - almost in unison.

Frank said, "I overheard some of your conversation, and remembered a discussion that I had with my squad one day in Nam. We were dug in one day during a lull in the fighting. One of my men said, that it was the kings, presidents' movers and shakers who make the rules of the world and the rest of us are just passing through."

Joe said, "Interesting comment."

Frank, "Yah. But I told him I thought that term "just passing through" was way too dismissive of the mark that we may make on the world – all of us. Few of us will ever know if what we did, what we said, the kind word that we uttered or the deeds that we did here or there, may have helped change the course of someone's life and if that change may have changed the course of an event or even the world. Our not knowing if it did or didn't does not mean that it didn't. We just don't know it, but it very well could have had a positive effect."

Joe pushed his chair forward and said, "A case in point was my best friend's mother. I had a fairly bad childhood."

Jim Interrupted, "Man, who hasn't?"

Lee said, "I didn't."

Frank said, ""I didn't either, but ahead Joe."

Joe, "As a boy I would get away from my house as often as I could to find somewhere where my brother, Charlie, couldn't put a cloud over my life. One such escape location was often the home of Mr. and Mrs. Marsden, my best friend's parents. At their house, I could just be a kid, and later, when I was a teenager, I could get away from the fear and drama that existed at my home. Mrs. Marsden never knew what she meant to me until her daughter, Judy, read a poem I had written for Mrs. Marsden's 90th birthday party. Had I not taken the time to relate the impact that Mrs. Marsden had on my life, she likely would have never known it. The fact that she would not have known it, though, did not change the fact that the impact on another person's life was made by her."

Lee said, "Thanks for sharing that, Joe. It is reasonable to expect that we all have made similar impacts on the lives of others, either positive or negative, so, as Frank said, the "just passing through" position is too dismissive of how each and every human may have positively impacted other people and thereby, the world. All of us have a chance to alter life and lives (both good and bad) by the manner in which we deal with others."

Jim offered, "I totally agree, but we have to be ready to acknowledge that our good deeds may not make a change in the outcome of some lives."

Joe said, "As my Great Grandmother Luci told me years ago, and she didn't want to believe it, "Sometimes there are just bad seeds in this world."

EPILOGUE

Divorce is a crushing reality throughout the world where virtually 50% of all marriages end up in divorce. So, half of the people who have said, "I do" and vowed to live their lives as a married couple until "death do (them) part," find their marriage so broken that divorce is the only reasonable path left open to them. They divorce, split the assets and go their separate ways. In advance, they will usually tell any children who they may have "that everything will work out fine and that mommy and daddy still love you, but we just can't live together."

Then the divorced parents usually "move on" with their lives and often find another companion or mate, and life goes on. But the break-up of the family, the selling of the home, the acrimony that accrues from the process is often devastating for any children that they may have and can wreak havoc with them long after the parents have resolved their issues.

This book was written not to condemn the parents for their action, the divorce, but rather to shine a light of hope for the children who must deal with the new reality of their lives. Despite the chaos that children will likely feel in their lives, they can emerge from that chaos to live successful, happy, fulfilled lives that may even include a successful and happy marriage.

Being able to be "whole" and live a happy life often depends on the attitude of the child. If the child is able to forgive the parents for the divorce and for the upheaval that is now their life, and let go of the anger that the child feels toward the parents, that forgiveness goes a long way toward the child being able to live and love again. The child need not forgive the parents face to face. Forgiveness can be given within one's own heart while the parent is alive or even when a parent dies.

If the child is not able to forgive the parent and move on with life, the child may end up permanently broken. Parents, grandparents and other caregivers must be alert to the warning signs that the child may give off and seek professional intervention to help the child deal with the loss of the life that the child knew.

Children must be taught and made to understand that each of us is or can become the master of our own fate regardless of our childhood circumstances. With our American freedom, we do not have to remain in the station in life in which we were born or which life's events, such as a divorce of our parents, poverty, may put us. All of us can rise to the level that our intelligence, desire, dreams, effort, native-ability, and opportunity can take us.

Chance does play a role in this. I define chance as a situation that arises unexpectedly, something that was not on our radar screen and we had no way of knowing that it (the situation) was going to come along. Not everyone has opportunities (chance) that just happen to come along. But, in order to take advantage of chance if and when it comes, one needs to be mentally, physically, emotionally (whatever) prepared to take advantage of the chance or opportunity if it is provided to them. For example, if you don't educate yourself, when an opportunity comes along that requires you to be educated, you won't be in any position to grasp onto that opportunity. But the point here is that we are in control of our lives and how we prepare for an unknown future is up to us.

Each of us is in control of how we prepare to overcome our present situation and how we go forward in life. Only we can look in the mirror and tell ourselves to "suck it up, and stop feeling sorry for ourselves.

We are the masters of our future, but only if we choose to be. If we fail to take control, if we dwell on what someone or something has done to us, and let it cripple us, then we are letting that person, who may have already done harm to us, continue to do harm. We are giving up control of our future and putting it in the hands of whomever or whatever has hurt us. The shame is on us if we let that happen.

As it concerns bullies, in this fictional novel, Joe took matters into his own hands to deal with a bully. This worked out well for Joe, but is not recommended by the author. If you are being bullied, please talk to an adult whom you trust - a parent, a teacher, a member of the clergy, a neighbor, a counselor, whomever. Your being bullied IS NOT YOUR FAULT. DON'T EVER BELIEVE THAT IT IS. It is the fault of the bully who is taking advantage of you. Take action by talking to someone you trust. Most people will make sure that the bullying that you discuss with them will be dealt with, and the bullying will subside or stop. Do not let your fear of the bully stop you from seeking help. Most bullies cringe when sunlight shines on their bullying behavior.

Author's note: This book is a historical fictional novel. Many of the events took place, some of them were embellished by the author for the interest of the reader, and some events were purely fictional. Any correlation between the book and the lives of any of the characters in the book is purely coincidental.